# CINEMA THEN AND NOW

# CINEMA THEN AND NOW

James Naremore

Conversations with
Craig S. Simpson

Sticking Place Books
New York

ISBN 979-8-89976-001-3

# TABLE OF CONTENTS

# WE CAN STILL BE FRIENDS
# BY CRAIG S. SIMPSON

I met James Naremore sometime in 2011, during my first year as Lilly Library Manuscripts Archivist at Indiana University. I recall the circumstances better than the date: I had listened to one of his lively, informative guest spots on the IU Cinema Podcast, looked up his email, and wrote what amounted to a mash note telling him that I enjoyed hearing his thoughts about movies. To my surprise, he replied soon after and invited me to lunch. We went to Lennie's Brewpub near campus in Bloomington, where he asked if I could assist with getting him a formal confirmation from the Lilly director of a donation he had made to the library. I did. He told me to call him Jim. I did that too.

Mostly we talked about movies, a deceptively simple interaction that extended in several unexpected directions and serves fourteen years later as the operating principle of this text. *Cinema Then and Now* is not a series of recorded interviews but rather one long interview that unfolded in an online document shared between Jim and me from May 2024 to March 2025. Occasionally we would discuss possible topics or kick around ideas by phone or email. A few structural changes aside, the official Q&A transpired exactly as it reads. Whatever this approach may have lacked in spontaneity, it more than makes up for in the breadth and depth of Jim's responses to my questions and the insights and surprises that he revealed about his life, his body of work, and his opinions about films over the course of approximately ten months of our collaboration.

Some factoids I knew beforehand. As anyone who has had the pleasure of reading his books, listening to his DVD commentaries, or attending his public presentations is likely aware, Jim's vast knowledge of cinema was honed by decades of teaching and research primarily at Indiana University, where he began in 1970, retired in 2007, and is now Chancellors' Professor Emeritus. Jim discusses his academic career across these pages, and fleshes out other points of interest when asked about them: he was born and raised under difficult conditions in Louisiana ("Looking back on it, I realize the town [of Sulphur] had adopted me," he reflects); he had been a magician (and years later received a phone call from the performatively mute Raymond Teller from Penn & Teller fame); he started as a literary scholar (specializing in Virginia Woolf) before transitioning to film; he has an interest in politics that is woven frequently into his writings about cinema ("Almost everything I've done has been affected to some degree by political life in America..."); he writes critical studies, not biographies, yet has a gift for sharing unassumingly relevant details about not only his subjects but himself. On the page, Jim's voice is identical to how he speaks: eminently quotable; disarmingly unpretentious; authoritative enough to swiftly dismantle a weak argument yet unthreatened by opposing views.

Driven by a rigorous intellect and a curiosity that still inform everything he does, Jim's eagerness to share opinions, ideas, and discoveries manifested itself regularly over my seven years at IU. I sensed these qualities before we met, on the aforementioned podcast episode, during which he pivoted seamlessly from discussing classical-era Hollywood filmmakers like Alfred Hitchcock to expressing his interest in seeing a new British sci-fi-horror movie called *Attack the Block*. (As I recall, he liked it.) In our sporadic conversations afterward, he tolerated my enjoyment in reading Pauline Kael (whose papers we had at The Lilly) and indulged my admiration of Robert Altman, albeit not without a little pushback. It was shortly after the release of the 2012 *Sight and Sound* poll when I mentioned that *McCabe & Mrs. Miller* would have been on my list of the ten greatest movies had I been asked to submit one. "I don't like that film," Jim said. "That's okay," I replied. "We can still be friends." He laughed. "Yeah, we can still be friends."

Divided into eleven chapters with a multitude of subheadings, our book (much more *his* book than mine) is roughly one-part memoir and three-parts critical analysis on a wide canvas of subjects both in his wheelhouse and brand-new territory—things that I've long wanted to ask him or which developed out of the flow of conversation. Jim is a consistently good interviewee (an online search reveals a pair of excellent in-depth interviews for Senses of Cinema and the World Socialist Web Site, among many others), and remarkably he avoids repeating himself. Part of it is his knack for expressing the same idea in a different way or from a new angle, and another is his ability to expand on prior assessments or even change his mind. I always learn something that I hadn't known before. One of many delightful revelations that came out of our interview was that "We can *never* be friends" is what Jim jokingly told his students if they disliked Max Ophüls' *Letter from an Unknown Woman*. Other particulars I'll let readers discover for themselves. (Suffice to say that Jim is wickedly funny, and his anecdote about delivering a speech at an event sponsored by The Optimist Club has a killer punchline.)

Exceptional though he is in the art of public speaking (a skill crucial to his life's trajectory), I was surprised to find that Jim feels more comfortable with lecturing than dialoging. While there are passages where he discourses at length (see his miniature case studies for Peter Bogdanovich's put-upon *Daisy Miller* and Sidney Lumet's forgotten *Deathtrap* as nuanced examples of cinematic adaptations of a novel and a play, respectively), in many others he encourages an interactive flow of conversation, sometimes even volleying a question back to me. Our lengthy chapter on his books and articles is a personal favorite not only because it showcases Jim's impressive array of interests but also because it gives him an opportunity to expand on (and I to ask about) the groundbreaking approaches that have defined much of his work.

It was Jim who brought to light Orson Welles' political ambitions and struggles (in *The Magic World of Orson Welles* and in his essay "The Trial: The FBI vs. Orson Welles"); who rose to the challenge of analyzing the nebulous art of screen performance (*Acting in the Cinema*); who yanked film noir from its well-worn American stereotypes of chain-smoking gumshoes, femmes fatales, and Expressionist shadows into an international history of a mutable concept (*More Than Night: Film Noir and Its Contexts*); who effectively applied "grotesque aesthetics" to the work of Stanley Kubrick (*On Kubrick*); who zeroed in on Charles Burnett's idiosyncratic humor rather than the customary, reflexive focus on neorealism (*Charles Burnett: A Cinema of Symbolic Knowledge*). Along with discussing these works in detail, he also reflects on his role in procuring significant film history collections such as the Orson Welles Manuscripts for The

Lilly and in heading the planning committee for the creation of the IU Cinema, inaugurated the same year I arrived under the brilliant stewardship of our mutual friend Jon Vickers.

We later explore—in another favorite section—types of film genres. Although musicals (*The Films of Vincente Minnelli*) and comedies (*Some Versions of Cary Grant*) were familiar terrain to Jim, it was fun to cover fresh examples, as well as venture into other genres (Westerns, horror films, documentaries) which his writings had hitherto not examined. Also threaded through our interview are his thoughts about at least several dozen movies. Some films mentioned—in detail or in passing—were analyzed previously in Jim's works (e.g., *Psycho, The Trial, Cabin in the Sky, To Sleep with Anger, The Awful Truth*), while others are more topical (e.g., *The Substance, Get Out, Anora, They Shall Not Grow Old, The Edge of Democracy*). Additionally, Jim's interest in television is reflected in his views on streaming series like Netflix's *Ripley*, Hulu's *Say Nothing*, and Apple TV's *Disclaimer*. I like two of those shows far more than the third (to his dismay, I also don't care for "Domestic Cary" Grant movies along the lines of *Room for One More*), but even when we end up disagreeing I always want to know what he thinks. Jim's opinions are so clearly, forcefully articulated that I regard them as Roger Ebert did Stanley Kauffmann's: "It's not that I assume he is right and I am wrong; it's that… I wonder if he was perhaps *more* right."

As evinced from our in-person exchange about *McCabe & Mrs. Miller*, Jim responds as agreeably to dissent as he offers it—debate engages him—and the intermittent junctures in the following text where I challenge or disagree with him or ask for clarity on this point or that derive from the unique circumstances of our relationship. My role in this project is not that of a scholarly peer capable of discussing Althusserian theory or rattling off the principles of *Gesampkuntswerk*; although, as a tenured faculty archivist, and having worked in academia for more than half my life, I can code-switch when the situation requires. Nor am I a former student influenced by Jim, many of whom are now distinguished scholars in their own right; although that gets closer to describing our dynamic. Rather, I occupy one-half of what has been described favorably in *The New York Times* and other publications in recent years as an intergenerational friendship—one developed during a serendipitous time when the IU Cinema became a haven where our enthusiasm for film converged.

Orson Welles was a key catalyst, starting with our membership on the planning committee for Indiana University's 2015 Welles Centenary Symposium, then continuing through other Wellesian endeavors. Jim asked me to join him for a Q&A following an IU Cinema screening of *The Lady from Shanghai*, recommended me to be a keynote speaker on *The Magnificent Ambersons* at a community event, and suggested to Oxford University Press that I write a bibliographical article on *Touch of Evil*. (These last two happened after he himself had been asked and declined.) I'll be damned if I know what I did to deserve such indefatigable support and generosity, including his inviting me to collaborate on this publication. I can only confirm that one of the perks of an intergenerational friendship is a refreshing lack of competitiveness (I'm part of Generation X—we have a lot of dubious priorities); another is a semblance of mentor/protégé rapport without a teacher/pupil hierarchy. Jim's touching tribute to his own mentor and "surrogate father," the late Joycean luminary Bernard Benstock, who taught freshman English at Louisiana State University the year Jim enrolled, is another highlight of our discussion.

In an effusive 1995 review in *Cineaste* of Jim's "idiosyncratic and progressive" book on Minnelli, Jonathan Rosenbaum offered some characteristics of the author that are worth revisiting: "The critical position of James Naremore is Frankfurt school auteurism, a seeming contradiction. That is, he shares the Marxist orientation of many Frankfurt school intellectuals but not their disdain for the artifacts of mass culture... As a consequence, Naremore's work shows an interest in style and pleasure that runs against the puritanical grain of most American Marxists, without ever losing sight of the social and political issues avoided by most American auteurists."

Thirty years later, I can vouch that Jim's political/aesthetic sensibility hasn't changed much, although his description may be phrased somewhat differently than Jonathan's. In *Cinema Then and Now*, Jim calls himself "an instinctive lefty" whose politics are "Social Democratic..." To this I would add that as virtuosic as Jim is with words, he considers them meaningless without action. He remains an overt supporter of political activism in general and student protest in particular, and I know he'd have sooner voted for Pauline Kael than Donald Trump. (Readers craving another tiresome polemic about wokeness or cancel culture—whippersnappers these days!—should find themselves another book.)

What has changed is that Jim no longer considers himself a pure auteurist (while still acknowledging the theory's foundational underpinnings), and in a late chapter he takes a fascinating deep-dive into the contributions of screenwriters, editors, production designers, composers, and other collaborators to film production. This critical stance isn't entirely new; his essay "Authorship, Auteurism, and Cultural Politics" in *An Invention Without a Future* posits that "anyone who functions in a creative job might, at least potentially, be viewed as an author." For our purposes, his emphasis on partnership extends to this collaborative work, though I should disclose that Jim suggested questions on occasions where I was unfamiliar with the subject. One example, which had not yet been published during our interview, is another of Jim's recent collaborations, *The Haunted Cinema of Pedro Costa*, co-authored by his wife Darlene Sadlier, a Professor Emerita of Spanish and Portuguese at IU, who is also a great scholar and a wonderful friend. Shortly before I departed Bloomington for San José in 2017, Jim and Darlene invited me to dinner, the entry to their home marked by (he pointed out mischievously) a Lynchian red door. "Let's keep in touch" is a clichéd response to one's departure that usually lacks conviction, but I'm gratified to say that it's borne out over the past eight years.

Near the conclusion of this book, Jim considers "Threats to Film History" with proper seriousness that is nonetheless bereft of—to put it colloquially—doom-spiraling. (Some may be surprised to read that streaming—the archnemesis of many cinephiles, and discussed in an earlier section—is something he values.) Nihilism is anathema to him; along with his palpable fondness for the artists of Old Hollywood, Jim's hope for the future of cinema (and American democracy, in spite of remaining clear-eyed about signs to the contrary) is, I suspect, what prompts him to resolutely support the young and seek out the new. That he also detests hagiography makes it a delicate balancing act to write an introduction that gives him due credit without causing undue discomfort, so I may as well concede defeat. To appropriate what Godard said about Welles, I owe Jim Naremore everything. And I'm glad that we're still friends.

March 17, 2025

James Naremore's website: https://jamesnaremore.net.

# BEGINNINGS

## Southern Childhood and Adolescence

*You were born in the South. What was that like?*

Memory is a tricky thing but I'll try to be as accurate as possible. I was born in 1941 and wasn't able to leave the South until my early twenties, when I was lucky to get out. I had loving parents but an unstable childhood. My first home was the small town of Bossier City in northwest Louisiana (right-wing congressman Mike Johnson, current Speaker of the U.S. House of Representatives, comes from there, which probably gives you an idea of the place). My father was in the Navy during World War II and came home to low-level white-collar jobs. Unbeknownst to me, my mother had contracted leukemia, and when I was about five we moved to Birmingham, Alabama, her original home, where she could get treatment. She died a couple of years later, and my father's life fell apart. He and I moved back to Louisiana, where I spent a few years living away from him with his two brothers, first in Bossier City and then in a town called Bunkie.

When he was on his feet, we moved to a newly built community called Maplewood in south Louisiana, then to a town called Sulphur, a few miles from Lake Charles. I much preferred French Catholic southern Louisiana to the Protestant north. But at roughly that point, when I entered high school, my father's alcoholism began to consume him. He lost his job and had to recover at a VA hospital. I spent most of my high school years dependent on the kindness of strangers, living with three different families in Sulphur who treated me well. Looking back on it, I realize the town had adopted me. These were good people, but my experience of that period left me with very complex feelings that I don't think I've ever overcome or fully analyzed.

My father died soon after I finished high school. I wasn't always unhappy and I enjoyed some of the things around me. I wasn't fully aware that the South was still like the Confederacy until around 1954, when the Supreme Court school integration case was announced and I saw the reaction of local citizens. That's when I realized that the South is another country.

*Did you see movies? Do you recall the first one you saw? Mine was* Godzilla vs. Megalon*. My parents said the first movie they took me to see was the animated* 101 Dalmatians*, but I have no memory of that experience.*

This shows the difference in our ages. I don't remember my first movie, but our home in Bossier City was a block from the only theater in town. I vaguely recall Saturday afternoon double features with Roy Rogers and Boston Blackie, and for some reason I was fascinated with the very young and pretty June Allyson, my first movie crush. But the first movie I vividly remember was a re-release of Disney's *Snow White and the Seven Dwarfs* (1937), which my mother took me to see. (In those days, there were many second-run pictures or re-released showings of successful older films.) When the Wicked Witch appeared, I was terrified and wanted to run sobbing and screaming from the theater. I suspect the early Disney features had similar effects on other children.

For many years as a kid, I also had a memory of a disturbing scene but couldn't recall what movie it was from. It was shot entirely from the subjective viewpoint of a man who walked up a stairway, entered a seedy operating room, and lay down on an operating table, where a creepy-looking doctor looked down at his (our) face and prepared him for surgery. It wasn't until I was an adult that I realized the scene was from *Dark Passage* (1947), in which Humphrey Bogart undergoes plastic surgery.

Despite such unsettling moments, I loved going to movies. Theaters were like a womb, especially when they were half empty. "It's Cool Inside," the marquees said, advertising air-conditioned escape from the clammy heat.

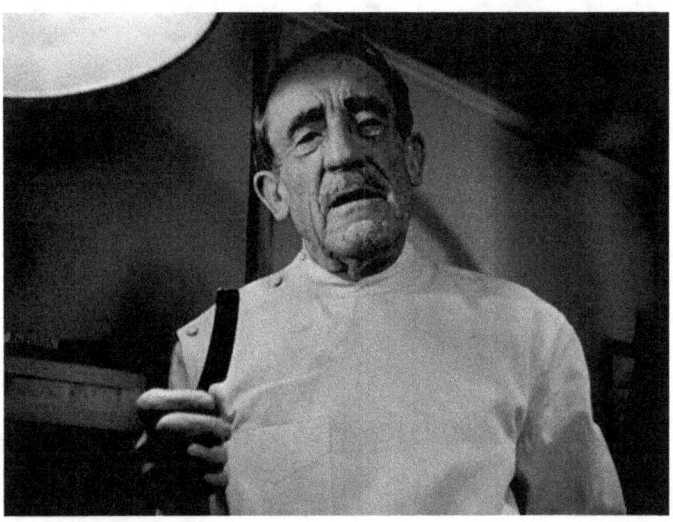

*Dark Passage*

*Living in the South, did you see any films with Black characters?*

In those days, Blacks in Hollywood played only supporting roles, usually as comic servants, so there was no problem in Southern theaters. When I was young I saw another Disney film, *Song of the South* (1946), a combination of live action and animation based on Joel Chandler Harris' Uncle Remus stories. The Black actor James Baskett played Remus and won an honorary Academy Award. I identified with the boy played by Bobby Driscoll and liked the film's animated stories about the clever Brer Rabbit. I went around singing its theme song, "Zip-a-Dee-Doo-Dah." I gather some critics at the time regarded the film as progressive, and in fact there's a sweetness about it. Later it was attacked as racist and is the only Disney feature film of the period that the company has never revived and theatrically exhibited. (It can be seen on YouTube.)

*Song of the South*

A few years afterward, I remember seeing a re-release of the Black-cast *Stormy Weather* (1943) in a Louisiana theater with a balcony for Black audiences only. Lena Horne's rendition of the title song made an indelible impression. I didn't see Stanley Kramer and Mark Robson's *Home of the Brave* (1949), which was about racism in the military and probably didn't get much distribution in the South. The first film I saw that depicted racism was Jacques Tourneur's wonderful *Stars in My Crown* (1950). Black actors sometimes played servants in Tourneur's films, for example in *I Walked with a Zombie* (1943) and *Out of the Past* (1947), but they were never comic and he always gave them dignity and intelligence. He's one of my favorite directors.

*Stars in My Crown*

*Did other films make an impact as you grew older?*

When I was seven or eight I saw a re-release of Fritz Lang's *Scarlet Street* (1945), which my aunt and uncle should never have allowed me to watch. It greatly disturbed me and only years later did I discover how good it is. Later, I saw King Vidor's *The Fountainhead* (1949), which was exciting because I had never heard people in a movie talk about ideas. I now realize the ideas were claptrap, but the film remains well worth seeing, mainly for Vidor's skill with eroticism. In addition to his many other virtues, he was very good at sexiness, as in *Duel in the Sun* (1946) and *Ruby Gentry* (1952). He repeatedly made films about strong women, one of the best of which is *Stella Dallas* (1937). He also wrote a memoir, *A Tree Is a Tree*, which made a big impression on me in high school and ought to be reprinted. One of his life-long aims was to create epic-sized films that told the story of ordinary Americans—films such as *The Big Parade* (1925), *The Crowd* (1928), and *An American Romance* (1944), the last of which was damaged by studio cutting. By any measure, he was one of Hollywood's greatest filmmakers.

As I neared adolescence I became a cinephile—in the lingo of the less pretentious, a movie buff. There were lots of memorable films in that period, among them Christian Nyby and Howard Hawks' *The Thing from Another World* (1951), which chiefly impressed me with its fast-paced, Hawksian dialogue; John Farrow's *His Kind of Woman* (1951), a very skillful mix of comedy and suspense; and Vincente Minnelli's *The Bad and the Beautiful* (1952), with three narrators and great black and white photography. The first subtitled movie I saw was Henri-Georges Clouzot's international hit, *Diabolique* (1955), which made my hair stand on end. The second was Roger Vadim's cinemascope *And God Created Woman* (1956), a daring movie for its day, which showed off Brigitte Bardot's body and made her a star. (There were Catholic pickets protesting the film outside the box office, which made it even more enticing.) Years later Godard derisively alluded to it in *Contempt* (1963), which opens with a cinemascope view of Bardot's naked derrière lit with the colors of the French flag.

Two other pictures that impressed me were Edgar Ulmer's *Ruthless* (1948) and Robert Rossen's *All the King's Men* (1949), both of which I saw in re-release. The Rossen picture is based on Robert Penn Warren's novel about a political figure who resembles Louisiana's Huey Long. I didn't know that at the time, but I later discovered more about Long and even worked one summer in the state capitol building that his administration had built in the 1930s. (It's a modernist skyscraper that looks a bit like the Chrysler building, and on a wall of the ground floor you can see the bullet holes from where Long was assassinated.) Long was treated as a proto-fascist by intellectuals during the Roosevelt years, but I was ambivalent about him. In grade school and high school I had free lunches and free textbooks because of Long. He built a beautiful campus at LSU because he had visited Stanford and liked the way it looked. He was also something of an enemy to the big oil interests in the state.

Hitchcock was on a roll: *Strangers on a Train* (1951), *Rear Window* (1954), and *The Wrong Man* (1956) made me recognize film style and the importance of the director for the first time. The last of these films, Hitchcock's most unusual and downbeat, had a shot that made a vivid impression on my young mind: an intense closeup of handwriting on a piece of paper, panning from left to right and stopping on a misspelled word. This note became evidence against the protagonist, Manny Balestro (Henry Fonda), a jazz-band musician wrongly accused of murder, who eventually gets out of prison to find his wife (Vera Miles) has gone mad. I also recall liking a couple of less famous pictures that are almost forgotten today: Jack Garfein's *The Strange One* (1957) and Douglas Sirk's *A Time to Love and a Time to Die* (1958). I think my taste was formed in that era.

*Did the towns in which you grew up have their own cinemas, or did you have to travel to larger cities to see movies that you wanted to see?*

In those days every town everywhere had theaters. Bossier City had only one but that town is just across the river from Shreveport, which had several. Birmingham had theaters with gigantic screens, one with an organist who played between features. (The biggest crowd I ever saw at a theater was at the Birmingham showing of *The Egg and I* [1947], where the line at the box office extended more than a city block; I don't recall seeing the movie, but it was a big hit, spawning the Ma and Pa Kettle franchise.) The little town of Bunkie had two theaters across the street from one another. Maplewood had one theater, Sulphur had two, and nearby Lake Charles had four. One of the Lake Charles theaters was a dilapidated place called The Majestic with smelly aisles and seats, specializing in re-releases and cheapo exploitation; I saw Capra's *It's a Wonderful Life* (1946) and Kubrick's *Killer's Kiss* (1955) in that theater. When I went to college in Baton Rouge, there were several movie houses, including a campus art theater where I first saw Godard and Bergman. I was occasionally able to visit New Orleans, where I remember seeing *Shoot the Piano Player* (1960), *Psycho* (1960) and *Lolita* (1962). One summer I had an arduous job in a shrimp-packing factory in the tiny town of Ponchatoula, Louisiana; it had one small theater, and on a rare day off I saw John Ford's *The Man Who Shot Liberty Valance* (1962). Those were the days when if you lived in a relatively small town there was a movie theater in walking distance.

## Movies, Magic, and TV

*Did you see an Orson Welles movie at that time?*

Not right away, even though I had become fascinated with Welles. This story needs some background. In my high school library I discovered a book by Deems Taylor entitled *A Pictorial History of the Movies*. Many years later I saw a

Martin Scorsese documentary, *A Personal Journey Through American Movies* (1995), in which he held that book up for the camera and said that as a kid he found it in a library and wanted to steal it. I was floored because I *did* steal it, or at least never returned it, and I still have it. A large format, slick paper volume, it's made up of excellent black and white stills from mostly Hollywood films, arranged chronologically, with informative captions. The 1950 edition begins with an optical toy from 1895 and ends with Rossen's *All the King's Men*. I had seen only a few of the movies it illustrates (there was obviously no way to see Griffith, Keaton, or Chaplin), but it made me yearn to see them. I practically memorized it, and at one point fantasied about becoming a contestant on a big TV show like *Twenty-One* and specializing in movie history. The book had two stills from *Citizen Kane* (1941) and it mentioned that Welles was not only a writer-director-actor but also a magician. That fascinated me because I was passionately interested in magic and had begun to perform it.

*I was surprised and delighted when you told me a few years back that you had been a magician. Talk about when and how you developed an interest in magic.*

I seem to remember that you were a magician, too. What was your experience?

*Not nearly at your level. I learned basic card tricks and such in my adolescence. It was really to develop my hand-eye coordination, which I struggled with as a kid (and on which I could use a refresher now). But I've never been interested in elaborate magic tricks, like David Copperfield making the Statue of Liberty disappear. I prefer the physical and verbal dexterity of Ricky Jay, or even the deconstructive magic of Penn and Teller. You've met or spoken with at least the non-verbal half of that act, haven't you?*

Yes, Penn and Teller were doing their act in Bloomington, and Teller called me on the phone. I thought it was a gag, but it turned out it was really him. He was an admirer of my book about film acting. We had lunch together in Bloomington and dinner in Washington D. C. when I had a fellowship at the National Gallery of Art and they were appearing in the city. When their act moved to Vegas, he sent me some very funny, surreal postcards. I was a great admirer of his talent and honored when he asked me to explain a special effect in the silent *Ben-Hur* (1925).

As for my own brief life as a magician, I had seen a couple of big illusionist shows on stage, which, like you, I didn't much care about (Penn and Teller, however, were excellent on stage). At some point I came across a book by Henry Hay called *The Amateur Magician's Handbook*. This was an intelligent book of instruction, not meant for people who want to do easy stuff. From it I learned a fair amount of sleight of hand (an art I never fully mastered and have almost completely lost) and also read about legendary performers like Cardini (cards) and T. Nelson Downs (coins). I subscribed to the journals of The Society of American Magicians and The International Brotherhood of Magicians and began to make a little money performing for things like the Rotary Club or the local Parrish Fair. In Lake Charles, I was on TV a couple of times, doing sleight of hand mixed with stuff you could get at magic shops. So naturally I was interested in Orson Welles. Maybe my love of movies has something to do with magic. The medium has been closely connected to magic since Méliès, though it has just as much in common with the Lumières.

In the mid-1950s my father bought a TV with an outdoor antenna. When the weather was right, you could pick up broadcasts pretty far afield. I first saw a Welles movie broadcast from a Galveston, Texas late show: *Journey into Fear* (1943), credited to Norman Foster but with Welles' fingerprints all over it—it not only has the Mercury players but also some of the same lighting, depth of field, and low-level angles as *Kane*. The first shot is a pre-credit sequence, quite rare in those days. The camera cranes up to a high window of an old building and goes through it into a shadowy room where fat Jack Moss (a non-actor who worked on the Mercury staff) winds up a Victrola and puts a record on it; as he carefully combs his hair, a scratchy operatic recording plays, getting stuck and repeating itself. When Moss is finished with his hair, he picks up a Luger pistol, puts it in his coat, turns off the record, and exits. Then the film's title appears.

This was like nothing I had experienced before. There was also a scene in which a magician (Hans Conried) gets murdered on stage during one of his big tricks. I never wrote about the film, but I've always been fond of it. It's evidence of what the Mercury unit at RKO could do with modest productions—the wittiest, most political of Hollywood's Eric Ambler adaptations. Welles' stock company has fun with it.

My chance to see *Kane* came a bit later. I knew it had been picked by critics as the best film ever made and I discovered that a re-release print was being shown at a

*Journey Into Fear*

theater in Beaumont, Texas, only about twenty-five miles from Sulphur. I don't recall how I got there—it may have been with a friend who had a car. I felt like a Catholic going to the Vatican. I expected to be completely overwhelmed, but to tell the truth I wasn't. I didn't dislike the film, but I didn't fully understand or appreciate it.

*What television shows did you watch back then? Did you ever see any other significant feature films for the first time on TV?*

I saw bits of two other Welles pictures—*The Lady from Shanghai* (1947) and *Macbeth* (1948). In those years TV wasn't as laden with movies as it is today, although beginning in the 1960s it acquired lots of old films and became the chief way for me and many others to learn about movies of the past. I don't remember much of what I saw on TV in the 1950s. I was much more a movie lover and book reader, but I recall being impressed by the first seasons of Jack Webb's *Dragnet* (1951–59) (later seasons were disappointing). That show began on radio, where it was excellent, partly because of Webb's voice and the documentary-like sound effects (when the cops ate lunch, you could hear them unwrapping the paper from sandwiches). The TV version was initially done almost entirely in closeups, maybe because of small TV screens, and was formally intriguing. Webb was an auteur. I admired most of his subsequent movies, especially *Pete Kelly's Blues* (1955). On TV I recall a couple of *Playhouse 90* dramas (one of them live) directed by the young John

Frankenheimer. I also liked a Sunday show called *Omnibus*, Edward R. Murrow's *Person to Person*, Sid Caesar's *Your Show of Shows*, and CBS' *You Are There*. The Army-McCarthy hearings were riveting. And of course I was a great admirer of *Alfred Hitchcock Presents*.

## Film Style in the 1950s

*The 1950s were a period of changes in theatrical movies— the age of CinemaScope and 3-D. Were any of those things important for you?*

Not at first. But looking back at it, the period was distinctive. Movies are obviously dependent on technology, and changes in technology always lead to changes in film style. Where the 1950s were concerned, Hollywood began to compete with TV by using wide screens, stereophonic sound, and 3-D. The first CinemaScope picture I saw was *King of the Khyber Rifles* (1953), a bad Tyrone Power vehicle. In shots of two characters talking, the actors were positioned at either side of the screen, and their voices came from left and right speakers. I thought this was lame. The first 3-D I saw was André de Toth's *House of Wax* (1953), which has fun emergent moments (moments when something jumps out at you and seems to break through the screen into the audience). That film is good even when exhibited flat. The best of the low-budget 3-Ds was underrated director Jack Arnold's *Creature from the Black Lagoon* (1954), not only because of Julie Adams in a swimsuit but also because underwater photography in 3-D really looks like three dimensions. Hitchcock's *Dial M for Murder* (1954) was the best of them all but wasn't exhibited that way because the audience for 3-D fell off pretty quickly. That film is very much worth seeing in 3-D.

In the long run, the most important new technology was widescreen, which changed the art of staging. There were fewer shot-reverse shots and directors had a broader area to block characters in the longer takes. The industry shifted almost completely to color, and photographers needed to find new ways of creating dramatic plays of light and shadow. Some directors—especially Minnelli and Sirk—were excellent with widescreen, and Russell Metty was a great photographer of shadows in color movies.

The French praised CinemaScope on the same grounds that Bazin had praised depth of field, but for its greater width rather than its depth of field. Several early films of the Nouvelle Vague, such as *The 400 Blows* (1959), were shot in a French version of widescreen and in black and white, a format I like very much. It's a rare format today, but see the Netflix series *Ripley* (2024), which is beautifully shot in a fairly wide black and white.

*Creature from the Black Lagoon*

*I'm intrigued by the divergent responses to the new widescreen formats by filmmakers during that decade: Orson Welles preferred Academy ratio (1:37:1) and wrote a famous takedown of CinemaScope and VistaVision ("Ribbon of Dreams"), yet many of his films seem bigger— wider—than they are; whereas Budd Boetticher (with DP Charles Lawton Jr.) lovingly shot* Ride Lonesome *(1959) and* Comanche Station *(1960) in CinemaScope, yet those films feel as claustrophobic as his earlier Ranown pictures. Do you have a preference in aspect ratios?*

Several of the older directors disliked Scope. I think it was Hawks or maybe Lang who said it was only good for shooting extra-long snakes and funeral processions. But Welles' *Immortal Story* (1968) was 1:66:1 and it still looks like a Welles picture. All his films look wide because he favored the wide-angle lens (and hated telephoto). Where Boetticher is concerned, I guess one reason *Comanche Station* seems claustrophobic to you is that even though it's shot in the open spaces, the action takes place in and around the station. Anthony Mann's *The Man from Laramie* (1955), a CinemaScope Western with James Stewart, was better at landscape.

As for me, I have a special fondness for the short-lived VistaVision, initiated at Paramount. This was 35mm film run horizontally through a camera gate; it had a 1:5:1 ratio and an image with an eight-sprocket width. When it was converted for use in regular movie theater projectors, it resulted in much sharper resolution than other formats. Hitchcock used it in the 1950s and Ford used it for *The Searchers* (1956). The last complete film to use it in the studio era was Marlon Brando's *One-Eyed Jacks* (1961), which is a movie I love. In 2024, however, it was revived for Brady Corbet's epic *The Brutalist*. I mostly enjoyed that film, but there were only a few scenes that seemed to me to have the effect of the old VistaVision. Maybe that was because it was digitally projected, like all films today. I was struck, though, with the mobility of the modern VistaVision camera. There are moments in *The Brutalist* when the camera looks hand-held, and there's a scene when the camera rapidly follows a character up two flights of stairs and back down again.

*Touch of Evil*

*Did Welles shoot* Touch of Evil *in 1:85:1? I have a vague recollection of some controversy about that, possibly when the 1998 restoration came out and I saw it for the first time in a theater, where I was blown away, in whatever aspect ratio it was.*

I imagine this will always be a controversy. I first saw it when it was originally released, and my recollection, which might be wrong, is that it was 1:37:1. That print is now known as the "theatrical" version. But a second, "prevue" version in 1:85:1 was later discovered. That was the ratio all Universal pictures had begun to use. The restoration of *Touch of Evil* is widescreen, as are most of the DVD/Blu-ray releases. Jonathan Rosenbaum and I did a commentary on a two-disc set that shows both the theatrical and prevue versions. I'm not sure how the original picture was shot, but Universal probably wanted Russell Metty to do it widescreen.

## Reading, Writing, and Filmmaking

*You've talked about reading books about movies and magic, but when did you first develop an interest in literature as a personal enthusiasm or academic endeavor?*

I've long enjoyed reading and my first encounters with important literature were outside the classroom when I was a junior or senior in high school. I had a part-time job as janitor in Sulphur's public library and learned a lot from dusting the books. (On my breaks, I hung out in the storage room, where I found piles of old *Time* magazines; the *Time* movie reviews—a few of them probably old enough to have been written by James Agee—were a godsend.) I also knew a lady who ran a small bookstore in Lake Charles and I liked talking with her about writers.

By the time I went to college I had read a fair amount of modern literature, including Faulkner's *The Sound and the Fury*, Joyce's *Portrait of the Artist*, stories by Kafka and Flannery O'Connor, and Eliot's *The Love Song of J. Alfred Prufrock*, which I only dimly understood. But non-canonical writings were especially important. In a rack of bus station paperbacks, I discovered Raymond Chandler's *The Simple Art of Murder* and fell in love with his style. And because of an interview with Ben Hecht that I saw on TV, I got a copy of his autobiography, *A Child of the Century*, which made a huge impact. I was swept away by the romance of Hecht's life as a Chicago newspaper reporter and Hollywood screenwriter—a life I fantasized about having. I read his and Charles MacArthur's wonderfully funny plays, *The Front Page*, *Twentieth Century*, and *Boy Meets Girl*, and because Hecht admired H. L. Mencken, I read him as well. Mencken was in some ways a conservative—he hated FDR—but he was a devastating critic of the Bible Belt, racism, and the booboisie. I had been raised a devout Baptist, and partly because of him I lost my remaining bit of religion.

During high school, my father got me a small typewriter and I tried writing fiction. *The Atlantic Monthly* had a feature devoted to first stories, and I sent something to them which was promptly rejected—it was probably awful and I can't remember the subject. I also wrote a couple of stories for the pulps, noir things with lots of cigarette smoking.

These, too, were rejected, but one of them had been read in its entirety: the misspelled words were corrected.

*Was there any way in those days to learn filmmaking?*

No, but I actually made part of a film! I don't recall how I got my hands on an 8mm home movie camera. Maybe my father won it in a bingo game. I had recently seen Alexander Mackendrick's excellent *The Ladykillers* (1955) and at the library's collection of records I heard Stravinsky's *The Firebird Suite*. For some reason these two things prompted me to experiment with the camera. I tried making a heist picture, though I never had time or resources to finish it. I bought several rolls of Tri-X black and white film, which was fast, cheap, and could be used in interiors with available light. With three friends as actors, I went before dawn to the empty streets of Lake Charles and shot the scenes of the heist (a smash-and-grab involving a briefcase). The results were noirish and moody—someone descending a dimly lit staircase, a hotel lobby, a barren street just at dawn, an escape in a car—and I was quite pleased. Somewhere I got a primitive editing setup that required glueing splices with a tiny brush. I projected the edited scene with background music from the recording of *The Firebird*, which worked well. It was only about five minutes long and I never had the time or the ideas to finish it. In my later travels I lost what I had shot. It probably wasn't as interesting as I recall, but I wish I had it as a memento.

*So do I! How old were you when you made it—14, 15? Welles was the ripe old age of 19 when he made* The Hearts of Age.

I think I was 16 or 17. But it was only a few minutes long and didn't have Welles' production values.

## Public Speaking

*Given that you were without a family, how did you manage to attend college? Did you have a strong academic record in high school?*

I was a lazy student with no aptitude for mathematics and no talent as an athlete. I liked reading and English courses, but what saved me was that I had a gift for public speaking. In some ways this was strange. Maybe because I was a semi-orphan, I'm shy in social gatherings and at a loss with small talk. But in front of a crowd I'm a lot better. When I was a junior in high school, I was in a debate club that travelled to a state tournament, where to my surprise I won a bunch of trophies: best debate team, best impromptu speaker, best first-year debater, etc. After that, my Speech and Civics teacher, Ms. Turner (she and her husband gave me a home for a year), entered me in contests I also won.

I'll always remember being in a speech tournament for young people sponsored by The Optimist Club, a businessman's outfit like the Rotary or Shriners. The finals were in Houston, Texas, and I won. Afterward, I was standing alone in an empty meeting room in the Shamrock Hotel, holding my trophy. An elderly Black janitor came in to do cleaning. "What went on here?" he asked. "It was the Optimist Club," I said. He looked at me and asked, "How old are you?" "Seventeen," I said. His response was, "You're seventeen and you're still an optimist?"

In my senior year I entered a nationwide oratorical contest sponsored by the American Legion, in which high school students gave speeches they had written about the U.S. Constitution, followed by short impromptu speeches about some part of the Constitution—Article IV, for instance. The impromptu topics were drawn randomly from a bowl of slips of paper. I won the State contest and was sent to the regionals in Ashville, South Carolina, which I also won. Then they put me on a train in Ashville and sent me to the national finals. I had never traveled farther than Alabama and Texas, and now I was on a cross-country train journey to Lodi, California, a relatively small town named after a racehorse, with a stopover in Chicago for most of one day to change trains. (While in Chicago I went to a movie: *Some Like it Hot* [1959].)

In Lodi, I won second place and was awarded $1,500. (Probably worth eight or ten times that amount in today's money.) I've sometimes joked that I missed getting first place because I quoted Adlai Stevenson in my speech to a bunch of Republican legionnaires. But that contest also gave me a good knowledge of the U.S. Constitution, something that isn't taught in this country's schools and ought to be.

As the national runner-up, I became a celebrity back in Lake Charles. My new speech teacher was flown to California to collect me, and she took me to San Francisco for a few days. I wanted to stay there forever. In addition to seeing the sights, I went to a bookstore and discovered *Agee on Film*, which, along with *Let Us Now Praise Famous Men*, is among my treasured possessions. When I returned home, my arrival was pictured on the front page of the Lake

*Some Like It Hot*

Charles newspaper, and well-to-do businessmen came up to me at public events and gave me checks to use at college. Governor Earl Long (Huey's brother) sent me a signed proclamation appointing me an honorary Colonel of the State of Louisiana.

Nobody in my family had ever gone to college. In my dreams I imagined going to some place like UCLA where I could learn to make movies, but there was no chance of that. Fortunately, Louisiana State University had low fees and admitted anyone who had graduated from a state high school. With the money from the contest, the various checks, and a variety of summer jobs, I was able to attend LSU.

*This topic—public speaking—gives me an opening to ask a question I've long wanted to: when did you lose your Southern accent? My great-uncle was a thick-accented Cajun from N'awlins (New Orleans), so I have a regional curiosity. When we first met, I assumed you were from the East Coast.*

Interesting. Like many people from Louisiana, I call it "New Orlins, Loosiana." In my recollection, south Louisiana doesn't have a deep southern drawl and the Cajun accent is unique. Some people in the environs of New Orleans sound a bit like Brooklyn. But I've always spoken with a pretty clear enunciation and when I was a teenager I consciously tried not to sound southern. My models were people I heard in radio, TV, and movies. I was (and am) a Frank Sinatra fan and liked his accent, though I never tried to imitate it. The patter I used as a magician often involved jokes, which have their own kind of inflections and accents. I'm told that I have vestiges of a southern accent—when I say "school," for instance, it sounds like "skool." I suppose I aspired to a higher social status.

# EDUCATION
# AND PROFESSIONAL LIFE

## A College Mentor

*Talk a bit about your experience at LSU. How did you settle on a major?*

When I arrived, I thought I would major in journalism and emulate Ben Hecht. The editor of the Lake Charles newspaper told me that studying journalism was unimportant, and when I took a course on the subject I agreed. What changed me permanently was freshman English. LSU had a test for placement in the required first-year composition classes. Depending on your score, you were assigned English A, B, or C. I ended up in B, which meant I would need an extra semester of composition. I must have had chutzpah, because I went to the professor's office and told him I didn't belong in B. Naturally he ignored me, and it was a good thing. He turned out to be the most influential person in my life.

Because no one in my family had gone to college, I thought of professors as old people with gray beards. My English teacher was Professor Bernard Benstock (eventually he told me to call him Bernie), a young New Yorker who had worked with *Stars and Stripes* in the Korean War. A conservatively dapper dresser, he smoked Gauloises and in one meeting of the class showed slides of his recent trip to Paris. The minute I saw him at work I knew I had found a vocation. I wanted to be like him and he became a surrogate father.

The first assignment Bernie gave the class was to write a short essay on your favorite aesthetic experience. I suspect some of the students had never heard the word "aesthetic." Of course I wrote about the movies, describing the beat-up Majestic Theater in Lake Charles, where I claimed to have seen re-releases of such classics as *The Public Enemy* (1931) and *King Kong* (1933). This wasn't quite true but it was true to the spirit. I got an A+ and my essay was published in the student newspaper. Bernie kept me in the class, saw to it that I wouldn't have to take a second composition course, and placed me in honors English. A few years later, when Jack Kennedy was assassinated, he came to my apartment and took me out for a drink. He knew I needed one. I had seen frat boys in Baton Rouge smirking at the assassination.

Bernie's Ph.D. dissertation on *Finnegans Wake* was published as a book, and he was especially interested in modern Irish literature. He also knew things about movies; he could quote the speed-limit conversation in *Double Indemnity* (1944) and the acid lines ("The cat's in the bag and the bag's in the river.") in *Sweet Smell of Success* (1957). I took several courses with him, including one on *Ulysses*, which for me is the greatest novel ever written. Because of Bernie, some of my early academic publications were about Joyce. He was very active in establishing *The James Joyce Quarterly* and in helping to organize international symposia on Joyce. In the seventies, as a young academic, I went to the ones in Dublin and Paris.

Bernie died unexpectedly in 1994, when he and his wife Shari were teaching at the University of Miami. He was writing a book about Dashiell Hammett and Lillian Hellman. It was a great loss.

## Graduate School

*What was your plan for graduate school?*

I was planning to attend grad school at Cornell, where I had a Woodrow Wilson fellowship, but my then wife and I discovered that she was pregnant. I now have a talented son who writes novels under the name of Jim (which sometimes causes confusion), and two grandsons, Alexander and Patrick, who work in film production—Alex in Chicago and Patrick in New York. We stayed an extra year at LSU, where I got an M.A., and then applied to the University of Wisconsin, where teaching assistants were fairly well paid. I was admitted in English, and she was admitted in Sociolinguistics.

But immediately before moving to Madison, I had an important educational experience. I got a summer fellowship from an organization called The English-Speaking Union, enabling me to attend a six-week course at the University of London for foreign speakers of English. This was a dazzling event. The students were grouped into seminars related to their interests and were assembled en masse to attend lectures. I saw and heard many distinguished English academics and literary stars. (Ted Hughes gave a reading of Philip Larkin's poetry.) I got to know London and went to the theater—in those days, balcony seats were cheap, and I saw a new Harold Pinter play. Also saw a couple of movies: *A Hard Day's Night* and *Marnie* (both 1964).

*Did you enjoy Madison?*

*A Hard Day's Night*

Very much. I'm still nostalgic for the cultural and political life of that campus in the late 1960s. When I arrived, I got a postcard from Bernie saying, "Welcome North." I was happy to see a statue of Lincoln outside the English Department but fearful of the northern winter, which I soon learned to enjoy.

The English Department had an old-style, *Beowulf* to Virgina Woolf curriculum and a terrifying Ph.D. final exam consisting of five four-hour writing sessions on five different literary periods. You couldn't have notes and were told to use pencils. You had no idea what questions would be asked, though they allowed you to see questions from previous exams. I still remember one of those questions, which consisted of six quotations from poems about sailboats and asked you to identify and comment on them. When I saw that I thought I could never pass. I spent every spare hour in the library doing extra reading.

The excitement of Madison was largely due to the extra-curricular environment. There was a lively film culture with a couple of film societies. Joseph McBride and Michael Wilmington wrote for the local papers. (I never got to meet them while I was there because I was so busy studying for the dreaded exams.) The university acquired a mammoth archive of 16mm films from Warner Bros., and grad students in the Communication Department established *The Velvet Light Trap*, which published major scholarship on the history of that studio.

*Did you see many movies in Madison?*

Not as many as I would have liked. I remember seeing Michelangelo Antonioni's *Blow-Up* (1966), and I was especially impressed with Sidney Furie's *The Ipcress File*

(1966), an anti-James Bond picture starring Michael Caine as a rebellious spy who wears glasses and seduces a woman by cooking her a dinner. That movie has remained a favorite of mine. I've watched it several times.

*The Ipcress File*

At one of the Madison film societies, I remember seeing Mario Monicelli's *Big Deal on Madonna Street* (1958), an amusing comedy about inept criminals, which has an all-star cast. I also saw Roman Polanski's *Knife in the Water* (1962). At the campus bookstore, I found Andrew Sarris' *The American Cinema*. My old, dog-eared copy of Sarris from those days is filled with notes indicating where I disagreed with his opinions, but he was enormously influential. In Madison there was also a daring off-campus theater, most of it directed by Stuart Gordon, who later had a brief career as a movie director. Besides all this, there was intensive anti-Vietnam War activity (a documentary movie was made about it, called *The War at Home* [1979]) and successful organizing for a graduate student union.

*Maybe this would be a good place to discuss politics, a prominent topic through much of your work. You had mentioned earlier watching the Army-McCarthy hearings on TV. Were you interested in politics then, or did your interest evolve at Madison?*

I've long been an instinctive lefty and would describe my politics as Social Democratic. Given my background, I don't know where my politics came from. I loved my father but had he lived longer I would probably have reached the point of not talking to him—he was against unions and a typical southern racist. But I didn't participate in protests until I got to Madison and have never been a political organizer. During my brief time as a grad student at LSU, before going to Madison, the university was integrated, and

I remember that in a composition course I taught the Black students chose to sit in the back row. I didn't stop them because I was reluctant to call attention to them by moving their group to the front.

My writings are primarily about art, but I gradually learned, beginning with my book on Welles, that art has a political dimension, just as everything else does. The cultural studies movement, plus Horkheimer, Adorno, Benjamin and all the usual suspects, had an influence on an anthology I did with my colleague Patrick Brantlinger (*Modernity and Mass Culture* [1991]) and on my book about Minnelli. My film noir book has a good deal to say about politics. Almost everything I've done has been affected to some degree by political life in America: the Civil Rights movement, the assassinations of the Kennedys and Martin Luther King Jr., Vietnam, the rise of feminism, and all the post-1968 events in society and film culture. I never anticipated the horror of Donald Trump, but I've always thought the country is about fifty percent fascist and susceptible to show-business politicians. Now that he's been elected a second time, I'm deeply alienated from my country and reminded of a remark by H. L. Menken: "American democracy is based on the idea that the people know what they want, and they're going to get it good and hard." If I weren't so old, I would probably try moving permanently to Britain or Portugal.

Unfortunately, the Vietnam protests at Madison culminated in violence from a bomb planted in a campus building, which, to say the least, was counterproductive. But Vietnam protests lasted throughout the war and affected university life everywhere. Bernie Benstock had just moved from LSU to Kent State, where the National Guard shot and killed four students. Soon after, he moved to the University of Illinois. I think you were at Kent at some point. You wrote a book about the protests.

*I was born in 1970, when the shootings occurred, but worked at Kent State from 2004–10, and my work on the Kent State Shootings Oral History Project led to a co-authored book on the subject in 2016* (Above the Shots: An Oral History of the Kent State Shootings). *This was before I met your wife, Darlene Sadlier, who was a student at KSU in 1970. I would have loved to have interviewed her.*

We should explain that Darlene is my second wife. My first marriage ended in a divorce in 1977. I was adrift and subject to depression for a few years, taught for a year in Germany on a foreign exchange program, and eventually met Darlene. She and I married in 1984. Now retired, she's Professor Emerita of Spanish and Portuguese, and was at one point chair of her department at Indiana. She's written very widely about the culture, literature, and film of Portugal and Brazil—most recently, an ambitious history of Brazilian documentary film. She's also the love of my life.

## Early Academic Publication

*What was your early experience as a professional academic?*

In 1970 I got my Ph.D. and was hired by the English Department at Indiana. Apart from occasional visiting professor gigs at the University of Hamburg in Germany, the University of Chicago, the Art Institute of Chicago, and UCLA, I've been at Indiana ever since. When I was hired at Indiana, they told me that they didn't pay as much as other Big Ten schools, but that they had great retirement benefits. I couldn't have cared less about retirement, but I ultimately realized that what they told me was true. If you retired at sixty-five, you were set. It was almost like golden handcuffs in the corporate world, making it somewhat difficult to leave. But even without a good retirement package or a big salary, tenured academia is one of the best of all possible jobs. I had enough laboring jobs to know that.

*What was your first impression of Bloomington?*

A fellow once asked me, and I said it was a bit like being in the South with fewer Black people. "Oh," he said, "the worst of all possible worlds." Bloomington was a much smaller town in those days, but it had a major state university with a fine English Department and five movie theaters. To get a sense of what the town was like, I would recommend Peter Yates' *Breaking Away* (1979), which was shot here a few years after I arrived. It's a charming movie about bike racing and town/gown relations (there's an annual bike race on campus called the Little 500). I used to show it in my classes, partly because it illustrates what Pudovkin called cinematic geography. Sometimes a character can be seen going down a street and turning right. When the film cuts to that street on the right the continuity is exact and the character seems to be continuing on the walk, but any Bloomington resident would realize we're in a different part of town.

Another way of getting a sense of Bloomington in the Seventies is to read the distinguished Indonesian writer Budi

Darma's *People from Bloomington*, a translation of which
has been published by Penguin Modern Classics. Darma got
a Ph.D. in English from Indiana, writing his thesis on Jane
Austen. His book of stories could only have been written
by a foreign student who was lonely and very observant
of the local weirdness; it's superb collection, maybe not as
good as Joyce's *Dubliners*, but far better than Sherwood
Anderson's *Winesburg, Ohio*. Even if you have no interest
in Bloomington, I would recommend both Peter Yates'
movie and Budi Darma's book for their intrinsic merits.

*Breaking Away*

I was hired as an expert in modern British literature
and knew that publishing would be a key to tenure.
(Besides, I liked to write.) My teaching in the early years
was on a variety of literary subjects at both undergraduate
and graduate levels. Because I now had a middle-class
income, I very briefly imagined that in my spare time I
would be able to make a 16mm movie. I wanted to loosely
adapt a Renaissance drama called *Arden of Feversham*,
generally attributed to Thomas Kyd but possibly also by
Shakespeare. It's a proto-noir crime story. Instead of doing
it in period, I thought it could be set in impoverished,
small-town, southern Indiana, but without verse dialogue
and maybe with a different title. My idea was to shoot it
neorealist style, with amateur actors and hand-held black
and white photography. I still think it would make a good
movie, but it was absurd to think I could manage it. I didn't
have enough technical knowledge of sound or editing, not
enough money, and no contact with the movie industry,
Besides, I needed to work at my job. My Ph.D. dissertation
was on Virginia Woolf, and within a couple of years I was
able to revise it for publication as a book called *The World
Without a Self*.

*Can you say a bit about that book? Does it have anything in common with your later writing on film?*

Most of my writing on film has a literary bent or shows literary training—I guess I could be called a literary intellectual. But the Virginia Woolf volume has only an indirect relationship to my things on film. It came about because one of my college teachers at LSU introduced me to a great book of literary criticism, Erich Auerbach's *Mimesis*. Auerbach covered the entire history of western literature, and his method was to quote a page or so from a well-known work, which he closely analyzed in terms of what he called historical changes in "the representation of reality." In graduate school I thought I might write a thesis applying a similar technique to James Joyce, but with a slightly different aim. I wanted to explain what was unique in Joyce's style, starting with close analysis of some pages. But I immediately realized that one of the things that makes him unique is that he has no single style. For a while I thought I might write on Joyce and Jonathan Swift, two Irishmen who have interesting things in common. I was interested in both modernism and 18th-century literature, and that made the topic appealing to me. But because of a seminar I took on Virginia Woolf (about whom Auerbach had written) my interest shifted to her. I tried to show what makes her unusual style not only distinctive but also expressive of her psychology and deep-seated thematic aims.

The title of the book is derived from a question raised by Woolf: "How describe the world without a self?" I was chiefly interested in the method of narration in her mature work, which constantly makes the reader ask a question raised by Auerbach: "Who is speaking?" She finds ways of giving her novels a watery feel, as if characters and narrator, inner and outer worlds are blended together. As a writer, she seems to have felt a need to escape the egos of a narrator and characters and have all life flow together. This aspect of her work has been linked by scholars to the time/space theories of Henri Bergson, but I don't think he was an influence. The important thing to emphasize is that Woolf's special aim was very different from early male modernists like Paul Valéry, T. E. Hulme, Wyndham Lewis, Ezra Pound, T. S. Eliot, and Ernest Hemingway, all of whom wanted a style that was precise, objective, and clear edged. She wanted to connect things, not separate them.

Little did I realize that, to use a Woolfian metaphor, the waves were about to hit the beach. There was rising interest in Woolf. My book was well reviewed and even got favorable mentions in places like *The Village Voice* and *Harper's*. I think the most important parts were the opening chapter analyzing a page or so from Woolf's first novel, and a later chapter explaining why, contrary to what most people thought, she wasn't a writer of stream-of-consciousness fiction. My major regret about the book is that I kept referring to "Mrs. Woolf." Nobody ever wrote "Mr. Hemingway."

If this book has a relation to my writing on film, it's because of my interest in close reading and style as meaning. In the chapter of my Welles book called "The Magician," I was trying to do more or less what I had done with Woolf—I picked a single scene from *Kane* (the boarding house sequence) and wrote a detailed description and commentary on the deep focus, the long take, the blocking of four actors, the pace of the dialogue, the single cut, etc. Then I used it as a springboard for other scenes, trying to show psychological/ideological implications of the style.

*Citizen Kane*

*How did you manage to become a writer on film, given that you were a professor in a literature department?*

Harry M. Geduld had established a nascent film studies program in Indiana's Comparative Literature department, and one of my colleagues in English was Charles Eckert, a brilliant writer of what became classic articles on film. Charlie and I were friends and discussed movies almost daily. I had just read Noël Burch's *Theory of Film Practice*, from which I learned a great deal, but Charlie was just as influential to my education. He was interested in the conjuncture of movies, politics, and money, and he wrote remarkable essays on those topics, among them "Shirley Temple and the House of Morgan" and "The Carole Lombard in Macy's Window." He died when he was at work on a book about the relation between Hollywood and Wall Street during the depression. It was another great loss.

Because I had a minor in Comparative Literature from Wisconsin, the English Department occasionally loaned me out to Comp Lit so I could teach film. My first course was on Welles and Hitchcock, who make a fascinating comparison and contrast. I continued to teach and publish on literature (articles on Woolf, the Imagist poets, Philip Larkin, and Dashiell Hammett) but I also began publishing essays on film (Huston and Welles). I was planning a book on contemporary British poetry, centered on what was once called the "Movement" poets of the 1950s. But everything changed when Harry Geduld and Ronald Gottesman offered me the chance to write a small book on *Psycho* for the *Filmguide* series they had established at Indiana University Press. After that, I concentrated almost completely on film criticism and scholarship.

# WRITINGS ON FILM

## *Psycho*

*Let's talk about your* Filmguide to Psycho *(1973), which I believe was your first monograph on a cinematic subject. What interested you in writing about that film, as opposed to other works by Hitchcock?*

The choice of film and the format of the book were determined by editors Harry Geduld and Ron Gottesman. I was pleased by the opportunity to write about *Psycho* (1960), a daring, influential, and important picture, easily one of Hitchcock's best. It's initial critical reception in the U.S. was qualified, but by 1970 there was great interest in it.

*On your website, you describe the* Psycho *book as "juvenilia." I think it's more than that, but I'm curious what you would do differently if you wrote or revised it today?*

For one thing, I would spell screenwriter Joseph Stefano's name correctly. I met him once and he informed me in a slightly unfriendly way that I had misspelled it throughout the book. (He also told a wonderful story. When he outlined his ideas for the screenplay during a story conference with Hitchcock, Hitch leaned back in his chair, smiled, and said, "We could kill the star!")

Maybe that mistake accounts for what I said on the website. There are other small mistakes I made because nobody knew differently. For example, I accepted Hitchcock's claim that he never looked through the camera. Many years later, Darlene and I had a pied-à-terre in Chicago, just up the street from the Ambassador East hotel, where scenes from *North by Northwest* were shot. That hotel had the best collection of movie star photos I've seen outside Hollywood, chiefly because its restaurant, the Pump Room, was once a stopping place for celebrities travelling between New York and L.A. One of the photos was taken in an alley across from the hotel, where Hitchcock and Robert Burks were lining up a shot of the entrance. The camera was at ground level, and Hitchcock was lying flat on his fat belly looking through the lens. When the hotel changed management and this photo was removed, I went to the manager and asked if there was any way it could be found so that I could buy it. He didn't know where it was.

Nevertheless, there are things about the *Psycho* book that I think are good. The introductory chapter, "Alfred Hitchcock and the Aesthetics of Repression," makes an argument that I wouldn't change much, and I think the scene-by-scene analysis still works because it was done with great care. In those pre-digital days, I had a rewind table with a ground-glass magnifier that enabled me to view silently every shot of a 16mm print. When I first began working with *Psycho*, I feared I was going to have bad dreams; the film had terrified me in the theater, but my fears went away as I studied it. I believe my description of its inner workings remains an accurate piece of close reading. If I had to do it all over, though, I'm sure I would add or change things, especially in the concluding summary.

*Toward the end, you express doubts about whether the psychiatrist's climactic explanation for Norman's condition is Hitchcock's idea of a (sick) joke, which is a popular interpretation. Do you still harbor those doubts?*

There may be sick jokes in *Psycho*, but this isn't one. My first viewing of the film was in its original release, in a large theater that was completely packed. It was such a carnavalistic and frightening experience (equaled only by the theater audience's reaction when I saw the opening run of *Jaws* [1975]), that the psychiatrist's explanation could barely be heard; people were talking nervously among themselves, trying to recover. When the shrink commented on cross-dressing, there were giggles, but I don't think Hitchcock meant the sequence to be amusing. He needed to give the audience information and do something to calm things down before the big ending. He claimed that he shot it in an offhand way. It's conventionally acted and directed, but it isn't a bad theory of Norman's psyche—it blames him as much as his mother.

*Seeing* Psycho *at IU Cinema ten years ago or so was an interesting experience. I had watched it many times before, but that was my first time with an audience. When Marion Crane got killed, nobody in the theater responded. It was as if they were expecting it, and they probably were, even if they'd never seen it before. But when Arbogast got stabbed at the top of the staircase, everyone jumped out of their seats. I bring this up because their reaction reinforces your description of Hitchcock's intent behind the "dreamlike" quality (enhanced by back projection) of Arbogast ascending and then plummeting violently back down the stairs, which emphasizes (again in your words) "the innocence, vulnerability, and complacency of a victim." Arbogast, like Marion, is a victim, but one who is very smart and resourceful. They get themselves killed because a madness like Norman's is beyond their comprehension.*

And because Norman, who is creepy, doesn't seem a killer at first, even to us. Both deaths obviously depend on Hitchcock's talent for shifting between suspense and surprise. (Also on his fondness for POV shots, which both scenes use.) The shower sequence is the most powerful surprise in cinema, although there's a sort of premonition of it in Val Lewton's *The Seventh Victim* (1943); it comes out of a relatively placid environment, preceded only by Norman's sneaky voyeurism and that strange house on the hill behind the motel. For viewers who don't know it's coming, it's frighteningly violent, protracted, and traumatic (also formally brilliant). I think the death of Arbogast is less surprising because it occurs in a haunted house atmosphere and has the buildup of a conventionally suspenseful walk up a stairway. But I expect you're right that the audience at that screening reacted to a cleverly designed jump scare. There was quietness building up to the sudden attack, and they hadn't heard about the scene in advance.

*Psycho*

*"Remaking* Psycho*," your article in* The Hitchcock Annual *about Gus Van Sant's 1998 version (which claimed to be a shot-by-shot remake but really wasn't), addresses the subject of viewer expectations: how, for you, it wasn't scary at all, unlike Hitchcock's original. You emphasize that the remake isn't a good movie, but is it accurate to say that you find it fascinating in an academic way?*

You've made me go back and reread that short essay, which I find is better than I remember. When I wrote it, I was interested in the theoretical issue of "original" versus "copy," especially in relation to adaptation and its close cousin, the remake. I have nothing against either. Hitchcock himself did a remake of *The Man Who Knew Too Mutch*

(1956) and wanted to remake *The Lodger* (1926). A great recent example of a director remaking one of his own movies is Olivier Assayas' *Irma Vep*, which was a feature film in 1996 and redone as a TV mini-series in 2022. I much prefer the remake, which is longer than the feature, makes better use of the Feuillade material, and stars Alicia Vikander, who is a knockout as a dancer.

There's no movie or piece of writing that isn't related in at least small ways to previous movies or writings. But even though Van Sant is a fine director, his remake is a failed experiment. The casting is weird—Vince Vaughn? Maybe it wasn't intended as a remake, but I can't figure out its purpose or why one should do it at all. *Psycho* and some other movies—*Duck Soup* (1933), for example—can never be satisfactorily remade. For anyone who knows the original *Psycho* (and who doesn't?) the surprise and suspense will be diluted. Formally, it can't be surpassed. A critic can perhaps make interesting comparisons with the original—color vs. black and white, different production design, etc.—which I tried to do in the essay. But in this case, even if they're formally relevant, they don't seem especially important. Van Sant's re-doing of scenes from Welles' *Chimes at Midnight* (1965) in *My Own Private Idaho* (1991) is more interesting.

*Roger Ebert wondered why nobody ever remade a bad movie to make a better one; in other words, that remaking a classic is doomed to failure. I suspect it was a rhetorical question, but any thoughts on that?*

As usual, I agree with Ebert, although I'm not sure remaking a classic, especially if the same director does both films, is doomed to failure. (The remakes of *King Kong* aren't bad, just not as good as the original.) It would be exciting if somebody remade a bad movie and turned it into a good one, but I can't think of an example. There are cases, such as the example of *Irma Vep*, where I think a remake is better than the original. Thorold Dickinson's *Gaslight* (1940) is a very good adaptation of a play, but for me George Cukor's *Gaslight* (1944) is better. One could argue about which version of *Dr. Jekyll and Mr. Hyde*, *Robin Hood*, and *Zorro* is better, but I'm not sure whether these films should be dubbed remakes or retellings of popular stories.

## Orson Welles

*A few years later, you pivoted from Hitchcock to* The Magic World of Orson Welles *(1978), frequently cited as the best critical study on Welles. (It should be emphasized that you write critical studies, not biographies, although you very deftly weave biographical elements into your analyses.) What was the inspiration or motivation for writing that book?*

As I've said, I've long been fascinated by Welles. For me, he's the most important filmmaker, and the first film course I taught was on Welles and Hitchcock.

Despite the *Psycho* monograph, some of the faculty in English at Indiana advised me to keep writing about literature, but nobody objected when I soon moved almost entirely to film. My original idea was for a book called *Orson Welles in America*, but my publisher, Oxford, rightly insisted that I cover his entire career. My title for that version was *Bright Lucifer*, but Oxford changed it to *The Magic World of Orson Welles*, which to me sounds sappy. Though it was a critical study, the biographical element was essential, not only to explain Welles' career but also to show his background, politics, theatrical interests, and embattled relationship with Hollywood.

*On the other hand, the title does connect between subject and author an interest in magic, albeit the text makes it clear that the focus will be on how Welles created his effects, as well as the interpretation of those effects. I don't want to know how magicians pull off their tricks (I mean, I do, but I can live without it), but your book is an illuminating discussion of the context and process for the making of each movie, the tone neither dismissive nor blindly reverent. Was that approach a goal that you had while writing it, especially given the existing literature on Welles at the time?*

Sometimes explaining tricks enhances appreciation of the movie, and I don't think filmmakers are shy or reluctant to reveal how their tricks are done. *Kane* was full of tricks—animation, for example, depth of field created by imperceptibly combining two images, and black art set design. Welles made brilliant use of RKO's special effects artists, especially of Vernon Walker, who operated the studio's optical printer. (There are many shots using that device. Notice the screaming cockatoo, or Kane's subjective view of Susan leaving him.)

*Citizen Kane*

My chief goal, though, was a comprehensive critical study, and I was primarily interested in Welles' films as art. As I've said, I wanted to give his work the same fine-grained descriptive analysis of style I had tried to give Virginia Woolf. Of course literary and film style are different because film is more like *Gesamkuntswerk*. Besides language and narrative poetics you need to talk about film stock, camera lenses, sound technology, cutting, special effects, dramatic staging, music, performance, etc. Even a director as much in control as Welles needs help with many things—sets, for example, or music.

I showed how some tricks were done, but my aim was always to show Welles' thematic interests and the meanings, some of them probably unintended, suggested by his style. (In his case, a certain romanticized Gothicism or Byronic theatricality, in potential conflict with a leftist political critique inspired by the Popular Front.) This involved discussion not only of his politics but also of his specific handling of depth-of-field photography, long takes, sound, staging, performance, and all the rest. I was able to use frame enlargements as illustration, and this was a great help.

The existing literature on Welles (Joseph McBride's book was excellent) hadn't put as much detailed emphasis on these things. Robert Carringer's *The Making of* Citizen Kane came out on the heels of my book and also talked about style, but our aims were different; he wrote a production history of the movie, giving credit to everyone but Welles and omitting the extremely important research he had done on the Welles/Mankiewicz screenplay. (His later book on *Ambersons* is an essential reconstruction.)

As with the study of *Psycho*, I went through the films shot by shot and discovered things others hadn't mentioned. For example, nobody seemed to have realized that the house in the first shot of *Ambersons* isn't the Amberson mansion but a bourgeois home across the street from the Amberson property. (It's framed nostalgically, but it shows us that "progress," in the form of streets and transportation, is already happening.) And writers on *Touch of Evil* hadn't mentioned the point at which we hear the offscreen sound of the Mexican shoe-salesman Sanchez being beaten during a police interrogation. The only feature films I didn't discuss were *Journey into Fear*, *The Other Side of the Wind* (still in production) and the aborted *It's All True*, which was a door I didn't want to open. Thankfully, Catherine Benamou later gave it a definitive book-length treatment.

*Were the sections on Welles' largely unknown-at-the-time newspaper columns from your initial access to his papers, then under the stewardship of Richard Wilson, before the first edition, or were they added after the collection was acquired by IU's Lilly Library (a procurement in which you played a significant role)?*

The discussion of the newspaper columns was in the first edition of the book and they were virtually if not totally unknown. I did a lot of research for the book, but one of my major discoveries was due to a student of mine, Joanne Eustis, who found those columns on microfilm at the IU library. They were enormously important to my commentary on Welles' politics. He had been involved in the Popular Front in the 1930s and his theatrical work with the WPA (the Harlem *Macbeth*, *The Cradle Will Rock*) and then with his own Mercury company (*Julius Caesar*, *Native Son*) was strongly anti-fascist. *Citizen Kane* made him lots of enemies in Hollywood besides W. R. Hearst, and it grew directly out of his politics.

By 1945, the year he wrote the columns, Welles had become an activist, engaged at one time or another in such issues as the Sleepy Lagoon case, in which Mexican teenagers were falsely accused of rape and murder, and in the blinding of Black war veteran Isaac Woodard. He took lots of risks to his showbusiness career and considered entering politics himself. The newspaper columns were overtly political, deeply concerned with what he saw as a renascent American fascism under another name and the growth of American capitalist colonialism in Latin America. They have an indirect bearing on *The Stranger* (1946), which is about an ex-Nazi posing as teacher at a New England boys' school (similar to the Todd School in Illinois, where Welles was a student), and on *The Lady from Shanghai*, which involves a journey to Latin America by a corrupt lawyer and his retinue, who return to America and arrive in San Francisco, where the newly established United Nations had recently held its first meetings. That film covers some of the topics and geography Welles discussed in his columns, and it also has a moment when Welles, in the role of the sailor O'Hara, recalls an incident involving sharks in Fortaleza, Brazil, thus alluding to the lost *It's All True*, which RKO had sabotaged for political reasons.

Where the Lilly collection is concerned, as part of my research for the Welles book I travelled to Los Angeles and talked with Richard Wilson, a film director who had worked as an associate producer for Welles and who kept the Mercury Theater files stored in a large room adjacent to his home near Malibu. He was a friendly and helpful source who told me useful things, but he was cagey about showing the files. (The only specific request I made was to see the cutting continuity for the ending of *Ambersons*, and he demurred.) When the book was published I sent him a copy with a letter. I told him that if he were ever interested in selling the files to a university, he should try Indiana's Lilly Library, one of the best rare book libraries in the country, which I assured him was as secure as the Thatcher Memorial. To my surprise and delight, he liked my book and approached the Lilly, which purchased his collection. (I heard indirectly that Welles was unhappy about this. I had written him when I began work on the book, asking if there was any way I could see *Don Quixote*. He never replied and didn't reply when I sent him a copy of the book.)

I haven't written a great deal about Welles since my book, though I did two or three essays and took part in some commentaries for digital editions of *Mr. Arkadin*, *Kane*, *Ambersons*, and *Chimes at Midnight*. I wrote my book without benefit of the Mercury archive and found that when I revised it for later editions I didn't have much to add. As a result I haven't done much work in the Lilly collection, and I expect you know more about it. You were a librarian at the Lilly and wrote a fine essay on the highly successful Welles exhibition you mounted for the centennial celebration of his career ["Presenting Orson Welles: an Exhibition Challenge," in Gilmore and Gottlieb, eds., *Orson Welles in Focus* (Indiana University Press: 2018).]

*Thank you. I should point out to readers that there are multiple Welles-related collections at the Lilly—the Welles manuscripts being the largest and most significant, but also papers of Arnold Weissberger, Peter Bogdanovich, and George Fanto (Welles' DP—one of them—on* It's All True *and* Othello *[1951]), among others—that I included in the exhibition. I also featured a terrific letter from Charlton Heston to you, which came from your own papers at the Lilly. Would you like to talk about that letter?*

Sure. For a brief time I had a telephone answering machine in my English Department office. I arrived one morning shortly before I was due to teach a class and found the phone's light blinking. I punched the button. A woman's voice said Charlton Heston would like to speak with me, and gave me his number. My class was about to begin (I don't recall the topic), so I went down to the classroom and announced that we would have a shorter session than usual because Charlton Heston had called and wanted to talk with me on the phone. I never said anything more and I left the students properly in awe. Burning with curiosity, I returned to my office and called. Heston's secretary answered, explaining that he was in a conference and would write me a letter. (This of course was before the days of email.) Not long after I got a charming letter from him, opening with an allusion to Lord Chesterfield: "I would have written shorter had I more time." He had read my book and wanted to correct what he thought were errors in the chapter on *Touch of Evil.*

Heston was justly proud of getting Welles a job as the director, something he mentioned in many interviews, but in my book I somewhat complicated his story by pointing out that the film's producer, Albert Zugsmith, who had recently cast Welles in *Man in the Shadow* (1957), claimed that he and Welles got drunk over a bottle of vodka and Welles offered to direct the "worst" script Zugsmith had to offer. Maybe both accounts are true, but Heston certainly deserves the major credit—as the star, he had more influence than anybody. In his letter to me he also said that I was wrong when I wrote that Universal ordered one of their house directors, Harry Keller, to direct a few small additional scenes in *Touch of Evil.* About this I was correct. Heston's memory had failed him. In any case, he was a gentleman about it.

*I should add that there are now significant holdings on Welles at the University of Michigan, including a letter from Welles to Wilson pertaining to the sale of his collection to the Lilly: "Now it's in the hands of the cineastes, God help us all," which made me laugh. Welles enjoyed conversing with college students (e.g., the footage from his* Filming 'The Trial') *but was suspicious of academics. Yet isn't it fair to say that academic scholars are responsible for some of the most significant reappraisals of his work?*

I blushingly agree. There was a time before enough serious criticism was given him when many believed Welles' only great achievement was *Kane*. Let me point out to his ghost, however, that "cineastes" are filmmakers, not critics or academics (though the term is sometimes synonymous with cinephile, which is clearly what Welles meant).

Let me also point out that one of Welles' many talents was as a pedagogue, and at a bemused moment in his later life he remarked that he might wind up teaching at a Midwestern university. (He could have come to Indiana!) With Roger Hill, he had written *Everybody's Shakespeare*, and his Mercury group did the first LP recordings of Shakespeare, which were aimed at school libraries. After World War II, he briefly planned to make 16mm educational films for schools. In a sense, there is a pedagogical aspect to most of his work.

But I can sympathize with him or any famous artist who is the subject of so much writing by academics. I'm sometimes suspicious of those people myself, even though they are one of the main reasons why older art of any kind survives. In my feeble defense, I believe the Lilly collection has a letter from Wilson to Welles, pointing out that I'm a nice guy.

*I have only read the 2015 Centennial Anniversary Edition of* Magic World. *Besides a new introduction ("Orson Welles at 100"), what is different about that edition compared to the 1978 and 1989 editions?*

You read the best edition. I was very disappointed in the Oxford original, which got great reviews but wasn't properly copy-edited and was printed with a missing page. (In a grim irony, it was the last page of the *Ambersons* chapter.) Illinois did a wonderful job with the Centennial edition, which has large print and excellent, large-size illustrations. I added a long new introductory chapter, newly available information about *The Other Side of the Wind*, and many new details elsewhere. I could have slightly embellished the critical commentary in a few places, but I felt couldn't do it without spoiling the fabric of argument. In retrospect I wish I had said more about *The Stranger*, and if I were doing the book again today, I think I would say something about A. J. A. Symonds' *The Quest for Corvo*, first published in 1935.

Back when I first began working on a book about Welles, I had read somewhere that the Symonds book was a source for *Citizen Kane*. I read it and couldn't see any connection, but I've since realized why it could be compared with Welles' film. It's an unusual biography of a literary artist, dispensing with the usual chapters on family and upbringing and instead becoming the story of the biographer's search for information. The subject is Fredrick Rolfe, a virtually forgotten figure who was a typical 1890s British aesthete. Rolf styled himself "Baron Corvo" and seemed flamboyantly gay, though he repressed his sexuality, trying unsuccessfully to become a Roman Catholic priest. He often lived in extreme poverty but had genuine literary talent. He wrote several books, two of which were published but sold very little. As years passed, he grew increasingly paranoid and ended his life in Venice, where his homosexuality broke free and he wrote letters to England asking people for money and inviting them to visit him so that he could serve as a pimp for local boys.

You might say, as I did at first, that this has nothing to do with *Kane*, and I doubt that Welles or Mankiewicz ever read *The Quest for Corvo*. But the Symonds biography, which consists of sometimes conflicting interviews with people who knew Corvo, is above all a quest narrative, a search for the solution to a mystery. The same can be said of Eric Ambler's spy novel *A Coffin for Dimitrios*, published in 1938, and of course of *Kane*, even though the film has never been described quite that way. It obviously involves a reporter/writer's search for clues to a mystery, some answers to which are revealed by interviews with people who knew Charles Foster Kane. This is part of its novelty.

*Your article "The FBI vs. Orson Welles," was published by* Film Comment *in 1991. I believe you obtained FBI records on Welles via FOIA (Freedom of Information Act) requests. (I got my copy bound from Amazon.) What were your takeaways from that research?*

You make me realize that I should have included more of that essay in the Illinois Press edition of my book. I was amazed that the FBI records eventually became available from Amazon. I had to write the government to get them. My major takeaway was that Hoover's FBI, originally egged on by William Randolph Hearst, was determined to brand Welles a communist agent. Their evidence was ludicrous, but Welles was clearly a left-wing activist (and, as the FBI suggested, a womanizer), and if he hadn't departed Hollywood for Europe after 1948 he would almost surely have been blacklisted—Hollywood had never liked him in the first place. The FBI tracked him all the way to Italy, where they found him hanging around with suspicious lefty types in Rome, but the federal agents decided he was broke and no longer a threat to Anglo-Saxon capitalism.

*By the late 1970s, when the Welles book was published, serious film criticism had taken a sharp leftward turn toward theory and auteurism wasn't in fashion. Did that affect your subsequent writing?*

Yes and no. Beginning with the Welles book, all my writing about film has a political or ideological argument running alongside a discussion of style. But after 1968, serious writing on movies in such journals as *Cahiers du Cinéma* and *Screen* began to turn almost completely against Hollywood, describing critical admiration for directors of the auteurist pantheon as naively romantic, and the viewing pleasures of commercial cinema as ideologically suspect. It mounted a critique of traditional humanism and in some quarters aimed at complete deconstruction of cinematic illusion. French novelist/filmmaker Marguerite Duras said that her aim in directing *India Song* (1975) was to "destroy" the techniques of commercial cinema. Meanwhile, Roland Barthes and Michel Foucault each wrote critiques of the idea of the author. Popular American cinema was out (except maybe for the French interest in Jerry Lewis and Frank Tashlin) and Godard, "third cinema," and counter-cinema were in.

Some of these aims were valid: Hollywood was and in many ways is still patriarchal, it had long been either consciously or unconsciously racist, and nobody has ever thought it isn't capitalistic or organized on industrial lines. Latin American, African, and counter cinema is certainly worth more attention. But I was ambivalent about the rise of theory and remained a humanist. I'm second to no one in my admiration for the brave, austere, avowedly Brechtian and political films of Jean-Marie Straub and Danièle Huillet, but I agree with Gilberto Perez, who wrote that *Screen*'s Althusserian discussion and praise of their work said too little about their art and threw the baby out with the bath water. I suspect many people have avoided their films because of what has been written about them.

I read plenty of theory in that period and occasionally dropped the names of Benjamin, Adorno, Barthes, Kristeva, Althusser, etc. I used an idea from Julia Kristeva and wrote about many other theorists in my book on acting, and I quoted Louis Althusser in the introduction I wrote for my Rutgers "Films in Print" book on *North by Northwest*. But I also wrote a defense of cinematic authorship entitled "Authorship, Auteurism, and Cultural Politics," which became the lead item in a collection of my essays, *An Invention Without a Future* (2014). In the essay I lamented that we had reached the point where the name of the theorist was more important than the name of the artist. It was as if some otherwise smart academics had embraced an occasionally unintelligible philosophical discourse and wanted not only to deconstruct cinema but also to obliterate its pleasures. I thought leftist French theory, for all its revolutionary claims, was a political failure. But there were theoretical writers in the period I truly admired, among them Laura Mulvey, whose writings on feminist issues were decisively important.

*I confess to having a few misgivings about auteurism—not the idea of authorship itself, which is perfectly valid, but how it's employed in some circles today. For example, in what used to be known as "Film Twitter" (now that Twitter has become Elon Musk's "X," I don't know what it's called), an amorphous collection of zealous young cinephiles—and some older ones as well—have used the auteur theory to promote a kind of mythmaking about their favorite filmmakers (e.g., Michael Mann, Wes Anderson, Christopher Nolan, David Fincher). If you think any of them have ever made a bad movie, you're out of the club, which recalls Groucho Marx's famous quip. But that's why I was delighted by your chapter on* The Trial *in* Magic World, *because I got the sense that you dislike that film. It's one of my favorite Welles films, but I appreciated your perspective and how your literary background shaped it.*

I don't do X or Facebook or social media. I cringe at the thought of them and their billionaire owners. I'm probably too much out of touch, and I'm not familiar with the things you mention. Seems to me every great director with a long career has made at least one bad or not so good film, and I don't see why that should count against them—as Joe E. Brown once said, nobody's perfect. All movie lovers like to recommend pictures or argue over them with friends, but the discourse on X sounds to me like fanboys. I wish a brilliant critic could write an evaluative book similar to Sarris' *The American Cinema* accounting for directors Sarris left out or misjudged and the many important directors since then. But the landscape is much larger and more diverse, and I doubt if such a book is possible or even necessary. Even if it were limited only to America, at a minimum it would have to include P. T. Anderson, Peter Bogdanovich, Charles Burnett, Tim Burton, John Cassavetes, the Coen Brothers, Francis Coppola, Sofia Coppola, Julie Dash, Carl Franklin, Greta Gerwig, Todd Haynes, Spike Lee, Jerry Lewis (whom Sarris thought was overrated by the French), David Lynch, Terrence Malick, Michael Mann, Sam Peckinpah, Kelly Reichardt, Martin Scorsese, Steven Soderbergh, Whit Stillman, Quentin Tarantino, and at least as many others.

I'm no longer an auteurist (which shouldn't be thought of as theory), though auteurism shaped my taste and interests and it still influences film history. I may never have been a pure Sarrisite, though in a fit of pique against High Theory I once called myself "an unreconstructed auteurist." In the article I've mentioned, I argued that auteurism was best understood as a relatively short-lived but permanently significant "movement." It was created by Alexandre Astruc and the critic-directors of the Parisian New Wave, by various writers at *Movie* in London, and by Sarris, Eugene Archer, and Peter Bogdanovich in New York. Like all movements it eventually splintered and dissipated. I would need to summarize the whole of my essay to fully explain why it was important despite its limitations, but let me point out its greatest achievement: we wouldn't still be talking so much about Ford, Hawks, Hitchcock, post-*Kane* Welles and many others if not for the auteurists critics. The auteurists created a canon that has survived, and not many critics can say the same. I'll just leave it at that.

Yes, I'm ambivalent about *The Trial*. There are very impressive, even brilliant things about it, but it's only partly Kafkaesque. Welles was convinced that you couldn't do Kafka after the Holocaust and as a result he changed the last third of the picture to something that would have been anathema to Kafka: rather than have K "die like a dog," he turns him into a rebel and has him speak out against the Advocate. He even introduces a critique of the modern theater of the absurd and action painting! I think it's okay to be unfaithful to the source, but not suddenly to overturn or contradict its implicit aims. It's almost as if Welles dislikes Kafka or is temperamentally opposed to him, and *The Trial* becomes a movie against itself. (I feel more negative, though, about *The Other Side of the Wind*.)

*The Other Side of the Wind*

*Would you like to talk about* The Other Side of the Wind? *It finally came out in 2018, three years after your Centennial Edition, so your remarks in the book are brief. But you did write an in-depth and very mixed review of the film in* Cineaste.

Yes, the story of the making of that film has been told in many places. The released version, which I discussed in *Cineaste*, was assembled from over a hundred hours of footage and edited by several hands, most importantly by Bob Murawski. It may or may not be what Welles wanted, but everybody who brought it to us deserves some kind of award. In stylistic terms, it's a brilliant pastiche of cinema vérité and "New Hollywood," and it's more complex than any film of its day. Primarily an attack on what Welles called "macho-ism," it's also a *film à clef* and a key example of other Welles themes. It gave him a chance to settle some old scores: with Ernest Hemingway (with whom he once had a fist fight), with Hollywood, with certain critics, and in a more complex way with Peter Bogdanovich.

Welles originally planned to make a film about an aging Hollywood director somewhat like Howard Hawks, who had been relatively ignored by critics but was discovered and idolized by a young generation. One of my chief problems is that *The Other Side of the Wind* doesn't convince me that Jake Hannaford, the very arrogant and unlikeable movie director who is the central character (well played by John Huston), is a talented artist who deserves the attention he's given. I'm not sure what to make of the film-within-the-film except that it fulfills Hannaford's sexual fantasies. A sour mood envelops everything.

# Film Acting

*Michel Ciment complimented you as one of few film scholars who is interested in acting and writes about it well. I suspect he was referring primarily to your next book,* Acting in the Cinema *(1988), in which you assess screen acting from Lillian Gish through Robert De Niro, or to* Some Versions of Cary Grant *(2022), which we'll talk about later. What intrigues you about acting in movies, and why do you think much of film scholarship doesn't go near it?*

I'm grateful to Michel Ciment for mentioning me. The acting book was well received in France, especially at *Positif*, which has often supported my writings. In 2011, Christian Viviani, a member of their editorial board, invited me to give the keynote address at a conference on film acting he organized at the cinematheque in Nice (a setting as spectacular as you might imagine), and then he translated my book into French. Viviani later wrote his own book about film acting, *Le Magique et le vrai*, to which I wrote a foreword. Today, French academics are responsible for a highly theorized rise in "acting studies," and as we speak they're organizing a large international symposium on the topic in Strasbourg. My acting book has been translated not only in France, but also in Italy, Romania, and China. It attracted little notice in America and took many years to develop a reputation, but to my surprise John Updike mentioned it in the acknowledgements of his 1996 novel, *In the Beauty of the Lillies*.

I'm convinced Orson Welles was right when, possibly in a fit of modesty, he said that actors are the most important thing in movies. And yet, while there are many books about stars and stardom, few writers have given close attention to the actual work of acting. I think there are at least four reasons why: A) Acting isn't medium specific and you don't need actors to make a movie. B) Performances can be manipulated or embellished by photography, editing, etc. C) Our culture puts too much emphasis on celebrity, and critics are right to be suspicious of the manufactured images of famous actors. D) Most significant of all, the analysis of acting is extremely difficult and sometimes impossible to do in writing.

At the most basic level, you can learn something about how to analyze acting by watching simple animated cartoons aimed at children. The expression of the character's emotions—amusement, puzzlement, fear, anger, joy, etc.— is largely a matter of what happens with the head, eyes, eyebrows, mouth, hands, arms, and legs. The quality of the voice is of course also important. But in movies with human rather than animated actors, the situation is complex. The expressive language is analog rather than digital. It's conveyed in degrees of more vs. less, and becomes subtle, always dependent on narrative twists and turns which the analysis needs to consider. Where the voice is concerned, just think of the variety of meanings you can suggest with different ways of saying something as simple as "Close the door" or "Thank you."

The actor's emotions are also suggested by the use of very simple things such as a cigarette, a champagne glass, or a hat, which become what I've called "expressive objects." Actors can draw attention to themselves with an object. As only one example, see a wide shot of a poker game in one of Vincente Minnelli's best pictures, *Some Came Running* (1958), when Dean Martin keeps doing a small flourish with his poker chips; his repeated, unostentatious move serves as a sign that he's a professional gambler, but it also pulls your eyes away from Frank Sinatra, who is sitting next to him—you can't stop watching him, and he steals the scene.

*Some Came Running*

But describing all this and much more in the form of close reading can be like walking on water, and many critics avoid it. In some ways digital technology has helped critics to quote clips or scenes for video essays, thereby avoiding description, but to me writing is more important for criticism. I think maybe what I did was not so much close reading as close description.

*The case studies follow a straightforward trajectory from Lillian Gish in* True Heart Susie *(1919) through Cary Grant in* North by Northwest *(1959). Then, after discussing* Rear Window *(1954) in Part Three ("Film as Performance Text"), you jump ahead three decades with a surprising analysis of Martin Scorsese's* The King of Comedy *(1983). I think many would have picked* Raging Bull *or another Scorsese picture and Robert De Niro performance; at the time of your book's publication,* The King of Comedy *had a mixed-to-negative reputation. It's held in higher regard now. What compelled you to write about that film?*

First let me say that the case studies were somewhat less important to me than the first section of the book, called "Protocols." I wasn't sure where I was going when I began the project, and Darlene saved me, indirectly making that first section possible. She went to the library and came home with some books she thought would interest me. Among them were Edmund Shaftesbury's *Lessons in the Art of Acting* (1889) and Charles Aubert's *The Art of Pantomime* (1927). Even more important was Erving Goffman's work on performance in everyday life, which was the key to everything. Goffman, Stanislavski, and Brecht were the pillars of my analysis and could be applied to any case study.

Among the case studies I chose, the ones I like best are on Gish, Chaplin, Dietrich, and Grant. I'm very pleased with the chapter on the entire cast in *Rear Window*, which deliberately never mentions voyeurism, a topic that had become central to Hitchcock criticism, and that allows me to more or less recapitulate the issues I discussed at various places elsewhere in the book. I limited myself to Hollywood because performances in a foreign language would have been even more difficult to analyze. There were many actors I wish I had been able to discuss, among them Myrna Loy and Barbara Stanwyck. If I were doing a more up-to-date version of the book today, I would probably write about Philip Seymour Hoffman and Denzel Washington, and certainly about Judy Davis and Tilda Swinton. (I cut a chapter I wrote for the book on Laurence Olivier in *Hamlet* on the grounds that all the other chapters were about Hollywood movies, and I was relatively negative about Olivier's acting/directing in that role. That chapter can be found on my website.) I ended with *The King of Comedy* because at the time it was a fairly recent film, and because it's *about* acting and performance. In that section, I was again writing about the full cast, not just De Niro, and again it allowed me to recapitulate certain themes.

*I think Jerry Lewis is great in* The King of Comedy, *but I would have trouble explaining why I think he is great. I could note that he's an example of Scorsese's love of casting Borscht Belt comedians (Don Rickles and Alan King in* Casino... *does Albert Brooks in* Taxi Driver *count?)*

*in dramatic roles. But you use André Bazin's concept of "doubling" as a framework for what Lewis is doing and how Scorsese is utilizing him.*

Yes, Bazin was writing about the technique of casting a well-known personality in a fictional role that resembles their real life self. In the case of *King of Comedy*, the role involves clever shifts between "Jerry Lewis" (whose birth name was Joseph Levitch) and "Jerry Langford." As he's walking down a street, someone shouts, "Hiya Jerry!" But to whom are they speaking? The most interesting moment in his performance, though, is the scene when Rupert makes an uninvited visit to Jerry's house. Jerry's mask of celebrity drops off completely and he seems tough, even dangerous, like no Jerry we've seen before.

I think we tend to forget what talented and versatile actors the comics can be. (Believe it or not, Lewis played a straight role as an elderly man suffering dementia who commits a murder in TV's *Law and Order: Special Victim's Unit* [season 8, episode 4, 2008]). And while we're on the subject, let me add that Lewis was a terrific director. For me, *The Bellboy* (1960) and *The Ladies' Man* (1964) are almost up there with Jacques Tati. When I edited the *Contemporary Film Directors* series of books for University of Illinois Press, one of the most fascinating and unexpected volumes was Chris Fujiwara's *Jerry Lewis* (2009). It's a brilliant critical study of the films Lewis directed and contains a lengthy interview with Lewis—the most informative conversation he ever did. Highly recommended.

*The Bellboy*

In regard to casting comics in off-beat ways, I'm reminded that Scorsese once said, "More than ninety percent of directing a picture is the right casting." A small book could be written on this topic. The job of full-fledged casting director in Hollywood didn't emerge until the Fifties, chiefly with Marion Dougherty, arguably the most important of them all, who was responsible for an astonishing list of what became major players in movies of the Sixties and Seventies. Scorsese worked with her and thought she should be given on-screen credit and an award. The Directors Guild of America long opposed that idea, almost surely because directors wanted to keep their reputations as auteurs. Casting is an art involving major decisions about the interaction between type and individual, which can involve fascinating permutations and creative choices. The light-weight comedy *In & Out* (1997), for example, gets over 50 percent of its immense charm from the great casting. So does *Spy* (2015).

*In the "Protocols" section, you include a footnote about one of your early childhood memories being asking your parents whether actors onscreen were actually kissing. You use that example as part of a larger question of whether acting involves imitation. Am I correct that your point was that, in cinema, illusions can feel more real than reality?*

No, but I'm going to give a long answer to your question because several readers of the book have commented on that footnote. I suppose it has unintended implications about pre-pubescent sexuality. I thought I was being clear in the paragraph where the footnote number is entered, but maybe not. The point I was making is simply that actors both imitate things (getting shot in the arm, having a bad cold, being drunk, suffering nausea, daydreaming, etc.) and *do* things. When they ride a horse, they're usually actually riding a horse. When they kiss, they may be pretending to be in love, but they kiss.

Of course my child's mind didn't know whether the kissing was real, nor how much work goes into kissing scenes in movies. The lengthy kissing between Cary Grant and Ingrid Bergman in *Notorious* (1946), for example, involves a kind of dance between camera and actors. The kisses are brief (Hollywood censors in those days had time-limit rules for kisses), but they're frequent and continuous, accompanied by murmured conversation and gesture, as when Bergman tickles Grant's earlobe. Sometimes Grant's face is favored and sometimes Bergman's, and the couple not only cross from a balcony to a room but also answer a telephone without letting go of one another. I've often wondered how many takes the scene required, but I assume Grant and Bergman had fun.

Contrast this with a kiss in a recent film, Catherine Breillat's *Last Summer* (2023), which tells the story of a steamy erotic affair between a married lawyer (Léa Drucker) and her teenaged stepson (Samuel Kircher). The first kiss between these two is shown in an intense closeup. I didn't time it, but it seems to last at least two or three minutes. It's open-mouthed, with lots of tongue work and passionate, pre-orgasmic breathing. I don't know if Breillat and the actors had the assistance of an intimacy expert, which movies sometimes employ these days for sex scenes, but the kiss no doubt involved rehearsal, revision, and careful management of emotion. Nevertheless, the couple is really kissing.

While we're on the topic, I should remind everybody that among the earliest motion pictures was Thomas Edison's *The Kiss* (1896), which was downright chaste by today's standards, and was executed by stage actors May Irwin and John Rice. The Roman Catholic church called it "disgusting" and called for reform, but the public didn't object. It was followed by imitations used to spice up the end of short film showings, among them *Something Good— the Negro Kiss* (1890). Ever since, countless Hollywood movies have ended with a kiss.

*The Kiss*

*Also in "Protocols," you mention one type of performance being "public figures who play theatrical versions of themselves." While you were referring to examples such as John Wayne and William Holden appearing on* I Love Lucy *as "John Wayne" and "William Holden," it made me think of a common criticism aimed at Wayne's (and other famous actors') dramatic performances—that he's "playing himself." I'm sure I'm not the first to point out that that rests on a couple of dubious assumptions: that it's easy to play yourself; and that the self that people choose to show others is always authentic.*

Exactly. It took work for Marion Morrison to create John Wayne, and in appearances as "himself" he was still acting John Wayne the movie star. (And who knew how much Wayne offscreen was like Wayne onscreen? Was he as boorish as he occasionally seems?) In a less purely creative and challenging way, it takes work for each of us to create a self that becomes our "natural" personality. Sociologist Robert Ezra Park said it perfectly in a comment I've long admired: "The word person, in its first meaning, is a mask... [E]veryone is always and everywhere, more or less consciously, playing a role... our role becomes second nature, an integral part of our personality. We come into the world as individuals, achieve character, and become persons." I think it's also true, as both Bertolt Brecht and Jean-Paul Sartre have noticed, that all of us—professional actors and everyday people—perform a variety of roles. A university lecturer behaves like a lecturer, and a restaurant waiter behaves like a waiter. When Chaplin cooks and serves a shoe in *The Gold Rush*, he acts like a cook, a waiter, and a fastidious diner, all within a few minutes.

*I was intrigued by your mentioning that you would have liked to have written about Richard Pryor's stand-up performances, and somewhere in the book you also mention David Byrne in* Stop Making Sense *(1984), Jonathan Demme's concert film. What would you say about their work in terms of acting or performing?*

I would have to talk at great length in order to be specific, plus I would need to study the films closely before saying anything. Pryor's famous stage show is in my opinion the greatest and most versatile display of acting, impersonation, and personation in the history of celluloid. When he imitated his mother punishing him with a switch and his childhood reactions, it brought back memories of a similar scene from my childhood and left me doubled over laughing. His routine is full of such things, and I found myself laughing so much my eyes teared. Because it wasn't a fiction film, however, I didn't include it—it wouldn't have fit the design of the book. *Stop Making Sense* gets my vote for the best of all concert films, mainly because of staging and the semi-acrobatic performances, but again it's not the kind of material that fit the case studies in the book, all of which involved star actors in fictional narratives.

*Actors in biopics are frequently showered with praise and awards. But is what they're doing more difficult or impressive than creating a character from the ground up?*

Not necessarily more difficult, but because their performances involve obvious imitations, moviegoers can see that they're acting. Imitation in a more subtle sense is a feature of a great deal of acting, but in biopics it's clearly there and it tends to lead to awards. Timothée Chalamet was recently nominated for playing Bob Dylan in *A Complete Unknown* (2024), but I prefer the great Cate Blanchett as Dylan in Todd Haynes' *I'm Not There* (2008). The same is true when well-known actors with established images play foreigners, alcoholics, or disabled characters—the work is visible and gets praise.

*Your book didn't discuss character actors until the last two chapters, when you were dealing with entire casts of films. Does analysis of character acting involve a special approach?*

I don't think so, but a book on the subject would certainly be worthwhile. It would first of all need to confront the question of what counts as character acting. In the glory days of the Hollywood studio system, the studios were rather like theatrical stock companies, with large numbers of versatile and sometimes eccentric players with familiar mannerisms who could be inserted as supporting players in a variety of genres. (See *Sunset Blvd.* [1950], when William Holden tries to pitch a screenplay to a producer, explaining that the plot could be used in either a baseball or a submarine movie, with contract player Bill Demarest in a supporting role.) Most of these players can be described as character actors in the sense that they played distinctive fictional types. The best of them gave an identifiable style to stock-company films by John Ford and Orson Welles. Ward Bond and Agnes Moorehead were among the greatest, most versatile character actors who ever lived, and so were Jane Darwell and Everett Sloane. There have been plenty more; any movie with Eve Arden, Thelma Ritter, Peter Lorre, or Akim Tamiroff is better because of them. Great character actors by the dozen appeared in the films of Preston Sturges, boiling around in a zany comedy that made those films special.

One could go on listing names, but there were also brilliant leading actors who played what might be called leading character-actor roles—"character" in the sense of a role that, while central, is a comic or low-level type like a gangster and not a heroic, glamourous, prime mover of the plot. (Sheldon Leonard was a gangster in almost every film he made, but never a lead.) For example, Orson Welles plays Falstaff in *Chimes at Midnight* (1966), a role that dominates both the film and Shakespeare's *Henry IV*, but a role that doesn't determine the action of kingship, politics. and warfare, which are the drama's central concerns as a chronical history. Falstaff is centrally important, but he's also old, fat, filthy, lazy, cowardly, comic, and in some ways lovably childlike—no character in history is more of a "character," and Welles, who usually took kingly roles, plays him definitively. I think Welles was right when he described Falstaff as "Shakespeare's good, true man," in contrast with the politicians around him.

Consider also the opposite case of an actor who usually played character types but could also take on the role of a tough leading man. The unhandsome Walter Matthau, a master of eccentric comic accents and movements, was a born character actor who played a variety of leading and supporting roles in comedy, but he also had the eponymous role in Don Siegel's great action thriller, *Charley Varrick* (1973), and he played that character to the hilt. The recent death of Gene Hackman must have reminded everyone of what a versatile performer he was. He began as a character actor in such films as *Bonnie and Clyde* (1967), but in the period of the New Hollywood, he and several others broke the mold of the matinee idol leading man. (Even Harry Dean Stanton was the lead in *Paris, Texas* [1984].) Hackman was not only a tough leading man in *The French Connection* (1971) but also a talented comic, as when he played Lex Luthor in *Superman* (1978), the dim-witted filmmaker in *Get Shorty* (1995), and a blind man in *Young Frankenstein* (1974)—"Wait!" he cries when the monster runs out of his house, "I was going to make espresso!"

It took a longer time for talented but unbeautiful women to do that sort of thing, but see Elaine May, who directed and performed with Walter Matthau in *A New Leaf* (1971), a movie which was taken from her control and defaced by its editors. Another example is Shelley Duvall, who had significant roles in Robert Altman's films and also worked unhappily as a stereotypical mousy wife (but a worm who turns) in Kubrick's *The Shining* (1980). An even better example is Melissa McCarthy, widely recognized as a great comic actor. She played a frustrated writer and forger of autographs in the non-comic *Can You Ever Forgive Me?* (2018), which is a film I like very much. Most of the others are in foreign or TV films. My pick would be the attractive but not glamourous Sidse Babett Knudsen, who plays the Danish Prime Minister in *Borgen* (2022) and more recently has a key role in the TV series *Prime Target* (2025). Like many important actors, she has a distinctive walk, a kind of march with arms swinging at her sides. She also has a beautiful smile.

*Besides your work for* Acting in the Cinema *and* Some Versions of Cary Grant, *you've written other things about famous actors. I'm thinking of your essays on Clara Bow and Humphrey Bogart.*

The essay on Clara Bow was written for the online journal Cine-Files some years after *Acting in the Cinema*. It could have easily been a chapter in that book because I was writing about a star in a single film: *Mantrap* (1926), an excellent silent picture directed by Victor Fleming. Bow was a unique personality, the quintessential It girl of the jazz age. Her life, however, was in some ways tragic. Born in Brooklyn to an abusive father and a mentally disturbed mother, she had only a seventh-grade education, but at the age of sixteen, against the will of her parents, she entered a "fame and fortune" contest sponsored by *Motion Picture Magazine* and wowed everyone. For her screen test, she was asked to walk on screen, answer a phone, laugh, look worried, and look frightened. One of the judges described her as "plastic, quick, alert, young, and lovely." She also had what college boys of the era called "pep," a liveliness suited for dancing on tables or jumping in men's laps.

By 1930, she had made nearly fifty films and become a major star at Paramount. Wide-eyed and expressively mercurial, she often did inventive, improvised things in her performances, things that her directors didn't anticipate. Her style suffered in the early, more slowly paced sound pictures, in which her lower-class voice was revealed. The Hayes Office, the tabloids, and the various guardians of morality made her the subject of gossip, chiefly because she was ill-educated, scandalously flirtatious, and had many affairs. In the comic *Mantrap*, however, she's wonderful, and at the height of her powers as an actor. The exact opposite of a 1920s sex star like Louise Brooks, she's amusingly spirited, naughty, flighty, slightly boyish, and lovably sexy. Though her character breaks many puritanical rules and seduces several men during the course of the film, she never seems a maneater. The only fully adequate way to describe her vivid movements on screen is to use frame enlargements.

*Mantrap*

I wrote about Bogart in several contexts and was chiefly interested in his trademark mannerisms: thoughtfully tugging his earlobe or lower lip, hooking his thumbs in his belt, and acting with a cigarette.

Although he had a relatively sophisticated upbringing and in his early appearances on stage played college types in tennis clothes, Bogart became a star in the role of a John Dillinger type. In the 1930s he played Warner bad guys who talked out of the side of their mouths, but beginning in the 1940s his work in *The Maltese Falcon* (1941) and *Casablanca* (1942) made him a romantic leading man. He could convincingly play intelligent, sophisticated characters, as in *The Barefoot Contessa* (1954) and *Sabrina* (1954), but one of his most interesting aspects was his tendency to pick unsympathetic roles that ran against the grain of his star image: the chief examples are the paranoid types in *Treasure of the Sierra Madre* (1948) and *The Caine Mutiny* (1954), and above all the disturbingly violent screenwriter in *In a Lonely Place* (1950), a film he produced, which completely undermines the tough Bogart persona.

*The Big Sleep*

## Vincente Minnelli

*Your next book was* The Films of Vincente Minnelli *(Cambridge University Press, 1993). What drew you to writing about him?*

I knew fairly little about Minnelli when I decided to write about him. *The Bad and the Beautiful* and *Home from the Hill* (1960) made a strong impression when I was young, and I remembered *Lust for Life* (1956) as one of the most impressive uses of color I had seen. Andrew Sarris had listed Minnelli among the laudable second rank of American directors ("the far side of paradise"), Victor Perkins had praised him, and Godard had alluded to him in *Contempt* (1963). He was famous for musicals, but he was also the subject of interesting essays on melodrama by Thomas Elsaesser and Geoffrey Nowell-Smith. These things piqued my curiosity and when I looked more at the films I realized he was a master of style with a penchant for what Sarris identified as a "vein of melancholy."

*Although the book is slightly over 200 pages, you have an ambitious theme—in your own words: "insights into the romantic imagination, American show business, and commodity culture." How does Minnelli's body of work align with those subjects?*

Sounds like everything, doesn't it? The format of the Cambridge series for which I wrote the book limited authors to a detailed discussion of only five films. I guess I was carried away in the long introduction, but I'll stick to my claim. Minnelli's films are certainly romantic in both the popular and ideological sense, and I was intrigued by the way his career followed the path of aestheticism and dandyism in 20th-century commodity culture. He began in Chicago, where he was a window dresser for Marshall Fields, then a fashion photographer, and then a designer of stage shows for the Balaban and Katz movie palaces. In New York, he became famous for the shows he designed for Radio City Music Hall and for a series of Broadway musical revues that were marked by sophistication and urbanity. He modernized entertainment and gave refinement to popular culture, borrowing ideas from art nouveau, impressionist and Post-Impressionist painting, and ultimately from surrealism. (To quote myself on art and commodity culture: "The descendants of the aesthetes became fashion designers, the impressionist paintings were bought by capitalist investors, and surrealism provided inspiration for television commercials.") It's no surprise that Minnelli became a valued director at MGM, the most prosperous of Hollywood studios. His success depended on the facilities of that studio, where the Latin motto on the logo translated as "Art for Art's Sake."

*In his review of your book, Jonathan Rosenbaum posits: "Naremore is interested in sketching out the ideologically charged battlefields where Minnelli's films and their artistic and social allegiances intersect with the contemporary issues of 'political correctness,' where questions of race, gender, sexuality, social class, and culture are repeatedly posed." Those battles keep raging more than thirty years later, but have your views shifted on any of Minnelli's movies? Which of his films was the most interesting or challenging to write about?*

Jonathan became a good friend and his review was typically elegant. I feel happy with what I said in my book about all the films I discussed, and my views of them haven't changed. The chapter on *Cabin in the Sky* (1943), an all-Black musical that was Minnelli's first picture, was the most carefully researched and complex in its social implications. My chief frustration was that Minnelli had made so many important films and I was limited to only five. For much of his career he specialized in three genres—musicals, non-musical comedies, and melodramas. I chose to represent the three types: *Cabin in the Sky* and *Meet Me in St. Louis* (1944) for the musicals, *Father of the Bride* (1950) for the comedies, and *The Bad and the Beautiful* and *Lust for Life* for the melodramas. I especially regretted that I had no room for *Designing Woman* (1957), *Gigi* (1958), *Some Came Running*, *Bells are Ringing* (1960), *Home from the Hill*, and *2 Weeks in Another Town* (1962). My head spins when I think of many others I like. It would have taken a very big book.

*George Cukor has been called a "woman's director," though I know Joe McBride's recent book on him makes the case that he was great with male actors too. But actresses frequently seemed at their best under Minnelli as well, and not just Judy Garland.* The Bad and the Beautiful *impressed me, Lana Turner and Gloria Grahame's performances in particular, as did* The Band Wagon *(1953), in which Cyd Charisse, as a blonde gangland moll sliding across the floor to Fred Astaire's leg, seemed never better.* Cabin in the Sky *showcases Lena Horne's terrific work, though you have to go to YouTube to see her bubble-bath number that was cut from the film.*

I wouldn't call Minnelli a "woman's director" and I think of Cukor as an "actor's director." But because Minnelli worked so much with musical theater and musical movies, he directed some of the most talented female singers and dancers in movie history. He knew and directed Lena Horne and Ethel Waters in New York before they came to Hollywood. He guided Judy Garland out of her prolonged adolescence at MGM, and just look at Cyd Charisse's conventional early work before musicals and Minnelli. He was probably responsible for the blonde and black wigs and especially the red dress she wears for the noir parody in *The Band Wagon*, also for the red tutu in her ballet number. But he didn't direct the slide across the floor—that was Michael Kidd, the choreographer.

His really surprising work with Charisse is in the nonmusical *2 Weeks in Another Town*, where she plays a sadistically sexy woman who makes Kirk Douglas go nuts, causing him a fit of automotive hysteria similar to Lana Turner in *The Bad and the Beautiful*. (There is nearly always a party scene in a Minnelli movie, even in *The Long, Long Trailer* [1954], where the crowded party takes place in a mobile home, but the modern Roman orgy in *2 Weeks in Another Town* was cut so much by the studio that Minnelli almost took his name off the picture.)

*2 Weeks in Another Town*

Gloria Grahame is good in any movie and *The Bad and the Beautiful* is one of her best. She's simultaneously sexy, troublesome, and touching. I once met Edward Dmytryk, who directed Grahame in *Crossfire* (1947), and I asked what she was like. He told me she repeatedly had plastic surgery for her nose and lips. Whatever the case, she's fascinating. The French dubbed her the definitive noir woman, and she deserves that title even though she never played a true femme fatale—the closest she came was the supporting actor bad girls in *Sudden Fear* (1952) and *Macao* (1952). There was always a suggestion of something vixenish and dangerous about her. For me, the only woman of the period that came close to her effect on screen was Diana Lynn, who never got the casting she deserved.

One of what Jonathan Rosenbaum called the "ideologically charged battlegrounds" in Minnelli's work has to do with sexuality. Everyone in Hollywood knew that Cukor was gay, but Minnelli was married for most of his life and was clearly the father of Liza. I suspect he was bisexual and I hinted that in my book. His taste and style were in sympathy with the bisexual/homosexual vein of the late 19th-century aesthetic movement—one of his early idols was James McNeill Whistler, and the French critic Louis Marcorelles has called him an "Oscar Wilde of the camera." Several of his films, most notably *Tea and Sympathy* (1956) are critiques of normative masculinity, and some of his male leads—Louis Jourdan, John Kerr, and George Hamilton—play either dandies or sensitive youths. The chief exception to the rule and the most important of his leading men, the hypermasculine Kirk Douglas, gave impressive performances for Minnelli as sexually conflicted, psychologically tormented men.

*The Bad and the Beautiful*

*I also love* The Clock (1945), *which captures Garland (and a wonderful Robert Walker) right at the nexus between innocence and adulthood. Am I wrong to see that movie as a precursor to films like Melvin Van Peebles'* The Story of a Three-Day Pass (1967) *and Richard Linklater's* Before Sunrise (1995)? *It appeared to have invented its own subgenre of "fleeting romance" in which there's tension between a couple's courtship and the compressed timetable it's on.*

I hadn't thought of the connection, but you're right, even if those other directors weren't aware of *The Clock*. The director MGM originally assigned to the picture was Fred Zinnemann, who would have made it less lyrical, less like a musical. Minnelli's rapport with Garland is evident and Walker is another of his sensitive young males. It's also a movie that shows Minnelli's love of the boom-mounted camera, which became his signature. Notice that the two films he made with movie directors as characters—*The Bad and the Beautiful* and *2 Weeks in Another Town*—show the director working from atop a crane.

One quality of Minnelli's work that I wish I had emphasized in the book, not so evident in *The Clock* (1945), is his impressive work with extras in crowd scenes. Just look at the barroom, nightclub, and street scenes in *Bells are Ringing*, or the fun-house dance number in *The Band Wagon*, where the many extras become individuated characters.

*I enjoyed* Cabin in the Sky, *although it really doesn't get cooking until the last half-hour at the nightclub with John W. Bubbles. I had forgotten that Georgia Brown, Lena Horne's character, doesn't show up until 45 minutes into the movie, but all the other characters talk about her constantly. She gets nearly as much build-up as Harry Lime, and then they cut her big entrance. I'm curious if Horne's bubble-bath number was in the original stage musical from 1940, or was it written specifically for her, not anticipating what the Production Code's reaction would be?*

I like several things in addition to Bubbles: Ethel Waters' singing, the Arlen and Harburg tunes, and of course the big Duke Ellington number with a dance choreographed by Busby Berkeley. The bubble bath wasn't in the Broadway show, which was extensively revised for the movie version. That bubble bath, incidentally, isn't a revealing flesh show. Horne's beauty was always kept under control by MGM. She was never made into a Josephine Baker type, and there was an unstated rule that she could only sing, not move around or dance much. The idea of her in a bathtub must have freaked out the censors, even though Minnelli made it modest. Too bad she didn't get a role in another musical for which she would have been perfect: the Julie Laverne character in MGM's *Show Boat* (1951).

*One last question about* Cabin. *After I saw the movie, a couple was leaving, and one of them said: "No way they could have showed* that *in the Deep South." It made me think of your mentioning earlier about seeing* Stormy Weather *at a Louisiana theater where Black moviegoers were confined to the balcony. Did you see* Cabin in the Sky *back then too, or did it come much later, or even when you were researching your book?*

I was too young to have seen it—I saw *Stormy Weather* in re-release and may have first seen *Cabin* on TV. As I think I mentioned in my book, *Cabin* did play the deep South (it was folksy enough to avoid southern ire) and was well received by overseas troops during the war. The chief reason it had been made was an effort by the government and Hollywood to have more Black representation in movies, especially when Blacks were fighting in the war. It was the lowest budgeted musical in MGM history and made a modest profit in general release. Reaction against it came not from the South but the North. It was understandably criticized as racist by intellectuals and Black newspapers, but in the end I think it works because of Minnelli's skill with design. He painted the mural in the nightclub, put a flower in Horne's hair (à la Billie Holiday), treated the folkloric qualities ironically, and imbued the film with a modernist Africanism redolent of Harlem rather than the South.

*Cabin in the Sky*

## Film Noir

*We're up to* More Than Night: Film Noir and Its Contexts. *It's my favorite of your books, both because of the subject and the unexpected way you approach it. You discuss some of this in your Introduction (*"This Is Where I Came In"*), but what compelled you to tackle an entire form after previous books mostly about directors and their films? (I'm using "form" instead of "style" or "genre," but correct me if that's not right.)*

I can't believe I started out as a Virginia Woolf critic and wound up as Guy Noir. But sometimes I think I was born to write that book. The first thing I published about film was an essay on Huston's *The Maltese Falcon*, and I've always loved the noir form or whatever you want to call it—people seem uncertain whether it's a genre, a cycle, a mood, or just a "phenomenon." Maybe we can't define it, but like pornography we know it when we see it.

I'm not sure why it took me so long to get around to noir. This was the most successful book I've done and one of the easiest to write. I got a couple of major fellowships to support the research, and when it was published it won an international book prize. It also sold extremely well for an academic publication and went into an expanded second edition.

The basic idea was generated when Laura Mulvey (the salt of the earth) visited Bloomington and I mentioned to her that I was thinking of writing a book about film noir. She said that as far as she was concerned noir was something created by critics. A light bulb went on over my head, like in the cartoons. I realized she was right: the best way to approach noir was as an idea or label originally thought up by critics, and I could start by writing a history of the idea. Ideas, like words, have meanings that change with usage over time, and the changes can be traced.

Writings on noir in this country invariably made it seem an American phenomenon based on hard-boiled fiction and German émigré directors. But nobody in Hollywood used that term when the films appeared. Its name was French, and I knew the idea of noir had generated there. France had a pre-World-War II cycle of films they called noir and were fascinated with post-war Hollywood films which they believed were similar to their own. The term noir had originated with the *roman noir*—the black or gothic novel, which in that period flourished in France in the form of paperback thrillers from Gallimard, many of them translations of writers like Hammett and Chandler. For French intellectuals, noir novels and cinema could also be viewed through the lens of existentialism and residual surrealism.

While in Los Angeles doing research I had lunch with Peter Wollen, who joked that the definition of film noir was any picture listed in Raymond Borde and Étienne Chaumeton's *A Panorama of American Film Noir* (which at that time hadn't been translated into English). He might have been joking but he was right—noir is usually defined ostensively, as a list of films. (Peter also tipped me off to the relevance of Boris Vian, whom I discuss at the beginning of the book.)

Among the first American films to be listed as noir by the French were *The Maltese Falcon* and *Laura* (1944), which have several things in common but are also different in many ways. Various writers, including J. R. Austin, Jorge Luis Borges, Jacques Derrida, Michel Foucault, George Lakoff, and Ludwig Wittgenstein, have shown that, contrary to the usual assumption, categories aren't made up of items with common properties; virtually every category has odd members that seem to raise questions. Writers on noir seemed unaware of that problem and handled the category awkwardly. People would say that film noir is an American phenomenon, but France and Italy got there well before Hollywood, and many other nations around the world have made films that could be described as noir. Some would say that noir involves femmes fatales (except when it doesn't), or shadowy lighting (except when it doesn't), or crime. At least one title listed as noir by the French, Wilder's *The Lost Weekend* (1945), isn't a crime picture. Almost always noir has been defined as a list of titles that have a considerable unacknowledged variety. If pushed against a wall, I would probably describe it with what Raymond Durgnat once called a branching tree-diagram, or maybe I would say it's movies that can be situated somewhere between horror and dystopian sci-fi.

*Many years ago, when I taught Humanities courses at a community college, I eagerly included a day or two on film noir as an example of a cinematic form or style. I'm embarrassed to admit that I also described it with the standard clichés about antiheroes and femme fatales and Expressionist shadows and so forth. Maybe that was the right approach at an introductory level. But your book simultaneously broadens and deepens the reader's understanding in historical, political, and aesthetic contexts. Were these ideas already in your mind when you started the book, or did they emerge as discoveries in your research?*

I forgive you for your description of noir. Nothing was wrong in doing it, especially for an introductory course. In a sense it's unavoidable because that's what almost everybody means by noir. I think, though, that you were describing what I would call "Forties-ness," or features of theme, characterization, narrative, lighting, and camera style that were rife in that decade, especially in the crime film, but that occasionally spilled over to every genre.

Where my book is concerned, once I began with the history of noir as an idea, everything fell into place like a winning poker hand and I knew the various contexts I would use. I moved from a chapter on critical writing about noir to chapters on modern crime fiction, censorship, politics, budgets, style, etc. Each chapter had a historical dimension and I tried to talk about noir as a world-wide phenomenon. But in discussing individual films in detail, I found that I stuck mostly to what you could call the beating heart of noir in 1940s Hollywood.

*In the chapter "From Dark Films to Black Lists," you make a powerful argument for reframing film noir in a political instead of solely aesthetic context, using both the Production Code and the Blacklist as examples of overt sources of pressure against which film noir managed to endure, even if many of its principal writers, directors, and actors did not, some of them tragically (e.g., John Garfield). Is that an accurate interpretation?*

Quite accurate. In the heyday of Hollywood noir, the Production Code Administration (known as the "Breen Office," after its administrator, Joseph Breen) was chiefly concerned with how films treated sex, violence, drinking, language, religion, legal authorities, clerical figures, and the fates of criminals. There were also censorship boards in individual states—in Ohio, for instance, people didn't see Wilmer kick Sam Spade in the head in *The Maltese Falcon*. For obvious reasons, dark crime films were scrutinized closely, but what's surprising is the degree to which major examples of noir were able to find ways to get around the censors. Noir not only blurred the line between sympathetic and unsympathetic characters but also in a few cases, such as *The Asphalt Jungle* (1950), made the criminals more admirable than the police and the respectable types. It depicted many homosexuals (but never made them attractive), plenty of heterosexual eroticism (with intercourse offscreen), and lots of booze. In *The Lady from Shanghai*, the legal system is corrupt and a trial becomes a circus in which the man charged with the crime escapes by exiting the courtroom with the jury; in *The Big Clock* (1948), managers of the media are murderous; and in *Ace in the Hole* (1951), a journalist is so unethical he might as well be a murderer.

Noir was always at the edge of what was permissible, yet the most famous public challenges to Code restrictions came from Selznick's *Gone With the Wind* (1939) and Howard Hughes' *The Outlaw* (1943), both of which publicized their minor infractions ("damn" and cleavage, respectively) to boost their box office. The Blacklist, which emerged on the heels of World War II, is another story, because it was about politics. It, too, wasn't confined to noir pictures: Howard Koch, who co-wrote *Casablanca* (1942) was "greylisted" because he also wrote *Mission to Moscow* (1943). Among the blacklisted were Dalton Trumbo, Walter Bernstein, Abraham Polonsky, and Waldo Salt, who had written a variety of non-noir pictures. Edward Dmytryk and Adrian Scott, who were among the Hollywood Ten, made *Murder, My Sweet* (1944), but also the non-noir *Tender Comrade* (1943). Of course the Blacklist also extended to many left-wing actors, composers, and technical workers. And while noir has no single politics, in the 1940s a significant number of directors connected with it were liberal or left wing: Welles, Huston, Dassin, Losey, Rossen, Ray, etc.

*Is it also correct to say that the Blacklist, far from "canceling" (to use an anachronistic term) film noir, inspired many classic examples of the form? To be clear, I don't mean this as a compliment, but as a byproduct of a tragedy.*

The Blacklist made certain kinds of noir dangerous for artists and was successful in canceling or driving many artists out of Hollywood. If it inspired anything, I would say it was a mini-cycle of right-wing noirs such as *The Woman on Pier 13* (1950, aka *I Married a Communist*). But perhaps in response to the HUAC hearings, left-wing noirs took an interesting turn in the late 1940s and early 50s toward social problems.

I think you could say that in the era of classic studios there were two significant moments of left social criticism. The first was at Warner Bros. in the early 1930s, with such pictures as *I Am a Fugitive From a Chain Gang* (1932), *Wild Boys of the Road* (1933), and especially *Heroes for Sale* (1933). The second was what Thom Andersen has called the *"film gris"* of 1947–51, by such directors as Rossen, Polonsky, Losey, Dassin, Berry, Endfield, and Ray, who turned noir toward social realism. Joseph Losey's *The Lawless* (1950), the story of a young Mexican in California accused of raping a white girl, is a key example.

*You discuss a little-known but compelling noir, Cy Endfield's* Try and Get Me *(1950), as an example of a political allegory released around the height of the Blacklist. It was the second film loosely based on the Brooke Hart murder and subsequent lynch-mob execution of his kidnappers and killers Thomas Thurmond and John Holmes, which occurred in San José, California in 1933; the first was Fritz Lang's also-compelling* Fury *(1936). (I'm marginally familiar with the case not only from having seen both movies but on account of our collection of newspaper records at San José State University on the Brooke Hart kidnapping.) I realize that it may have been a while since you've seen either film (me too), but I'm curious how Endfield's version seems to be generally considered film noir yet Lang's isn't, if aesthetics or timeframe don't play a part (or play less of a part) in defining these admittedly imperfect, retroactively imposed categorizations?*

Thom Andersen suggests that *Try and Get Me* is a "presumptive allegory." It's the most disturbing film I've seen about lynch-mob violence—sometimes preachy but excellent in its treatment of social class and low-rent areas around Phoenix, Arizona.

You could say there's a Hollywood subgenre about lynchings in America: *They Won't Forget* (1937), *The Ox-Bow Incident* (1943), *Hang 'em High* (1968), *Till* (2022), etc. *Fury* is only one example, and if anyone wants to call it noir that's okay with me. (They usually don't, probably because it was made in the 1930s and mostly lacks the style associated with the 1940s and 50s.) But most of these films are about the lynchings of white people. Hollywood didn't have the nerve to deal with lynchings in the South, especially where many of those lynchings were happening.

But *Try and Get Me* (aka *The Sound of Fury*) is exceptional in other ways. It's better than *Fury* because the lynching succeeds and is horrific. A mob led by a bunch of fraternity boys charges the jail, overwhelms the police, seizes the white perpetrators of the crime (whom we know are guilty, one far more than another, because we've seen them do it), and hauls them off to be tortured and killed. All this is shot on location in neorealist style and is very different from Lang.

*I'm also fascinated by how some motion-pictures found ways to subvert the Production Code, as you pointed out. Using your examples of* Double Indemnity *and* Detour *as a possible jumping-off point (you discuss them in a different context in the book), were "A-movies" or "B-movies" more likely to get material past the censors? In other words, was a film attached to a powerful producer or director given more leeway than one that wasn't, or did "mainstream" films noirs invite more scrutiny than noirs from Poverty Row?*

It's appropriate that you mention those two movies because Edgar G. Ulmer, who directed *Detour*, tried to capitalize on the success of *Double Indemnity* by writing a script called *Single Indemnity*, which was never filmed. Ulmer was by far the most talented director of low-budget movies, and *Detour*, his masterpiece, has things in common with James M. Cain's fiction. In *Double Indemnity*, Billy Wilder had tried to challenge the PCA by having the murderous couple die by their own hands rather than by the police; Phyllis shoots Walter and Walter shoots her. This wasn't enough for the censors, who wanted the law to punish somebody. Wilder took a sort of revenge by filming a detailed, accurate scene of Walter's death in the California gas chamber. Both Paramount and the PCA were shocked and influenced his decision to have it cut, though he later claimed it was one of the best scenes he ever filmed.

*Detour*

It's certainly true that influential studios or producers could occasionally skirt the rules, as with Selznick and Hughes. I've seen the PCA report on *Double Indemnity* but not on *Detour* or other extremely low-budget pictures produced at Poverty Row studios like PRC, so I can't speak with authority. But I think *Detour* didn't break the rules—the unreliable narrator-protagonist doesn't get away with inadvertently causing a death, and is a victim of what he thinks of as "fate." But *Detour* does many unglamorous things that an A picture would never do, for fear audiences might recoil. The atmosphere throughout is seedy, and Ann Savage's performance as Vera, the potential femme fatale, is something you would never see at Paramount or MGM. Ruthless, slatternly, half-crazed (no actor's real name was more appropriate to the character), she spends a lot of the film in a bathrobe, snarling and downing bourbon. She gets my vote for a Lifetime Academy Award, and I love it that Guy Maddin, who called her performance in *Detour* "feral," brought her out of a long retirement and cast her as his mother in *My Winnipeg* (2007). It was her last role.

*In the book, you proceed to complicate the binary of "A-vs.-B" movies by discussing "intermediate" (B-plus?) films. One example you use is Joseph H. Lewis'* Gun Crazy *(1950), which I think I like more than you, but I certainly see how its production elements and other elements are at a higher level than* Detour's. *This falls outside when* More Than Night *was published, but do you think that digital restorations of authentic B-movies have in some ways done their job too well? I remember seeing a crummy print of* Detour *years ago on TV and practically smelling the stale atmosphere of the diner where we meet Tom Neal's doomed protagonist. When the restored version began making the rounds in 2018, many thought it impressive but also almost misleadingly respectable.*

In the book I point out that the A and B distinction arose in the Depression, when theaters offered two pictures (a double feature) for the price of one. The B picture wasn't necessarily low budget—it was the second feature because exhibitors thought it would be less popular. The term B later became associated exclusively with low budgets and Poverty Row, although there's no exact definition of it. *Gun Crazy* doesn't have an extremely low budget or a Poverty Row studio—it's financially intermediate, but because of its title and story, it seems pulpy to some viewers and critics. For me it has a few problems artistically but also has great moments, especially the long take from the back seat of a car as the lovers/gunslingers make a getaway, ad-libbing for most of shot. I hope I made clear that I like it very much. The chapter where it's discussed is largely about critical reception of low- and medium-budget pictures, so maybe that's what created the wrong impression.

The low- to medium-budget pictures that got the best critical reception in the 1940s were Val Lewton's RKO horror movies, which I suppose can be described as noir, though I didn't discuss them. As far as I know they weren't exhibited as parts of a double feature, but RKO publicized them as far more horrific than they were. Lewton, a great producer, knew that if he followed studio rulings on titles and promotion and if he worked on low budgets with a small but talented unit of artists, he could maintain control and do something special. He certainly did. These are unique films with haunted moods, intelligent scripts, and sensitive characterizations.

*Gun Crazy*

You've made me realize that I've never seen a "restoration" of *Detour*. The film studies program at Indiana had an excellent 16mm print and I used that. The picture has obvious low-budget qualities but it isn't at all badly photographed and has a good music score. It seems to me you saw a degenerated print. Where digital restorations are concerned, I have mixed feelings. Most of them are good, but they give a certain over polish to the old B movies, in some cases making them look more glamourous. I have more problems with the restoration of *Citizen Kane* than with *Detour* because the digital "timing" seems to give it more light than I originally thought was there.

*I was also pleased to see you discuss DTVs, or direct-to-video movies, which is now largely an antiquated term (or conflated with streaming, but that's a topic for later) yet were quite common when you were writing your book. You mentioned two of my favorite examples,* Red Rock West *(1993) and* The Last Seduction *(1994), both directed by John Dahl, and rereading your thoughts corrected an error I've held for thirty years that* The Last Seduction *was released before* Red Rock West. *I may have seen* The Last Seduction *first and got them turned around in my head. That film premiered briefly on HBO before a fairly successful run in theatrical release, which is what controversially made Linda Fiorentino's performance ineligible for Oscar consideration. (Gene Siskel and Roger Ebert went to bat on their show for both the film and her performance.) But since Dahl was scolded during production by a distribution-company executive for making an "art film," I'm curious if you see DTVs as descendants of B pictures if even in the tenuous sense of lacking respectability even when they earned it?*

I thought *The Last Seduction*, which was intended for TV, went straight to theaters, so I stand corrected. I'm a big fan of John Dahl, whose first movie, the excellent *Kill Me Again* (1989), had a brief run in theaters. But one of my favorites of his films was *Rounders* (1998), a relatively big-budget, underappreciated picture starring Matt Damon and Edward Norton. (I like everything with Norton, who was the star and director of *Motherless Brooklyn* [2019], a grossly underappreciated noir.) Most of Dahl's later work seems to be as a writer or director of episodes in TV series. It's interesting to think of DTVs and made-for-TV movies as descendants of B pictures, especially in the case of Dahl, who must have experienced critical condescension in some US quarters, but like many of the unsung noir directors in the 1940s was embraced in Europe. Today Hollywood is more complicated and A vs. B doesn't exist. Movies made for TV can have very big budgets.

*A year or so ago, we had a lively discussion about "neo-noir." The Criterion Channel's use of that term for a series of films newly programmed at the time of this writing prompts me to ask your thoughts on whether or not its current usage is accurate?*

I was on the verge of inventing an equally useless new term: neo-Western. For starters, I would have listed *The Missouri Breaks* (1976), *Heaven's Gate* (1980), *Once Upon a Time in the West* (1968), *Dances with Wolves* (1990), and fifty or sixty others. But to my dismay, I discovered Neo-Western is already being used! The very likeable TV series *Dark Winds*, about a modern-day, native-American law officer, has been described as a Neo-Western. I guess it could also be called a Neo-Western-Neo-Noir.

Neo-Noir is now universally accepted and everybody knows certain of the films it points to, so I may as well give up. But I still feel as I did when I wrote my book. It's not a question of accuracy, it's just that Neo-Noir as a category isn't needed and is every bit as difficult to pin down as film noir, which didn't have a widely recognized name in this country until the original period was over and the supposed Neo-Noir was beginning. What's the first Neo-Noir? Is it a film in color? There were already color noirs in the old days. Is it post the old Production Code? That Code died off well before so-called Neo-Noir, but the term is always related to a cycle of films such as *Body Heat* (1981), which is a sort of *Double Indemnity* with the clothes off. Paul Schrader's early history of noir says it ended with its "epitaph," *Touch of Evil,* in 1958. Does that mean that *Cape Fear* (1961) and *Johnny Cool* (1963) aren't noir? Everybody seems to think *Pulp Fiction* (1994) is Neo-Noir, but Quentin Tarantino says, "I don't do Neo-Noir."

The one place where I think "neo" is appropriate is in French crime fiction. The French term for the American hard-boiled novel was the *"polar,"* but by 1970 the great French writer Jean-Patrick Manchette argued that the *polar* "had its day" and that while it could still be honored one needed to take "a new social reality into account." Hence the term *"néo-polar."* I don't think the so-called American neo noir ever took enough account of the new social realities, but Manchette certainly did. He's an extraordinary artist, as noir as they come. He translated Donald E. Westlake and Ross Thomas, two of the greatest American writers of crime fiction (who usually wrote from the point of view of criminals), and then he wrote a series of dark, violent thrillers about alienated characters, some of which have been translated into English and published by City Lights Books and The New York Review Classics. If Freud and Marx walked into a bar, they would find Manchette mixing the drinks and he would introduce them to Guy Debord on a nearby barstool.

As far as I'm concerned, Hollywood noir has never died and was never reborn, although the industry, the technology, the culture, the critical discourse, and the meanings associated with the term have changed. "Neo-Noir" seems to me little more than a marketing concept that refers to a relatively small group of films. Do people still make Neo-Noir, and if so are we supposed to call every crime TV show or movie since 1980 a Neo-Noir?

I prefer "historical noir" if we really need a term for films of the 1940s and 50s, just as critics have long used "historical avant garde" to distinguish early 20th-century art from the contemporary avant garde. In the expanded edition of my book I have a chapter on noir in the twenty-first century, where I talk about films by Michael Mann,

Robert Rodriguez, Mike Hodges, David Lynch and many others. These are fine movies, different in many ways from Hollywood in the 1940s, but I don't call them Neo-Noir because I don't think a new term is necessary. I suppose I should give up. As an English professor, I should know better than complain about changes in language.

*Prior to that chapter, you discuss some interesting examples of noir (or Neo-Noir) in the 1990s, which address explicitly or implicitly the racism, homophobia, and misogyny of some examples of the original noir cycle (attributes certainly not confined to film noir). Carl Franklin's* Devil in a Blue Dress *(1995) starred Denzel Washington in an ambitious adaptation of Walter Mosley's debut mystery novel of Black detective Easy Rawlins and set in 1948 Los Angeles. The movie was a much different thing than* Shaft *(1971) or other crime pictures in the Blaxploitation era of the 1970s, but audiences rejected it, which in turn shut down a possible series of Easy Rawlins detective movies. The movie has its admirers, but I would be hard-pressed to name many more contemporary noirs that have centered Black characters in the years since. If Denzel Washington can't do it, who can?*

Somebody probably will, but more likely on TV. *Devil in a Blue Dress* is an exceptionally good film and as you suggest there should be more like it. But in the current commercial environment, any film that follows in the path of *Chinatown* (1974), as with *Miller's Crossing* (1990) and *Devil in a Blue Dress*, both of which are excellent pictures recreating the world of Hammett and Chandler, is likely to have only a modest impact in theaters. I suppose you could call Denzel Washington's *Equalizer* trilogy noir, despite its quasi-superhero action and spectacular beatdowns of villains, but I don't think so.

*One of my main takeaways from your book is the mutability (if not indestructibility) of noir, and in the current century it's worth noting the success of telenoirs, namely Vince Gilligan's* Breaking Bad *(2008–13) and* Better Call Saul *(2015–22). Allen Glover and others have traced noir on television back to the days of live TV. But these more recent series could even be called (to blend part of your term with Glover's) Neo-Western-TV-noirs, which take advantage of location shooting in Albuquerque—and its surrounding, foreboding desert—to conjure a fatalistic atmosphere. Near the end of* More Than Night, *you quote the CBS network chairman in 2005 saying, "Americans don't like dark." Why do we seem more comfortable with dark themes or antiheroes in our TV programs now (i.e., in our homes) than in mainstream feature films (i.e., in theaters)?*

I hope we don't call anything Neo-Western—I was only kidding. I'm probably not good at answering your question, but things we could call noir (before it had that name in America) have long been around in American mass culture, and not just in film. Narrative formulas or genres tend to spread and evolve across all the available media. There was once plenty of pulp fiction, and there were tough TV detective shows even before hits like *Mike Hammer* and *Peter Gunn*—I remember a live or kinescope Mike Hammer on the Dumont TV network in the early 1950s. Well before that, noir was on the radio. Howard Duff was very good as Sam Spade, Gerald Mohr was Philip Marlowe, Dick Powell was Richard Diamond, and Orson Welles did a radio version of Hammett's *The Glass Key*. More important in the 1940s was the CBS radio show *Suspense*, which starred major Hollywood actors in adaptations of pulp writers. Lucille Fletcher's "Sorry, Wrong Number" was written for that show and later became an excellent film noir. There were also very good, even daring, noir comic books from the EC publishing company, until a Senate investigation shut them down as a dangerous influence on American youth.

And yes, one of the major arguments of my book on noir has to do with what you describe as mutability. Noir can be called a genre, but if we do that we should be aware that "genre" has an etymological connection with "gender," and that Hollywood films are often trans-generic or hybrid. Their generic features combine, merge, and overlap; there are noir Westerns (or Western noirs if you prefer), noir musicals, noir melodramas, and noir comedies or satires. The Name of the Genre is unstable, open to even more critical deconstruction than the Name of the Author. The problem of definition is the same in all the generic categories. There are always marginal examples that threaten clear definition. What's a horror film, for example? Recent writers on horror have given up trying to define it by anything but affect, but even that runs into problems.

I'm no television historian, but the CBS executive you mention was speaking of pre-streaming network TV, which was more family oriented and subject to moral/political scrutiny. *Breaking Bad* was a hit in a very different media environment and I doubt it had a bigger audience than old network shows like *I Love Lucy*. Where theaters are concerned, today's Hollywood needs large audiences who pay for expensive tickets. Dark, serious, or downbeat films—not just noir but thoughtful drama—are a risk at the American multiplex unless they hike up casting, sex, and violence.

That being said, current TV provides plenty of opportunity to stream shows we could call film noir. One of the best, and still available, is Britain's *Cracker* (1993-96), starring Robbie Coltrane as a chain-smoking police psychologist whose personal life is a wreck. There are also newer British and European crime shows which, allowing for differences in today's culture and visual technology, are analogous to and sometimes far better than the average noir pictures Hollywood turned out in the 1940s and 50s. For recent examples, see the 2024 Danish series *Follow the Money* (2016–19), the Swedish series *Beck* (1997–2025), the British series *Line of Duty* (2012–21), and especially the German series *Dark Rivers* (2020–22)

## Stanley Kubrick

*The first edition of* On Kubrick, *another of my favorite books of yours, was published in 2007, less than ten years after his passing. What was the general critical/scholarly consensus about Stanley Kubrick at the time, and what did you hope to add?*

The consensus then was much the same as now. He was highly regarded. I imagine his individual films may have gained or lost critical approval in today's environment, but he remains canonical. What's interesting about Kubrick's critical reception is that although he was in almost complete control of every movie he made (except for *Spartacus* [1960]) and although he had an easily recognizable style and set of personal interests, the auteurists didn't like him. (Andrew Sarris eventually changed his mind.) He was also disliked by Victor Perkins, Pauline Kael, David Thomson, and Anthony Lane. Probably no great filmmaker had so many influential critics who said he was overrated. But he also had important supporters—notably Michel Ciment in France and Alexander Walker in England—and there was a good deal of academic as well as professional interest in him. (John Dahl had said that what made him want to be a movie director was seeing a Kubrick picture.)

It seemed to me that the critical dislike of Kubrick had to do with the tone or emotional effect of his work, which Kael described as his "arctic spirit," along with his overwhelmingly masculine interests and pessimism about human relations. He eschewed sentiment or melodrama except to put ironic quotes around them, and with almost no exception he didn't allow audiences to root for his characters. (The biggest exception is Kirk Douglas in *Paths of Glory* [1957], which was controlled by Douglas.) I thought I could improve on the critical literature by dealing with the unusual qualities of tone, affect, and theme in his films. I also wanted to write a thorough critical study of the individual pictures. Fortunately, the book was successful and I recently had the opportunity to do a revised and expanded edition that elaborates on what I call Kubrick's "cold modernism" and belief that human society is founded on violence.

*You spend more time than many critics and scholars delving into Kubrick's early years as a photographer. What elements in that early work can be found in his filmmaking?*

I guess I should remind some of our readers that as a very young man Kubrick took up photography and was so good at it that he was hired by *Look* magazine—next to *Life*, the biggest mass-circulation photo-news journal in the nation. He knew members of New York's Film and Photo League and he socialized with the New York School photographers, among them Diane Arbus, Robert Frank, Lee Friedlander, and Arthur Felig. He later hired Felig, aka "Weegee," to do publicity photos for *Dr. Strangelove* (1964). Examples of his work during that early period can be seen in Rainer Crone's coffee-table sized book, *Stanley Kubrick: Drama & Shadows* (London: Phaidon, 2005), and in Christiane Kubrick's *Stanley Kubrick: A Life in Pictures* (Boston: Little, Brown, 2002).

Movie directors often start as writers, theater directors, or actors, but Kubrick began as a still photographer, which determined his approach to his art. As a director, he sometimes quoted famous photographers: the subway scenes in *Killer's Kiss* are derived from Walker Evans, and the eerie twins in *The Shining* are inspired by a Diane Arbus photo. By the same token, his early photos for *Look* foreshadowed the unorthodox, slightly creepy sensibility of his films—they show an interest in automata or simulacra, a flair for surrealist juxtaposition, and a kind of sublimated grotesquerie.

As a director, Kubrick was always intensely concerned with the techniques of photography, which he knew as well as any of his DPs. He photographed his first two features, but in Hollywood he wasn't allowed to operate the camera because he wasn't a member of the ASC. Even so, he photographed the hand-held shots in his films, such as the attack on Burpleson Air Force Base in *Dr. Strangelove* and the shot of an ape tossing a bone in the air in *2001*. On his first Hollywood picture, *The Killing* (1956), he overruled the experienced DP Lucien Ballard and essentially told him how to shoot everything. His mastery of technology was legendary: the front-projection system in *2001*, the NASA lens for candle-lit scenes in *Barry Lyndon* (1975), the early use of the Steadicam in *The Shining*, and the innovative use of zoom lenses in the films he made with DP John Alcott.

Kubrick's imagery has a lapidary quality, but equally important it's influenced by still photography. Unlike Welles, whose films are busy with camera movement and have a fine frenzy of visual information, Kubrick likes a relative stillness. Many of his shots, like art photos, have what George Toles has called "the lucid character of a firmly articulated thought," and when reproduced as stills they have an iconic force: Major Kong riding the bomb, the Star Child floating in space, Alex leering at the audience, etc.

*Dr. Strangelove*

*You also discuss another fascinating subject I don't recall seeing raised by many other writers: "the grotesque." What is Kubrick's relationship to grotesque aesthetics?*

When I began the book I did some reading about the grotesque, which in ordinary parlance means simply "hideously ugly" but in the history of art has a more complex meaning. As far as I know, movie critics and historians have seldom if ever discussed the grotesque as an artistic mode, even though examples of it can be found in Buñuel, Eisenstein, Sternberg, Welles, and many comic films.

The term originates in the 16th century and has been written about by such important art historians as

John Ruskin, Wolfgang Kayser, and Philip Thompson. Thompson describes its emotional effect as unresolved tension or uncertainty between laughter and an unpleasant emotion such as disgust or fear—a fear often related to the lower regions of the body or a confusion between the animate and inanimate.

Kubrick's films are filled with grotesque effects, and I devoted a whole chapter to the topic. There are many moments in his pictures when one feels unsure how to react emotionally. How are we to respond when Strangelove shouts, "Mein Fuhrer, I can walk!", or when Alex smashes the Cat Lady's head with a ceramic penis, or when Jack complains about "the old sperm bank" he has married? How are we to respond to everything Lee Ermey does in *Full Metal Jacket* (1987)? In every case, there's emotional push-pull between humor and revulsion, and it's everywhere in Kubrick. The chief difference between *The Killing* and Huston's *The Asphalt Jungle* is that Kubrick's picture is a festival of grotesque effects. (This is true even in the casting:; see Tim Carey and Kola Kwariani.) From *Killer's Kiss* to *Eyes Wide Shut* (1999), one finds instances of bodily grotesque and confusion between the animate and the inanimate.

In the expanded version of my book, I elaborated on this argument by showing the relationship between the grotesque and three other artistic modes in Kubrick: black humor (a tension between laughter and horror), the Freudian uncanny (a tension between the ordinary and the fearful), and the fantastic (a tension between reality and the supernatural, which Michel Ciment has intelligently discussed). Together, the four modes account for Kubrick's "cold modernism."

*Some of the conversation around how Kubrick uses actors has felt reductive. ("He hates actors," "He uses them as pawns on a chessboard," etc.) But now that Shelley Duvall has passed away—and I suspect I love her work for Robert Altman more than you do—how would you evaluate her performance in* The Shining, *or how Kubrick "uses" her, if you were to explore it as a case study?*

I'm not so much an admirer of Altman as you are, though I grant he does interesting things with genres. I like Duvall's work with him very much, especially in *Popeye* (1980), which most critics hate. She had a gangly body and a somewhat goofy face, but as an actor she could evoke sexiness, ditziness, or pathos—sometimes all at once. In *The Shining*, which is not one of her best roles and not one of my favorite Kubrick films, she's cast as Wendy, a drab housewife with a string-bean body and a trailer-park twang. According to his notes on Diane Johnson's screenplay, Kubrick was unsure what motivated Wendy to stay with her mismatched, eventually psychotic husband. Kubrick could also be rough with some of his actors if they didn't follow directions or debated with him, which may have been the case with Duvall. As a result, he took a satiric approach, cutting some of her scenes and dialogue, turning her into an almost laughably fragile, skittish, and fearful character who eventually triumphs over the monster she's married. During the production he seems to have treated her in dismissive fashion, quite opposite to the way he treated Jack Nicholson. In Vivian Kubrick's documentary on the film, his on-set interactions with her suggest near contempt or disregard. Maybe he wanted to motivate the nervousness of her performance, but he keeps pushing the film itself near to overt misogyny. (He was also a director who took more unexplained retakes than anybody since William Wyler, which might have driven her and all his actors crazy.)

I once wrote an essay on acting in Kubrick and Welles, who are among the rare American directors to impose an identifiable acting style on their films. In Welles, the acting is theatrical; he believed actors could "project" as much as they do in theater, as long as they paid close attention to the placement of the camera. In Kubrick, the acting almost systematically oscillates between underplaying and overplaying. The underplaying is evident in parts of *Barry Lyndon*, in *Eyes Wide Shut*, and especially in *2001*, where the humans are almost robotic. ("Open the pod bay doors, HAL.") The overplaying is most obvious with Malcolm McDowell in *A Clockwork Orange* (1971) and Jack Nicholson in *The Shining*. In an interview, Kubrick once said that prospective film directors should read Stanislavski, but when Jack Nicholson tried to do Stanislavskian realism, Kubrick told him, "Real is good, interesting is better." He got something that was not only interesting but wild and crazy—a parody of Jack Nicholson played cleverly by Jack Nicholson.

*Your comments on* The Shining *lead me to ask: do you think Kubrick is a misogynistic director?*

He was certainly a masculine director and most of his fans are male. He made films about war and technology, and in private life he liked guns, American football, and computers. With the notable exception of Diane Johnson I'm not aware of women who have admired his work or come to its defense. But I would point out that one of his abiding interests is male sexuality, which he treats in extremely unflattering, mostly Freudian terms. *Dr. Strangelove* and *Full Metal Jacket* are savage critiques of phallus worship and sublimated fascism. He treated the nuclear family in three films, and all three are critical of the patriarch (*The Shining* is almost the only horror movie in which the monster is the father in a family). In *Eyes Wide Shut*, which is probably his most personal film, his treatment of conventional marriage is one of the more complex in the movies.

*I don't remember if you discuss this in the book, but I'm interested in the frequency of voiceover narration in his films. How does Kubrick typically employ the device? Are these unreliable narrators? Contrapuntal? Or is he doing something else?*

I don't think he uses narration a great deal more than certain other filmmakers, but his use of it varies from film to film and is always interesting. I can never decide whether the narration in *The Killing* is as satirically intended as it seems. It's spoken by Art Gilmore, a well-known radio and TV announcer, who sounds as stiff and official as the voice of *News on the March* in *Citizen Kane*. (And for all this narrator's careful attention to the timing of things, he makes a couple of mistakes.) James Mason is an amusingly bothered and bewildered narrator in bits of *Lolita*, which I think is one of Kubrick's most underrated films. Of course Kubrick famously cut the elaborate narration for *2001*, deliberately making the film enigmatic. I think his best use of narration is *Barry Lyndon*, my favorite Kubrick picture. He abandons the first-person narration of his source, a little-known Thackeray novel, and gives us a God-like narrator in the spirit of 18th- and 19th-century fiction. Michael Hordern's voice is beautiful and his reading nuanced. His comments are sometimes in counterpoint with what we see, sometimes a complement to the images, and sometimes informative about things we don't see. Lofty and cosmopolitan, he speaks directly to the audience, often in maxims or truisms. He also makes wry or satiric judgements. He's as important as any character.

*A Kubrick film that doesn't use voiceover (i.e., doesn't explain its mysteries, as* 2001 *refused to do) was his last:* Eyes Wide Shut. *Were you among those who were disappointed when that movie first came out, or were you always as impressed with it as your chapter on it indicates?*

I've been ambivalent about several Kubrick films, but they tend to grow better with passing time and closer viewing. At first I wasn't sure about either *Full Metal Jacket* or *Eyes Wide Shut*. Where the latter is concerned, when I read Schnitzler's *Traumnovelle* and thought about the film in relation to Kubrick's marriage and his Mitteleuropa family origins (also his interest in Freud), it became fascinating. It has some flaws for me, I think mostly due to Kubrick's death before his final edit, but I find it extraordinary.

*Authorship is another interesting, at times tricky subject with Kubrick. I remember reading about Anthony Burgess' objections over the title* Stanley Kubrick's A Clockwork Orange. *But I'm curious why, in your book, you choose not to discuss* Spartacus, *a film about which there has been some debate about the level of Kubrick's involvement, but there is a chapter on* A.I. Artificial Intelligence (2001), *for which Kubrick famously laid the foundation but I would consider to be a Steven Spielberg film?*

There are several instances when screenwriters, novelists, and historians have said that Kubrick took too much credit for film scripts. According to Kirk Douglas, Kubrick offered to take credit as the writer of *Spartacus* in place of the blacklisted Dalton Trumbo; Douglas instead gave the credit to Trumbo, thus breaking the Blacklist for good. Kubrick also seems to have undercredited Jim Thompson for providing only dialogue in *The Killing*. Calder Willingham and Terry Southern claimed they did more for him than he acknowledged on the screen. Nobody, however, has challenged his work as a producer/director. He wrote *Barry Lyndon* and there is little doubt that he supervised or collaborated with the writing of scripts for his other films — he certainly did as much supervision as Hawks and Ford had done in the old days.

As for the prolific and multitalented Anthony Burgess, my feeling is that he did protest too much. At the time the film was made, he said that his novel, which got poor reviews in Britain and no royalties for Burgess when the rights were sold to Kubrick, was a sub-par dystopia written when he was ill. I've got problems with the film (it seems to me a bit too amused or comfortable with "ultra violence" and rape), but it was Kubrick who wrote the adaptation, which differs significantly from the novel and is certainly a Kubrick movie. If it hadn't been advertised as *Stanley Kubrick's Clockwork Orange*, it would never have gotten a large audience and eventually turned the novel into a big seller for Burgess. (Ditto with Stephen King's complaints against *The Shining*, which seems to me something of an improvement over the novel and certainly over the awful version King did as a TV movie.)

My book explains why I didn't do *Spartacus*. It was Kubrick's most disappointing experience as a director and little of it seems like a Kubrick film. He lost control to producer/star Kirk Douglas and DP Russell Metty, and in interviews he pretty much disowned the picture. He told Michel Ciment that as history it was "dumb." Furthermore, I've never liked it much. Afterward, Kubrick briefly worked with producer/star Marlon Brando in the development of *One-Eyed Jacks*, a title he supplied along with casting and writing suggestions. I admire that movie but he soon left it. These experiences soured him on Hollywood and motivated his move to England. He was immensely successful at manipulating the Hollywood system from a distance.

I don't think *A.I.* should be described as simply a Spielberg movie. It's dedicated to Kubrick and derived from a project he had been working on for well over a decade. But I wasn't especially concerned about the authorship question when I wrote the chapter—in fact I believe auteurist arguments over Spielberg vs. Kubrick are a waste of time. *A.I.* is a great film that throws light not only on the differing interests of Kubrick and Spielberg, but also, perhaps more importantly, on the topic of A.I., which is on everybody's radar today. I believe that chapter is the most intellectually ambitious and significant part of the book, partly because it ranges afield of the two author/directors. Though readers may not agree with me (they certainly don't agree about the quality or authorship of the film), I'm fond of it and regard it as one of the best things I've written.

*Kubrick is often compared to Welles, but one important difference seems to be that he didn't leave behind any "incomplete" works that I'm aware of (unless one counts* Eyes Wide Shut*), which have become a veritable cottage industry among some Wellesians. Seeing that Kubrick is an established pantheon director still actively discussed, and re-releases of his films still widely seen (e.g., the magnificent restoration of* 2001*), what unexplored avenues or directions do you foresee opening in Kubrick studies?*

I agree about Welles/Kubrick, but I'm afraid I don't have an answer. My interests moved on to other projects and I haven't given thoughts to unexplored avenues regarding Kubrick. No doubt others will find them. There will always be more writing about any major artist, but I've had my say about him.

## BFI Film Classics: *Sweet Smell of Success* and *Letter from an Unknown Woman*

*Let's discuss your pair of monographs for the BFI Film Classics series together—* Sweet Smell of Success (2010) *and* Letter from an Unknown Woman (2021). *How does that series work? Do authors suggest which films they would like to write about, or does the BFI recruit authors for films they have in mind?*

Authors propose films they they would like to write about, and editors at the BFI determine whether the title fits their list. I proposed both of those titles.

*I remember your introducing* Sweet Smell of Success (1957) *at IU Cinema, with, I believe, a relative of James Wong Howe in the audience. A leading question, but how significant was Howe in realizing Alexander Mackendrick's visual design?*

Howe was versatile and all his work was important. *The Thin Man* (1934), for example, has much more effective imagery than its sequels. He didn't have a single style and could be equally good with a colorful romantic comedy like *Bell, Book and Candle* (1958) and a tough realistic picture like *Hud* (1963). *Sweet Smell* gave him special problems because much of it was photographed in very cold Manhattan weather, usually after midnight or before dawn, in an effort to avoid crowds. (Mackendrick wanted more exterior scenes than in the original Ernest Lehman script.) Two details can give you a sense of Howe's skill with the interiors: Mackendrick suggested that in the role of J.J. Hunsecker, Burt Lancaster should wear glasses, as Lancaster did in real life. In the restaurant scene at the 21 Club, Howe photographs Lancaster with a wide angle lens and a hard spotlight above his head, throwing shadows down from the glasses and over his cheekbones, making him look hooded and reptilian. In that same scene, screenwriter Clifford Odets suggested that Howe use a crab dolly to encircle the table where five characters were sitting. Probably at Mackendrick's suggestion, Howe uses the dolly sparingly, but at just the right moment.

*Sweet Smell of Success*

*What discoveries did you make about* Sweet Smell *in the Clifford Odets manuscripts at The Lilly Library?*

First I need to take this opportunity to correct an awful error that makes me cringe. Odets was a major left-wing playwright whose post-war career in Hollywood ran afoul of the HUAC investigations. In the book I said that he named names for the House Committee, just as Elia Kazan had done. In fact he didn't, and I deeply regret my mistake. I made clear, though, that Odets was perfect casting for this film, which enabled its left-wing contributors to get revenge on media celebrities like Walter Winchell (the model for J.J. Hunsecker), who had destroyed major careers during the Blacklist.

I did most of my research for the book at the Herrick Library in Los Angeles and at the Lilly in Bloomington, which has a major archive of Odets' work. The Lilly was a goldmine. Odets had inherited Ernest Lehman's script for *Sweet Smell*, and though he preserved much of Lehman's plot, he altered almost every scene. He did eleven extensive rewrites and scores of revisions to individual scenes, some with as many as a dozen versions. He also gave the copious dialogue its best lines, plus some verbal motifs involving animals, food ("you're a cookie full of arsenic"), and even the Bible. A fair amount of this was composed while the film was being shot in sequence. Tony Curtis, who played Sidney Falco, recalled walking around the set in bitter cold at three or four in the morning and hearing the sound of a typewriter from the property truck. He entered to find Odets in an overcoat typing "The cat's in the bag and the bag's in the river."

Peter Bogdanovich, who as a young man directed a successful New York stage production of Odets' *The Big Knife*, once told me that Odets' only advice to him was "play it fast." That's exactly what Mackendrick does, and later in his life, when he became a teacher of film production at Cal Arts in Los Angeles, he paid tribute to Odets. His Cal Arts lectures, posthumously published and edited by Paul Cronin under the title *On Film-Making: An Introduction to the Craft of the Director* (New York: Faber and Faber, 2004), ought to be required reading for every aspiring filmmaker or critic. A full chapter of the book is devoted to *Sweet Smell*, using Odets' screenplay to show how a skilled writer develops "density and subplots." As Mackendrick shows, Odets was especially good at creating scenes with a "triangulation" of dialogue between three characters, and he was a master of what Mackendrick calls "ricochet" dialogue, or scenes in which A speaks to B but is really speaking to C. (The major example is the scene at 21, when Hunsecker speaks to a Senator but is really aiming parts of the speech at Sidney Falco, who sits just over Hunsecker's shoulder.)

*Let's turn to* Letter from an Unknown Woman *(1948). Had you written about Max Ophüls prior to this book?*

No, but I much admired Ophüls, a great director of actors and a virtuoso of camera movement who created sensitive, in some ways anti-romantic pictures about women. I once taught a class on Lang, Ophüls and Wilder as European émigrés, and a few times in other classes I showed *Letter from an Unknown Woman*, which is one of my favorite movies. I jokingly told students that if they didn't like it we could never be friends. I assumed young people would resist the film because it was a period melodrama centered on a woman in love.

*What is a "recognition plot"?*

I may have used that term in reference to *Letter*. I certainly talked about recognition, but I'm not sure there's something called a recognition plot. Recognition *scenes*, on the other hand, have been an important element in every kind of plot there is—comedy, tragedy, farce, satire, melodrama, etc. They can be found in such various places as *Oedipus Rex* (1967), *Othello*, *Tom Jones* (1963), *The Shop Around the Corner* (1940), and *Chinatown*.

The term "recognition" in narrative stylistics derives from Aristotle's *anagnorisis*, which in the *Poetics* he defines as a dramatic change from ignorance to knowledge. There are many scholarly debates about the term: is it a change in the knowledge of a character, an audience, or both? How is it related to catharsis, which can be a purging of dramatic tension derived from understanding? Whatever the case, Terence Cave and Peter Brooks have written impressive books on the topic, showing that recognition is especially important to melodrama. (Also to psychoanalysis, which is fundamentally about recognition.) At its climax, *Letter from an Unknown Woman* has one of the showiest recognition scenes in the history of Hollywood.

*You delve deeply into Stefan Zweig's novella. Is Ophüls' film a faithful adaptation, however one may define that, or does it take liberties and change meanings?*

The Zweig novella involves a successful forty-one-year-old author who returns home to Vienna after a vacation and finds in his mail a letter from an unknown woman. She tells him she has loved him all her life. When she was young and poor, they met and had blissful sex. He soon forgot her, but she had become the mother of his child, spending her subsequent life as a shopgirl and then as an upper-class prostitute. He never remembered her, she says, and in a later sexual encounter he didn't recognize her. Her child has died, she is ill, and by the time he reads the letter she will be dead. "I do not believe in God anymore," she writes, "I love only you." When the author, who has had many sexual conquests, finishes reading this letter, "something broke open inside him and he thought of the invisible woman… as one might think of distant music."

Ophüls' film retains the central plot but makes many changes. Zweig's narrative is told from the close first-person point of view of the woman's letter, framed by the close third-person point of view of the anonymous author who reads it. The film adaptation by Howard Koch and Ophüls names the central couple Lisa Berndle (Joan Fontaine) and Stephan Brand (Louis Jourdan). Brand becomes a glamorous concert pianist appropriate for the "melos" of melodrama, and Lisa ultimately becomes the trophy wife of an aging military officer. We hear Lisa's letter as offscreen narration, but at the same time the film brilliantly dramatizes her world with a breathtaking mobile camera, creating a full picture of Viennese society at the turn of the century. There are moments, such as the early scene when the young Lisa sees Brand's possessions being moved into her building, that are among the most impressively executed and meaningful crane shots in the movies. At the ending, the film abandons Zweig's ironic, subdued recognition scene, giving us recognition with melodramatic force. All this may not be faithful, but to me it's an improvement over the already excellent source.

*Letter From an Unknown Woman*

*Many writers struggle with writing plot description, and many readers struggle with reading them, but you describe* Sweet Smell *and* Unknown Woman *very elegantly and hold one's attention in more or less half the length of each book. Have you any tips for how to do that?*

Thanks for the praise, but I have no tips. I worried that the *Sweet Smell* volume had too much blow-by-blow description. With *Letter*, I didn't have that problem because an overview of the film led to progressive discussion of important issues: point of view, audience identification, critical reception, melodrama, recognition, etc. My method in each case was to do background reading and then view the film carefully, taking scene-by-scene notes. That led to a somewhat chronological account, which isn't always the best way of doing things. I'm relieved that I kept your attention.

*Since Charlton Heston quoted Lord Chesterfield to you, I'll appropriate that quote for one more question: is it harder to write a short book?*

No, I think a short book is easier. What Heston meant is that it takes time to write concisely and well. A hasty first draft (a characteristic of most student essays) is almost always awkward or prolix. It's not uncommon for me to spend a day revising a paragraph. Even when the writing goes smoothly, to make something good takes time.

## Charles Burnett

*In the acknowledgments to* Charles Burnett: A Cinema of Symbolic Knowledge *(University of California Press, 2017), you mention that Burnett is the first filmmaker you've written about whom you've met personally. Did that have an impact on your approach to the topic? And did you receive any feedback from him after publication?*

I usually avoid trying to meet the filmmakers I'm writing about because I want to retain a critical detachment— I don't want my work to seem "authorized" or influenced by friendship. I do research in libraries or film archives, and once or twice I've interviewed people who worked in secondary roles on films by Welles and Hitchcock. The great Brazilian director Nelson Pereira dos Santos became a friend because my wife Darlene had written a book about him. I've interviewed or appeared alongside Peter Bogdanovich at a number of events. I'm fond of Guy Maddin and had fun in public conversations with him. Because Jon Vickers invited so many legendary directors to IU Cinema, I met several of them. (You probably did also.) I especially enjoyed having dinner with Bette Gordon and Jim Jarmusch. And I've come to know and enjoy conversation with Pedro Costa, about whom Darlene and I have just written a book.

But Charles Burnett was the first exception to the rule. I had begun writing my book about him when he was invited to IU Cinema. I gave the Bloomington audience an introduction to one of his films and afterward he and I went out for coffee, where I nervously announced what I was doing. He hadn't read any of my things and knew nothing about me, so I imagine we both felt a bit uncomfortable. But he's a quietly unassuming person and a pleasure to be around. I was deeply impressed by his films, and that probably made me shy or inhibited when we talked.

I maintained a distance because I didn't want to pester him and because I was writing about his films, not his life. Carolyn Schroeder, his producer on *The Glass Shield*, helped arrange for me to have lunch with him in Los Angeles, where I was able to ask him some questions, and as I wrote the book he answered more questions on email. He gave me two of his screenplays—*Bless Their Little Hearts*

(1984) and the equally excellent but unfortunately unfilmed *Man in a Basket*, which is his adaptation of a Chester Himes novel. Jon Vickers also enabled me to view a screener of his rarely seen *The Final Insult* (1997), a fifty-five minute semi-documentary on homelessness in Los Angeles, which was originally shown on ZDF television in Germany. That impressive film seems to have fallen through the cracks of the table of contents in my book and has been seldom viewed in America. I wish I had given it more emphasis.

My book was supported by a grant from the Academy of Motion Picture Arts and Sciences, which, as part of the award, invited me to give a lecture on *To Sleep with Anger* (1990) at the Mary Pickford Theater in LA. On the day of the talk, Charles' honorary Academy Award had just been announced. He and many of those who worked with him were there, and he let me give him a hug. We never became close friends but I very much liked and admired him. I suppose my admiration couldn't help influencing what I wrote, but I'll stand by my critical judgements. I sent him a copy of the book. He thanked me, but we never had a conversation about it.

*I detect in the book an interest in one transplanted Southerner by another. Burnett didn't live in the Deep South as long as you did, and his circumstances were obviously different. But you emphasize Burnett's experiences with discrimination while growing up in Watts and you suss out Southern themes and motifs that recur in his films.*

That has more to do with the films themselves than with my growing up in the South. I've never felt transplanted because I was too glad to get out. But only a few of Burnett's pictures are without Southern themes, simply because he was part of the Southern Black diaspora that moved to Los Angeles after World War II. The people he knew as a young man were what he called a "displaced community," often grimly poor and separated from the rest of the city by de facto apartheid. Burnett sometimes shows us the reactionary and chauvinistic elements among them, but his films never make simple judgements of Black characters and in general are loving portraits. It took a long time for the Black southern community in L.A. to become more or less assimilated, and one way they survived was to hold on to important Southern customs, religion, and folkways. This is an obvious issue in *Killer of Sheep* (1973), *My Brother's Wedding* (1983), and *To Sleep with Anger*. Burnett's later pictures—especially *Nightjohn* (1996) and *Nat Turner: A Troublesome Property*

(2003)—deal with the historical South because that subject is absolutely necessary for understanding Black experience in America.

*The Black Arts Movement from roughly the mid-1960s to the mid-1970s advocated Black Pride and Power in creative works in literature, poetry, painting, and on stage, but tended to dismiss similar achievements in Black cinema and television, and scholars have followed suit (erroneously, Lars Lierow has argued in recent publications). By and large, the movement didn't recognize the gifted Black filmmakers who emerged out of the "L.A. Rebellion," which happened concurrently, although the term, as you point out, wasn't coined until 1984. You also point out that Burnett, the most prominent of the Black directors to come out of UCLA, tended to focus on the domestic sphere instead of making overt political statements. Do you think that's why his work hasn't been more widely recognized?*

Elyseo Taylor, one of Burnett's most influential teachers at UCLA, was a proponent of the Black Arts Movement and directed a fifteen-minute color documentary on Black painting. The movement seems to have been concerned with inculcating a Black point of view in various forms of high or respectable art. There was a general distaste among socially committed Blacks, including Burnett, for the Blaxploitation movies of the Seventies, and that may have played a part. But filmmakers like Bill Gunn were also overlooked.

I would say that in later years Burnett's work has been very widely recognized by critics and filmmakers, and his reputation has grown steadily. Even so, he's relatively little-known to the Black or White popular audience. No filmmaker has more seriously and devotedly depicted the Black underclass, but Burnett isn't widely famous because he hasn't made the kind of movies that would interest your average producer. His films have never gotten truly big budgets and wide distribution. It's true that he doesn't make typical social problem films—I think this is a point in his favor—but social problems are evident everywhere in his work. As he once put it, his pictures are less about winning than about survival. He once lamented that "if the socially oriented film is finally made, its showing will be limited and the very ones it is made for and about will probably never see it."

*To say that* Killer of Sheep *has held up would be an understatement. I recall your deeming it the greatest student film ever made. Martin Scorsese has spoken to its influence*

*Killer of Sheep*

*on subsequent generations of filmmakers. But I didn't know until reading your book that it received some dismissive reviews upon its original release.*

First I should say I've just learned that Milestone has produced a 4K edition of *Killer of Sheep* that will be shown at theaters around the country in 2025 and soon after be distributed by Criterion, along with many extras.

It certainly counts as a student film. It was Burnett's 1973 MFA thesis at UCLA and was shot in 16mm black-and-white on weekends in Watts with a cast made up partly of local residents. It turned out to be a major achievement and one of the most original films ever made in America. In the late Seventies it had limited showings in this country but in 1981 it won a prize at the Berlin Film Festival, followed by another limited release that got dismissive reviews from *The New York Times* and *Sight and Sound*. (Even J. Hoberman of *The Village Voice* disliked it, though he later changed his mind.) But its reputation grew steadily and in 1990 it was one of the first films picked for the National Film Registry at the Library of Congress. Nearly thirty years after it was made, Milestone Films, Steven Soderbergh, and UCLA's Ross Lipman restored the print, converted it to 35mm, and gave it proper theater showings and a DVD. As you say, it has held up.

*My favorite of his films is* To Sleep with Anger, *and the demonic Harry is my favorite of Danny Glover's performances. I was surprised to read in your chapter that*

*Burnett almost didn't offer the role to Glover because he was rumored to prefer playing younger characters. (The running gag in the* Lethal Weapon *movies from the same era is that Glover is always on the verge of retirement — even though the actor was only in his early forties in the first two installments — and his catchphrase is "I'm too old for this shit.")* To Sleep with Anger *has many qualities worth discussing, but it seems like a particularly good example of what you describe as Burnett's unappreciated sense of humor.*

*To Sleep with Anger* is also my favorite and I agree it's Glover's best performance. When it was shown in conjunction with the talk I gave at the Mary Pickford Theater, the director-photographer John Bailey, who was then President of the Motion Picture Academy, told me he hadn't seen it before and was especially impressed by its complex mixture of tones and moods. I think that's exactly right. It has the domestic and the supernatural, the sinister and the comic, the quotidian and the dream, the troubling and the sweet. It even verges on comic absurdism when Harry falls dead on the floor and the family can't move the body. (The trouble with Harry is that once he's in your home you can't get rid of him.) Maybe the dominant tone of the film is comic, in the sense that everything ends harmoniously, with dangerous family tensions resolved and the Harry Man, who brought the tensions to the fore, no longer a problem.

*To Sleep With Anger*

I think quiet humor is an important element in Burnett's work, even when his films are about grim subjects. One of his pictures, *The Annihilation of Fish* (1999), is a flat-out comedy starring James Earl Jones and Lynn Redgrave, with a plot that was very risky for Hollywood: it involves a romance between an older couple of different races, both of whom are schizophrenics. In other films Burnett pays a good deal of attention to children, who can be innately humorous, and to a kind of situational humor. In *Several Friends* (1969), one of his early UCLA student films, there are comic moments when two pals struggle mightily with moving a refrigerator and repairing a car. A third friend arrives and berates them because he's brought along a couple of women for a date. The two guys are un-showered and stinking and will make a bad impression. One of them says defensively, "at least we ain't hippies."

*I gather* The Annihilation of Fish *has recently been restored and released.*

Yes, the original showing of the film had such a negative review in *Variety* that it never got a distributor. I had to view it at the UCLA film and TV archive. That original review was wrong, but I thought the recent NPR review somewhat overpraised the film (and it should have mentioned that sex is the potentially controversial basis of its comedy). Although I do like the film, I think Margot Kidder is miscast as a landlady, and I think the production design makes everything look too prosperous and pretty, unlike the film's literary source, which is a story by Anthony Winkler. I suspect these problems weren't due to Burnett. His treatment of minor characters or semi-extras is one of the best things about the picture, and the clearest sign of his directorial presence.

*Do you think that* The Glass Shield *(1994) ultimately overcomes Harvey Weinstein's patented tampering before its initial release?*

I think it's an unusual and excellent film. Miramax's tampering was mainly with the ending, in which the young cop J. J. Johnson has a despairing conversation with his fiancée. Burnett told me the original version was deemed "too long," and was edited a bit at Miramax's insistence. Producer Carolyn Schroeder told me it was "tamped down" but in her view that didn't damage the film. The real problem was in Miramax's promotion and marketing. Instead of exhibiting the picture in adult or art film venues, they created a shoot-'em-up preview and action-oriented advertising aimed at teenaged Black audiences, who were no doubt attracted by Ice Cube in a key role. It's the farthest thing from an action-packed gangster picture and kids hated it. Partly because it was booked in the wrong theaters, the reviews were mixed and some critics didn't realize what they were seeing. *The Glass Shield* is about police and judicial corruption, but it isn't like Sidney Lumet's *Serpico* (1973). The style is often expressionistic and the central character isn't a professional but a callow young Black man who naively joins a criminally racist police unit and whose misplaced idealism causes him to betray his values and damage others.

*Which of Burnett's relatively recent works do you find particularly noteworthy?*

I highly recommend *Nightjohn*, one of his very best pictures, which as we speak is available for streaming on Amazon. It's about slavery in the antebellum South, centering on the extreme danger of literacy among slaves. A young girl is secretly taught to read by a rebellious slave named Nightjohn, whose name derives from his teachings in the deep of night. This causes trouble among both the slaves and their overlords. When Nightjohn is discovered, his forefinger and thumb are chopped off by the plantation owner so that he can never write again. The film is based on a young adult novel and was produced—believe it or not— by Disney and Hallmark in the period of after school TV movies for the young. Inevitably it compromises in showing the grisly, violent terror of the slave system, but it remains a powerful film and got deserved critical praise.

I also highly recommend *Nat Turner: A Troublesome Property*, produced in association with KQED Public Television. A unique combination of talking-head interviews and dramatic episodes in which six different actors play Nat, it's absorbing and educational in the best possible sense. And I have a soft spot for *Warming by the Devil's Fire* (2003), which is part of a seven-picture series on blues music produced by Martin Scorsese for PBS. That series had some distinguished directors, including Scorsese, Wim Wenders, Mike Figgis, and Clint Eastwood, but Burnett's offering is by far the best. In some ways autobiographical, it's an impressive archive of great blues performers. Finally, I would strongly recommend *When it Rains* (2007), which is among the finest short films I've ever seen. "We live with contradictions," the narrator and leading character says, "how do you mix jazz and blues together?" The film shows you how, and is a sometimes humorous, sometimes downbeat portrait of a community.

*I spent an hour with Charles when he visited the Lilly, and showed him some highlights from the collections. It was during that hour that he offered a critique of John Ford, in his inimitably softspoken manner, that was nonetheless so powerful that I wish I had written it down. The point of this is not one's opinion of Ford, but rather recognizing that the force and clarity yet elusiveness of Burnett in person (my not remembering his exact words but vividly his meanings) is what draws me to his films. Would you describe that quality as more from his lyrical/poetic side than the much-discussed influence of neorealism?*

That's a perfect description of Charles' personality, which usually gave me the feeling of still waters running deep. I would love to know his opinion of Ford and wish you'd been able to write it down. (I'm sure he was critical.) I always felt he was a gentle person with strong and admirable convictions, and as you say there's a lyrical/poetic element to his work. To me the neorealist description of his early films is overstated. By the Seventies, when Burnett began, there was no reason to describe every on-location picture with non-professional players neorealist. I think Burnett had more in common with the early Brazilian Cinema Novo (whose films he knew), and he once praised Jean Vigo, a poetic filmmaker if ever there was one.

## Cary Grant

*Some Versions of Cary Grant (Oxford University Press, 2022) feels in some ways an extension of Acting in the Cinema, specifically the latter book's chapter on Grant's performance in North by Northwest. But you're also doing something very different in breaking down an actor's body of work into different types of performances. To attempt this with one of the most famous of movie stars, one frequently thought to be playing himself (whoever that was), is especially bracing for the reader. How did you get the idea for the book, and how did you decide on your approach?*

The book came about almost by accident. In Bristol, England, the birthplace of Archie Leach, there's a biennial Cary Grant celebration, and in 2020, the event was scheduled to take place simultaneously in New York and Bristol. Because of my chapter on *North by Northwest* in the acting book, I was invited to give a talk in New York.

The New York conference was cancelled due to the Covid pandemic, and Professor Charlotte Crofts of the University of the West of England in Bristol invited me to give the talk to their audience via Zoom. When I wrote that talk, I realized it could form the basis of a short book, which was fun to write because Cary Grant is fun. The "versions" approach was inspired by William Empson's great book *Some Versions of Pastoral* (1935).

*In your introduction, you even suggest that Grant was an auteur. Could you explain what you mean by that?*

I wrote "a kind of auteur." Like several of the major stars in the last decades of the studio system, Grant perfected a style and a set of thematic interests that could serve as a personality and a brand in his films. He was an intelligent actor who contributed to his scripts and watched the rushes closely, and to a remarkable degree he chose the films in which he appeared. In his late years he had his own production company in partnership with Stanley Donen. I think all this qualifies as a kind of authorship.

Grant made some good and bad choices, only selectively picking roles that were markedly different from his usual image. Among the pictures I wish he hadn't turned down was the Cukor version of *A Star is Born* (1954), in which he would have played a fading, suicidal movie star. He was good friends with Clifford Odets, but he seems also to have turned down a proposed film of Odets' *The Big Knife*, where again he would have played a suicidal star. (I hasten to add that Grant wasn't suicidal, but he wasn't inclined to be critical of Hollywood or his stardom.)

*I know you don't mean for your five versions of Cary Grant to be the only way to assess his acting, but in your chapter on "Farceur Cary," I appreciated that you not only praised his comic performances as significant instead of trivial, and highly disciplined instead of tossed-off, but you break down even further how Grant is giving different comic performances in (to use two of your examples)* The Awful Truth *(1937) and* Bringing Up Baby *(1938). How does he calibrate his performances in those movies?*

Grant's early theatrical training was in an all-boy group of Bristol comics who did slapstick and acrobatics. That experience, plus his innate good looks, made him unique as a movie star. *The Awful Truth*, which more than any of his early films helped him become a star, shows his ability to be

*The Awful Truth*

what Andrew Sarris described as a "well-tailored romantic gentleman with the physical gifts of a baggy-pants comedian."

In *Bringing Up Baby* he's even more physical, but instead of a sophisticated man about town he's an awkward, absent-minded professor in glasses (modelled on Harold Lloyd) who keeps saying "uh" and "oh" while running and tripping in the wake of Katharine Hepburn. The third farcical film I discussed was *His Girl Friday* (1940), in which he plays a dapper, unscrupulous newspaper editor with a gift for fast-paced repartee with Rosalind Russell, who plays a reporter ex-wife. These are three very different but equally funny roles.

*While my favorite version of Cary Grant is Farceur Cary, my favorite "Cary Grant movie" is also one of my top-three Hitchcock movies:* Notorious *(1946). How does that film and* Suspicion *(1941) reflect what you call "Dark Cary," even though he never played a villain (as even Jimmy Stewart did early in his career in* After the Thin Man) *or even an antihero (as Stewart did in some of his Westerns for Anthony Mann)?*

Hitchcock directed both of those movies and Grant was a perfect actor for him. Grant could do the simplest, in some ways most difficult things (opening a door, crossing a room, taking a chair) with consistency and precision, and he could calibrate his glances offscreen in ways that suited Hitch's editing schemes. But Grant had a screen presence that David Thomson has accurately described as the ability

*Bringing Up Baby*

to be attractive and unattractive at the same time. In *Suspicion*, he plays a man who, at least in the source novel, is a wife killer. The film was supposed to resemble the novel, but RKO refused to have a famously romantic star be a murderer. As a result, Hitchcock made Grant innocent but irresponsible, untrustworthy, and in some ways sinister. The key to the performance is a sustained ambiguity, a charm mixed with a touch of menace. Some critics have seen the film as a portrait of a woman who neurotically fantasizes that her husband is a killer, but as Tania Modleski has pointed out, there are good reasons why the wife (Joan Fontaine) should be suspicious. It isn't one of Hitchcock's best films, but Grant certainly doesn't qualify as a hero.

In *Notorious*, Grant is a neurotic good guy, a U.S. government agent who begins by thinking Ingrid Bergman is a promiscuous alcoholic, then falls in love with her, then out of hurt pride enlists her in a scheme to marry a Nazi. He's just as insecure and prone to jealousy as Claude Rains, her prospective husband. For me this qualifies as a slightly dark character in a darker film. I should also point out that in his first major picture, *Blonde Venus* (1932), Grant plays an unsavory character. He's a criminal, albeit sometimes likeable, in *Sylvia Scarlett* (1935), and in *Mr. Lucky* (1943) he's a crooked gambler who reforms.

Maybe I should also note that in *The Bishop's Wife* (1947), he plays an angel. I sometimes think I should have had another "version" called "Perfect Cary."

*For "Romantic Cary," my thoughts turn first to Stanley Donen's* Charade *(1963), in which Grant stars with Audrey Hepburn. Or even* Only Angels Have Wings *(1939), in which you'd have to Venn Diagram the multiple love triangles between Grant and Jean Arthur, Grant and Rita Hayworth, and (perhaps the emotional heart of the film) Grant and Thomas Mitchell. But you choose another Leo McCarey movie, the popular* An Affair to Remember *(1957), and a different Stanley Donen movie, the relatively not-remembered* Indiscreet *(1958). How do those films showcase Grant as a romantic leading man?*

Most classical Hollywood movies of the studio era could be called romantic because they have attractive male/female parings and happy endings. *Only Angels Have Wings* is certainly romantic in that sense, but it's also a Hawksian action-adventure film with traces of a Dark, even misogynistic Cary. You can call *Charade* romantic, but it's very much a Hitchcock-style thriller. I was speaking of films that are *primarily* centered on heterosexual romance—films that involve an attractive but ostensibly mismatched couple who meet by chance, fall in love, encounter impediments to their relationship, and ultimately achieve happiness. That's what classic Hollywood meant by a romantic movie, which could be dramatic or musical in form. *An Affair to Remember* and *Indiscreet* are pure Hollywood romance—boy meets girl, boy loses girl, boy gets girl, without suspenseful action-style elements.

*I forget who said it, but I read somewhere that the key to Grant's romantic appeal is that he rarely chased women in his movies—he let them chase him. Do you think there's truth to that statement?*

I'm not sure who first said it, maybe Pauline Kael, but you probably read it in my book because I said it there. I also quoted Andrew Britton, who wrote that Grant represented "a male heterosexuality which is so different in tone from that of the action hero, and which is arrived at through a different kind of relationship with women." From the moment when Grant was invited by Mae West to come up and see her, his movies usually let the woman take the lead. You wouldn't see him grabbing the woman and carrying her upstairs to bed, à la Gable in *Gone With the Wind*.

*This is where I must confess a dislike for "Domestic Cary"—not your chapter on the subject, but what I derisively call "Cary Grant with a Bunch of Urchins" movies. I don't care for the premise in general, from* Cheaper by the Dozen *(1950, with Clifton Webb and Myrna Loy) to* Yours, Mine and Ours *(1968, with Lucille Ball and Henry Fonda). But other than* Father Goose *(1964)—which you don't use as a case study, but has an edge to it that I enjoy and gives us a Cary Grant gone amusingly to seed in Peter Stone's script— they don't work for me. That probably says more about me than the movies themselves. But what am I missing?*

Maybe it says something about you, but I agree the two non-Grant pictures you mention aren't good. Obviously, however, I like the films I chose for that chapter, which maybe you didn't see or should watch again. *Mr. Blandings Builds his Dream House* (1948) is excellent, and *Room for One More* (1952), which nobody would pick as one of Grant's best, is worth defending.

When I wrote about domestic Cary I was reminded of W. C. Fields' advice to thespians: never play scenes with children and animals. You probably agree with Fields, but Grant upends that advice. He's very good with kids, maybe because he liked them, or maybe because he began as a teenage comic. In *Monkey Business* (1952) he plays a scientist who takes a serum and regresses to childhood. In *Mr. Blandings* his interactions with the two pre-teen girls are always amusing because of the way he lets the girls get the better of him. "Just one morning I'd like to have breakfast without *social significance*," he says to the older one, whose school paper is critical of "middle-class people." When the younger daughter says "bicker, bicker, bicker" to Grant and Myrna Loy, Grant can only respond with, "Drink your milk."

I can't believe you don't like Grant's scenes in *Room for One More* with "Foghorn" George Winslow, a unique child actor who a year later worked alongside Marilyn Monroe in *Gentlemen Prefer Blondes* (1953). Grant had spotted Winslow on TV and insisted on him for the film. In this respect it's worth noting that when Grant was just starting out in New York theater, he knew, admired, and studied George Burns, and as a result he was skilled in comic reaction shots and in scenes where he plays the straight man—in *Room for One More* he plays straight man to Winslow while at the same time making a chocolate cake that ends up being eaten by the family dog.

*My struggles with understanding "Cockney Cary" also undoubtedly have to do with my not having seen those movies, but how do you see that version in the overall picture of Grant as an actor and star?*

Unlike Claude Rains and Michael Caine, Grant wasn't a Cockney. Bristol is a long way from the East End of London, which was the historic home of poor and working-class people who were called Cockneys. Lots of actors have played Cockneys in movies, usually in comic pictures—even Bogart did one. Probably in order to understand what I meant, you need to see George Cukor's *Sylvia Scarlett* and Clifford Odets' *None But the Lonely Heart* (1944), two of the films in which Grant played a Cockney character. The first was a box-office disaster that nevertheless convinced critics he could act. (It has an important afterlife as a favorite of the LBGTQ community.) The second is probably Grant's most personal film, a kind of tragedy reminiscent in some ways of his childhood. It got him an Academy Award nomination but is seldom shown today.

These two films represent a version of Grant, and the chapter about them brings into focus my use of William Empson for the title of my book. Unlike most of the films in Grant's career, they have what Empson describes as a "pastoral" quality, by which he means a story that gives humanity and complexity to outlaws or the working class. Grant uses a Cockney accent in both films. In the bittersweet comedy *Sylvia Scarlett*, he's a charming thief, and he exaggerates the accent, dropping an initial "H" at every opportunity. In the realistic *None But the Lonely Heart*, he plays a vagabond who is alienated from his impoverished London neighborhood, and he modulates the accent. Grant didn't always have to behave as if he belonged in a well-appointed drawing room. He was more like Archie Leach in these films, both of which deserve more attention.

*With all the impressions of Cary Grant on talk shows and by stand-up comics and in movies over the years (you cite a memorable example: Tony Curtis' in* Some Like It Hot*), do you think that developing an identifiable persona is one thing that separates "classic" Hollywood movie stars such as Grant from contemporary famous actors? I ask because, while Leonardo DiCaprio, Joaquin Phoenix, and others are big box-office draws, I would be hard-pressed to think of an accurate or amusing impression of them, because what would that look like? A few years ago, Ryan Reynolds and Jason Bateman starred in* The Change-Up, *a body-switching comedy together, and my first thought was: how could you tell them apart?*

Curtis' impersonation of Grant, with whom he had recently acted, is the best of the lot, but it's cunningly exaggerated for comedy. (It's interesting that Billy Wilder was a great fan of Grant and kept trying to get him for a movie, with no luck. Grant would have been wonderful in *Love in the Afternoon* [1957]). Comic impersonation is usually exaggerated, and dramatic impersonation tries to be realistic. Both are modern developments, dependent on media celebrities known to a very large audience. But as you say, contemporary Hollywood stars are less subject to impersonation because they have a broader range of roles and don't develop easily identifiable mannerisms.

Some very good films have required actors to do realistic impersonation. I admire Larry Parks in *The Jolson Story* (1946), Clint Eastwood as John Huston in *White Hunter Black Heart* (1990), and Philip Seymour Hoffman in *Capote* (2005). Christian McKay is terrific as Orson Welles in *Me and Orson Welles* (2009), and I suspect the British actor Tom Burke , who appeared as Welles in *Mank* (2002), could probably play him anywhere without half trying. Keven Spacey does a virtuoso imitation of Bobby Darin in *Beyond the Sea* (2004), but to me it doesn't quite work because Darin was younger than Spacey and Darin's talent as both actor and singer was immense, almost beyond imitation. A boatload of women have impersonated Marilyn Monroe, but I think the best of the lot is the amazing Michelle Williams in *My Week with Marilyn* (2011). I can't count the number of Elvis impersonators, who blur together.

To my knowledge there has been only one film that features a realistic impersonation of Grant: the TV miniseries *Archie* (2023), with Jason Isaacs in the title role. There are fleeting moments in that show when Isaacs seems like Grant, but most of the time he doesn't. I can't get involved with the film because the very attempt by an actor to play Cary Grant realistically creates an alienation effect. There's a danger of this in any film involving non-comic impersonation, no matter how good it is.

*What is your favorite version of Cary Grant?*

Like you, I like Farceur Cary. I think Grant's skill as a comic was almost the equal of Charlie Chaplin's, an actor with whom he had surprising things in common.

# Pedro Costa

*It hasn't been published at the time of this interview, but you have written a book about the great Portuguese filmmaker Pedro Costa. It's notable for being your first co-authorship with your wife, Darlene Sadlier. Would you like to talk about that project?*

By all means. The book is titled *The Haunted Cinema of Pedro Costa*, scheduled for publication in Summer, 2025. I collaborated with Darlene for several reasons: working together with her is enjoyable, she's fluent in Portuguese, and she knows more than I do about the cinematic/social/ artistic history of Portugal. We're both great admirers of Costa, who in my opinion is the most unusual and important contemporary filmmaker. We got to know him, had a memorable visit with him in Lisbon, and throughout he's been very helpful to us. The book is a departure for me not only because it's a collaboration, but also because it's about a foreign artist.

*How did you go about collaborating? Did Darlene write some chapters and you others?*

No, we wrote every chapter together. Sometimes I wrote the first draft and sometimes she did. We passed each chapter back and forth, making revisions and additions until we were satisfied. This was an easier process than it might seem because we have adjacent studies in our home. We seldom argued about anything. We made individual contributions to the book, but it's impossible to say that any chapter is the product of a single author.

*Although Costa has many admirers, his work isn't widely known. How would you describe his films and explain their importance to people who haven't seen them?*

I'll start with the title of our introductory chapter "Who is He and What is Cinema?" We chose that title because when we told friends and colleagues we were writing about Costa, they sometimes asked, "Who is he?" The question wasn't surprising. Costa has never received wide distribution in America and is best known at festivals, metropolitan art cinemas, and museums. Many of his films were made with minimal equipment and crew, which is the best way of maintaining artistic control, and the best way for most people to see them is in a boxed set from Criterion or in Blu-rays from various distributors. These relatively low-budget pictures are set in unfamiliar places and are sometimes deliberately elliptical and disorienting, without the signposts or expository information moviemakers usually give audiences.

That being said, Costa has a fairly wide range of work, beginning with a moody black and white noir called *Blood* (1989) and an impressive color film called *Down to Earth* (1991), shot on a volcanic island in Cape Verde. The second film led to a career-long interest in the lives of Cape Verdean immigrants in Portugal. He's diverged from his major interest only twice, in a couple of documentaries about artistic labor: *Where Does Your Hidden Smile Lie?* (2001), which is a loving and amusing portrait of Jean-Marie Straub and Danièle Huillet as they edit one of their films, and *Change Nothing* (2009), which is a portrait of French actress and chanteuse Jeanne Balibar as she performs and works on an album.

Costa's most revolutionary films were shot in tight spaces with non-professional actors and compact digital equipment, but they're also the products of a great pictorialist who creates beautiful films about unglamorous lives in impoverished locations. In certain ways he provokes André Bazin's famous question, "What is Cinema?" When digital cameras, CGI, and digital post-production were first introduced, some theorists argued that the abandonment of celluloid was the death of cinema—an untenable argument few would make today, and that Costa's work clearly refutes. Other arguments are more difficult to resolve. Is Costa's *In Vanda's Room* (2000) documentary or fiction? The people in the film play themselves, using their own words and daily experiences. When they smoke heroin or inject it, they're actually doing it. But the film doesn't seem like direct cinema or a fly-on-the-wall documentary; the images are artfully composed, the scenes were often re-shot many times, and the soundtrack was manipulated for diegetic music and effects.

The collaboration between Costa and the performers is so intense that one can also ask, what is the authorship? Our answer, with necessary qualifications, is Costa, though he gives his players more freedom than Robert Bresson, a director he admires. Should his performers be described as actors? We say yes. Costa's chief actors, one could even say his stars, are Vanda Duarte in *Bones* (1997) and *In Vanda's Room*; Ventura in *Colossal Youth* (2006) and *Horse Money* (2014); and Vitalina Varela, the eponymous heroine in *Vitalina Varela* (2019). All three are non-professional but unforgettable inhabitants of either the drug-ridden Lisbon casbah, Fontaínhas, or the public housing projects outside

Lisbon, constructed for "urban renewal." The films in which they star occupy a fascinating liminal space between poverty and beauty, narrative and non-narrative, documentary and fiction, auteur and collective, acting and being.

*Why does the book describe Costa's cinema as "haunted"?*

He doesn't make horror films, but the atmosphere of his pictures, which aren't without sweet and comic moments, often seems haunted. In some cases his characters are troubled by memories and have conversations with ghosts, but the ghosts don't at all seem strange or spectral—we only retroactively realize they were ghosts. His major characters also have another kind of liminal quality, a hovering between life and death. It's significant that *Down to Earth*, one of his early films, was inspired by Val Lewton and Jacques Tourneur's poetic horror picture *I Walked with a Zombie*. Most of Costa's chief characters have a Zombified existence—they're drug-addled, or in the case of one of his greatest films, *Horse Money*, tormented by schizophrenia, confusion, and frightening memories. The result is a strange kind of cinematic poetry.

*Horse Money*

*A quality that stands out in your bibliography is that you rarely repeat yourself. You've written a book, edited a book, and published articles all on Welles, but by and large there are surprising transitions, from* Psycho *to* Welles *to acting, from film noir to Stanley Kubrick to Charles Burnett, and now Pedro Costa. Is it a conscious choice to take on different subjects?*

There are some academics who spend their whole lives writing about Virginia Woolf or participating in the Hitchcock industry, but I've never wanted to specialize in a single author or topic. Actually, my publishing range hasn't been as wide as it might seem because I've written mostly about Hollywood. If I had remained an English department specialist in modern British literature, the situation might have been roughly similar. I probably would have written about a variety of authors, but I would have remained in the boundaries of that historical period.

I always feel I've burnt a bridge behind me when I finish a book and am somewhat fatigued by the subject. The acting book came about when an editor suggested I write a book about movie stars, and it became something different from what I initially proposed. The Minnelli book happened when the editor of a series on directors suggested I write one of the volumes (my first choice was Andy Warhol, who had already been picked). The Kubrick was prompted when Rob White, a fine editor at the BFI, offered me a chance to write about *2001* for their Film Classics series; I didn't want to do that and instead proposed a book on Kubrick's whole career. The Charles Burnett originated when I was editing the *Contemporary Film Directors* series for University of Illinois Press—a series that published roughly thirty-five volumes and is still going with a new editor. I repeatedly tried to get a Black scholar to do a volume on Burnett but couldn't find one who was available. As a result I decided to write a longer, different kind of book myself—I admired Burnett greatly and thought somebody should do it.

I've long harbored a desire to write about foreign and art films, and I wish I could have been more cosmopolitan. In my later years, as a "writer at large" at *Film Quarterly*, I wrote an annual column picking my ten favorite pictures of the year. I listed very few Hollywood pictures in that column, and none from Hollywood were my top choices. The book on Pedro Costa that I've just written with Darlene is an outgrowth of my desire to escape the Hollywood-centric quality of my work and to put emphasis on a great artist from abroad.

# TEACHING

## Classroom Experiences

*When I was a teaching assistant, my mentor, Dr. Ron Zupko, a brilliant professor of history, initially didn't like that I was emulating his style to a certain extent. He seemed somewhat mollified when I explained that it was natural for a greenhorn in any profession to look to a veteran for inspiration (it's common with filmmakers too) and that I would eventually develop my own classroom persona (which I did). Did any of your mentors influence your teaching style? And did that style change over time?*

As I've said, my most influential teacher was Bernard Benstock. My literary specialization was due to his influence, and I liked his personal style outside the classroom. Bernie was a world traveler and bon vivant who could cook a mean coq au vin. I never imitated his style, but it inspired me. This being said, I can't think of anybody whose style in the classroom I tried to imitate—I had almost no bad teachers, but there was nobody I wanted to copy when speaking from the front of the room. This was especially true when I began teaching film courses, for which I had no models. I'm sure my teaching style and technique evolved over time, but I wasn't conscious of it. I think Professor Zupko gave you good advice. Teachers, like writers, can have influences (not of the anxious kind posited by Harold Bloom), but they need to find their own voices.

*You've been retired from teaching for some years. Do you miss it?*

No, I'm happy to be retired from teaching—not to be free of the classroom but free of grading student papers and attending faculty meetings. Sometimes I miss the contact with young people, which can be enjoyable, enlightening, and refreshing. I was lucky to have that experience and I also had moments in the classroom that gave me ideas for writing. But since retiring I can jog every day, take naps, and reserve much more time to write. I can't believe I wrote my early things while teaching. I composed by hand and copied what I had written on a typewriter, sometimes using scissors and paste to rearrange or add things. The Indiana English Department had a good typing pool and I could pay someone to make clean copies for me.

Indiana is a research institution so my teaching load was light compared to many places. I taught two courses per semester, mixing undergraduate and graduate classes. But the teaching eventually became onerous. When I switched to film I had large enrollments, not only in the undergrad lecture courses where I had teaching assistants, but also in the smaller courses, which sometimes had up to forty students with no teaching assistant. I didn't give short-answer exams and spent a lot of time grading essay papers. Things were a bit easier when I did guest teaching in Hamburg, Chicago, and UCLA.

*How were the guest teaching jobs different?*

For one thing, I was free of the many jobs regular faculty members have in addition to teaching. I didn't have to attend faculty meetings, administer graduate degree exams, direct dissertations, or work on various committees inside and outside the department.

I loved the year in Hamburg. The city and its culture were exciting and the teaching was relatively easy. I knew very little German, but I was in the University of Hamburg English Department, where I lectured in English. I picked up a fair amount of what you could call street German. (My accent was bad. People would sometimes ask me, *Bist du Franzose?* [Are you French?]). I taught a course on *Ulysses*, and because this was the pre-digital world I hauled a 16mm print of *Citizen Kane* all the way to Germany so I could teach a course on that. The local art cinema, the Kommunalen Kino, also known as the Metropolis, was showing a retrospective on Kubrick and because students could go there cheaply I taught a lecture course on him in a big auditorium. To my astonishment, there were over two hundred students in the class and no assistant. I was very worried until it was explained to me that nobody had to write anything unless they wanted — they were mostly there to hear me speak English.

At Chicago and UCLA I taught courses on Minnelli, Kubrick, and film acting. I've offered the acting course in several places but always felt it was unsuccessful. These schools were difficult for me only because they are on the quarter rather than semester system, which means that graduate students have very little time to write term papers. Maybe I should mention that I also enjoyed teaching one-week guest seminars for English-speaking graduates in Spain, Italy, and Norway, plus a one-month course for university teachers at a Lilly Endowment event in Boulder, Colorado. In those places I lectured about pedagogy and talked about Kubrick, Welles, and in one case *The Best Years of Our Lives* (1947). There was no paper grading, which added to the pleasures of the visits.

*You say the acting course never felt successful. Was that because of you or the topic? Do you think you had strengths and weaknesses as a teacher?*

It was probably my fault but it was also because of the topic. Writing about acting is difficult, and the student term papers weren't productive enough. These were graduate seminars with seven to ten students, and I always felt my role in any seminar was to establish readings and films, not to lecture. I tended to sit back and moderate discussion, then give the students advice about writing papers. It worked in most seminars, but not so much in seminars on acting,

When I offered an acting seminar at Indiana, though, I had an interesting experience. One of the students told me he wanted to write his term paper on Montgomery Clift. I told him fine, but because I had read biographies of Clift, he should be careful to write about Clift's art, not his tragic life. In my view Clift was an enormously talented actor, more gifted than James Dean. His major early films— *Red River* (1948), *The Heiress* (1949), and *A Place in the Sun* (1951)—were three quite different roles and together they established him as one of the most versatile and also beautiful stars in the movies. (Young Stanley Kubrick took great casual photos of him in *Look* magazine.) As he grew older and lost his beauty, rumors circled around him: supposedly his face was ruined in an auto accident, he had become a drug addict because of a Dr. Feelgood, and he was gay. Only the last of these claims was accurate. Clift's life was short, but in some of his late films—*Judgment at Nuremberg* (1961), *The Misfits* (1960), and especially *Wild River* (1960)—he gave us dramatically insecure characters and showed that he had lost none of his talent.

I was concerned that my student should treat him as an artist. "Don't worry," the student said, "Montgomery Clift was my uncle." He was Robert Clift, who now teaches film production at Pittsburgh and has become a fine documentary filmmaker. He's made an excellent documentary about his uncle, debunking the biographers: *Making Montgomery Clift* (2018).

Another failure in my eyes was a literature seminar on pulp fiction, which, apart from Hammett and Chandler's short fiction, is chiefly about studying plots. I think I realized that too late and could do a much better job of selecting readings today, especially if I broadened the topic to the history of the crime novel.

I always thought I was much better as a lecturer than as a leader of discussion in small classes. I found it difficult to get students talking or debating with one another. Success in the smaller graduate classes was more frequent, but it depended on the topic and the quality of the students. One of my most successful seminars was based entirely on *Casablanca*. Two students in that class later wrote important books on film: Rebecca-Bell Metereau's *Hollywood Androgyny*, which deals with cross-dressing and androgynous sexuality, and Robert B. Ray's *A Certain Tendency of the American Cinema*, which is an ambitious ideological and critical study of the classical Hollywood forms and genres. I was fortunate in having several other talented and successful students who went on to publish books on film, among them Jonathan Cavallero, Guerric DeBona, Michele Hilmes, Kathleen McHugh, Neepa Majumdar, Justus Nieland, Veronica Pravadelli, Jacob Smith, and Juan Suárez. In my library there's an entire shelf of volumes they've written.

*A general question about teaching film. Do you think it's helpful for film students, especially those who study production, to be familiar with other art forms, such as literature, painting or music, or be interested in real-world concerns such as politics?*

I don't think it's necessary for film students to be interested in politics. Some of the best writing on film is formalist in nature. But if you go beyond formalism and want to say something about the politics or ideological implications of movies, you obviously need to know more than movie history. It might also be useful to know about not only politics but also political economy.

Maybe because my training is in literature and most of my teaching has been in literature departments, I believe film students should have a good knowledge of the humanities, and there are certain directors one can't fully understand without wide reading and awareness of political history. Welles, for example, can't be properly written about or studied without understanding that his American career began in the period of the WPA—also that much of his best work was politically engaged and was often literary adaptation. People who write about him need to brush up their Shakespeare. Filmmakers, however, sometimes need only their imagination backed by general knowledge. They don't necessarily need an education, just a passion for an art form and a creative gift.

I can't tell you how often in my first decade of teaching students came to my office and asked me where one should go to learn filmmaking. This was in the years before Indiana had a production school. I told them there are many production schools where in two years you can get your hands on equipment and learn the technical basis for making a film. It also helps if the school has some ability to connect you with job opportunities in the industry. But I always advised students to get an undergraduate degree or a few years of study in the humanities before going to a technical school.

I'm reminded of something I once heard Werner Herzog say. A number of years ago, when Jon Vickers was director of the Indiana University Cinema, he invited many celebrated filmmakers to Bloomington, among them Herzog. During that visit, I attended a luncheon for Herzog organized by Michael McRobbie, then President of the university and a great supporter of the cinema. This was at a moment not long after my retirement, when film studies was about to be moved from Arts and Sciences to a newly created Media School. During the lunch, one of the administrators at the table asked Herzog what sort of university training an aspiring filmmaker should have. His reply was emphatic, almost a shout: "Read, read, read!"

The two directors I've most written about are Welles and Kubrick, neither of whom went to a university or a film school, but who were omnivorous readers. Welles was educated primarily in theater at the Todd School for Boys in Woodstock, Illinois, where he learned Shakespeare by heart. His prodigious talent on stage and in radio enabled him to make movies, but even before he went to Hollywood he had taught himself about movie technology. He made *Hearts of Age* as a teenager, and later his Mercury Theater company made *Too Much Johnson* (1938), an impressive silent movie pastiche with a naughty title, which was designed to be shown as part of a comic stage production. For his part, Kubrick was an indifferent high school student but a prodigy as a photographer. His earliest films were independently produced short subjects and his first two features, *Fear and Desire* (1951) and *Killer's Kiss*, were virtually handmade products that he not only directed but also edited and photographed. He was self-taught as a filmmaker and a remarkable autodidact who read psychology, science, and literature. Both Welles and Kubrick also knew art history and music. Their imagery is indebted to Renaissance perspective and the scores of their movies are unusual—Welles ranged from Waldtufel to Satie, and Kubrick from Strauss to Ligeti.

The Media School here at Indiana has taught many young filmmakers whose work I admire, but as a general rule I think the artists of cinema are best when they've read widely, whether or not they use what they read for movies. I agree with someone who once said, "Reading doesn't make you smart. It makes you human." Unfortunately, in public universities across the nation the humanities are under assault and the emphasis is on job training rather than becoming human. At Indiana, there's a new university administration that's also putting curbs on free speech and student protest. It's depressing.

*Did you enjoy teaching film more than literature?*

To a degree, but I worried about whether the subject of film was adequate for an undergraduate humanities education. I wasn't concerned about the graduate courses, which are aimed at professional education and training. My goal in those was to give the students an opportunity to do research and write term papers that might become essays in an academic journal or seeds for a dissertation—this would help them get an academic job, assuming there were jobs to be had. The undergraduate film classes, on the other hand, were popular as electives, often with students who weren't bright and thought film would be easier and more fun than literature—plus there wouldn't be a lot of assigned reading.

Nobody was going to get a job from the courses I taught, but I hoped I could make the relatively unsophisticated students become more thoughtful and critical viewers of film. Because I was lecturing about old movies, they could also learn some history. (I once taught a big undergrad course on Warner Bros. in the 1930s, which was ideal for learning not only about film but also about the history and politics of the Depression era.) I had enthusiasm for teaching film and maybe that helped. I also put emphasis on writing short essays, a useful skill that I hope I enabled some students to acquire.

*Did you gain any experience as a teaching assistant in graduate school, or did you plunge right into teaching courses as a regular faculty member?*

I was a teaching assistant at both LSU and Wisconsin, at first in elementary composition courses that were taught in small groups of fifteen to twenty students. Even though I had lots of experience with public speaking, teaching for the first several years always gave me butterflies. It was a captive audience, I was young, and I wasn't sure I knew what I was talking about. At Wisconsin, new graduate assistants were given a bit of training in how to grade and comment on student papers. I remember they handed out a sample student paper and asked all of us to assign it a grade. The paper got everything from an A to an F. That was amazing, and I never found out what the faculty thought the grade should be. We were taught that the comment you wrote at the end of the paper was more important than the grade. I agree, although as time went by I felt that students weren't reading my comments.

At Wisconsin the large undergrad courses on literature had discussion sections taught by graduate TAs. I taught several of these, sometimes for courses in which I had to teach two or three classes a week on a given text. That was immensely educational for me, not for learning techniques of teaching but for gaining intimate knowledge of the literature. If you taught Faulkner, Dos Passos, Yeats, or Dickinson two or three times in a week, you got to know them well and you developed ideas.

The first time I taught my own courses was at Indiana. I was hired as an expert on modern British literature, but for a couple of years they gave me undergraduate courses on things that weren't my specialty. One semester the department chair asked me if I would teach a freshman-level course on creative writing, which was an elective somebody had recently created. I knew zero about how to do such a course, but as a new faculty member I wasn't going to turn anything down. The result was like a basket weaving class taught by a blind man. I had no idea how to grade papers and gave passing grades to everybody. I also gave them freedom to write whatever they wanted, as long as it was a story or a poem. One of the students wrote a poem on traffic safety.

The English department later developed a large MFA program in creative writing. Distinguished writers have taught in it, but I remain skeptical of courses on the topic at the undergraduate level. I should note, however, that my son, who got an advanced degree in creative writing from Boston University, is a talented and award-winning novelist. I'm sure it's important to have training in the fine arts, ballet, classical music, theater, film, and even video game design, but I'm not sure everything needs an MFA. I probably sound like an old fogey.

# Student Responses

*Did you have interesting or memorable student responses to your teaching?*

In my own schooling and for several years after I began teaching, there were no student evaluations of faculty. I recall that in one of the graduate courses I took at Madison, the teacher asked us to evaluate the class using a questionnaire that he passed out to us. I thought this was odd and self-serving, because it never occurred to me that students should grade their teachers, even if their teaching was bad. I didn't think it was my place to pass judgement. As time went by, however, the faculty in the English Department at Indiana were required to have students anonymously evaluate their classes using a standard evaluation form. The scores on these forms were one of the things the department used to determine tenure and promotion. I've never liked this policy. In my own case, I found that I didn't fully appreciate some of my own teachers until many years had passed. I also think the student evaluations contribute to grade inflation. I'm pretty sure they did.

But I've had some memorable reactions to my teaching. One course I taught in my early years was a giant freshman or sophomore-level lecture class. Because it was required, it enrolled over a hundred students and was aided by graduate assistants. The course was thematic in nature, involving a miscellany of readings from different historical periods. The teacher was required to have an overall theme, but could determine both the theme and the texts. I was cynical about the themes other faculty members had used—"The Search for Order," for example. In rebellion, I titled my class "Sex and Money," on the theory that most literature is about one or both of those things, and maybe I could do Freud and Marx 101 along with the novels and poetry. About halfway through the semester a student came to my office and told me he was dropping the class. "You know your shit," he said, "but I can learn more about sex and money on the street." He wasn't an especially good student but I had to admit he had a point.

A lot of my early teaching involved experiments in essay topics for students. I remember teaching a sophomore course in English that required me to assign a mix of poetry, novels, and drama. In the poetry phase, I tried something similar to I. A. Richards' famous experiment with his Cambridge students: I made typewritten copies of five or six short poems without telling my students who wrote them, and I asked the students to write a short essay on the poems they liked best and least, explaining their reasons. I deliberately picked what I regard as one of the worst poems ever written: Alfred Joyce Kilmer's 1914 "Trees," which begins, "I think that I shall never see/ a poem as lovely as a tree." It has a rocking-horse meter and is every bit as wince-inducing as a sentimental greeting card. I also picked a poem that I thought might fool the students into thinking it was sentimental or corny: John Crowe Ransom's "Janet Waking," which is about a very young girl who awakes one day to find that a bee has stung Chucky, her pet chicken. Poor Chucky is dead. The poem starts as if it might become bad, but doesn't have the see-saw rhythm and rhyming in "Trees." The first line is, "Beautifully Janet slept/ till it was deeply morning." It ends with a gut punch as Janet weeps uncontrollably, "and would not be instructed in how deep/ was the forgetful kingdom of death."

None of my students said they liked the Ransom poem, but a few of them said their favorite was Kilmer's "Trees." I suddenly felt helpless as a teacher. How could I explain what I believed were their misjudgments without seeming snobbish and superior? From then on I always explained why I liked certain things and encouraged but didn't force them to express their opinions about quality.

*Students' reactions to the films noir I showed in classes were interesting. (Bear in mind this was over 20 years ago; the new generation might have different reactions and different tastes.) They typically enjoyed* The Maltese Falcon *and* Double Indemnity. *The most hostile reaction was toward* Kiss Me Deadly *(1955); they didn't like the eccentric flourishes, and they hated the apocalyptic climax, although the one they saw was the more abrupt version than the slightly longer one restored not that long ago by Criterion.*

*Did you have any memorable class reactions to films noir, positive or negative? I don't think Joe McBride would mind if I shared a related anecdote. A few years ago, I was delighted when he asked me to sub for him in one of his film studies courses that he teaches at San Francisco State University. That day's topic was John Frankenheimer's* The Manchurian Candidate, *a favorite of both Joe's and mine, and it's covered in your book on noir as well. I screened the movie and then led a fun discussion with his students, one of whom, who had remained silent and scowling, seemingly lost in thought, finally raised his hand and asked, "Did people back then think solitaire was scary?" Joe told me later that you never know what students are going to fixate on, but at least that*

*Kiss Me Deadly*

*question was original. Some students, however, can be quite perceptive.*

I suppose anyone who has taught movies as long as I did is intensely aware of students' limited historical knowledge and unpredictable generational changes in taste. (According to Borde and Chaumeton, when they showed a revival of *Murder, My Sweet* at the Toulouse Cine Club in 1953, scenes that had once seemed avant garde no longer worked; when Marlowe kept sinking into the black pool of unconsciousness, the audience laughed.)

But one of my earliest memories of a reaction was an important learning experience. Often you can learn from students. I had just shown *The Maltese Falcon*, and a young woman in the class said she disliked it because of its misogyny. Why hadn't I thought of that? This was before the first wave of feminist writings on noir, but the student was of course talking about the treatment of Brigid O'Shaughnessy, Iva Archer, and Effie Perine (at one point Spade compliments the loyal and brave Effie by saying she's "a good man"). Of course the film could also be criticized because its four villains are a femme fatale and three homosexuals. I realized it was important to discuss sexual politics, especially in a good film that may have questionable elements.

Some of the reactions over the years were more amusing. I can remember when students broke out laughing at the scene in *Touch of Evil* when a character behind a wall whispers about a "Mary Jane." I haven't shown the film for a class in many years, but I suppose students today wouldn't recognize the term. I also recall when *Out of the Past* seemed humorous to students because of the trench coat, the numerous cigarettes, and the many noir tropes; to them, it was almost a parody. It's one of my favorite films, so I was very disappointed.

I guess I can understand why some of your students didn't like *Kiss Me Deadly* (I didn't like it much when I saw its original release), but why be hostile? I used to warn students beforehand that it's a brilliant movie with a style worth examining, but it also has dated, over-the-top aspects (the super-duper reel-to-reel answering machine in Mike Hammer's apartment, and the ballet barre in the apartment of his secretary, Velma). It has jaw-dropping moments, as when the femme fatale opens an atomic Pandora's box—a scene you could describe as "Va-Va-Voom!" The ending is great, but so outrageous it can inspire a laugh. The upside-down credits at the opening should tip them off that something unusual is in store. I suspect they need to be told about the Mickey Spillane craze and how this film both supports and subverts it.

*It's heartening that you considered your students' responses in terms of* why *they felt that way about* The Maltese Falcon. *I know that the term "woke" didn't exist then with the pejorative meaning that it has now, but the current and incessant use of it as a blanket dismissal or knee-jerk condemnation grows tiresome. A friend of mine, who is one of the few Black film critics writing for a mainstream publication, and who also attends the annual* Noir City Festival *in the Bay Area, told me that he was a visiting speaker to a college-level class recently, and that when a student asked what he thought about "problematic" movies, he replied: "It's okay to like movies that are problematic, and it's okay to dislike movies that are problematic. Just don't think that you're the first to point out the problems." I thought that was an effective way to frame an approach to films in general, but especially film noir, which, as your examples illustrate, frequently contains elements that may be jarring today.*

The Republican right wing, oversensitive when some of their racist or sexist attitudes were called to their attention, became angry and defensive. They made woke a pejorative, sneered at the politically correct, and whined or yelled in faux outrage about being cancelled. I would rather be awake and correct, though we could always argue about what that would mean and whether it's appropriate in specific cases.

If noir is sometimes problematic, however, it isn't alone. In one way or another, everything from Shakespeare to the most sanitized Hollywood musical has problematic aspects. (Mel Gibson's movie about Jesus is certainly problematic, even if it seems like holy writ to many.) In the noir book,

I have a chapter on censorship and politics in which I argue that the puritanical Hollywood Production Code of the 1940s and 50s made many noir movies politically problematic for anyone aware of reality (crime doesn't pay, legal officials, churchmen, and cops are always good, etc.). Thankfully, many films found ways around this. You could almost see the traces of censorship and what it tried to hide.

I'm aghast at the idea of burning books or films, but some films strike me as not just problematic but evil. This makes me wonder if something morally or socially reprehensible can still be art. It's an issue we might discuss later because it takes us afield from the topic at hand.

*You've mentioned teaching several courses, including ones on Kubrick, Minnelli, and acting as a guest lecturer at other institutions. What were some of your favorite courses at IU, both undergraduate and graduate level?*

As I've already noted, the first film course I taught was on Welles and Hitchcock, who make a great comparison/contrast—Welles the exhibitionist vs. Hitchcock the voyeur; Welles the critic of American plutocracy vs. Hitchcock the expert on ordinary people in suspenseful situations; the motel in *Touch of Evil* vs. the motel in *Psycho*, etc. At the time there were few readings to assign, so I required only Joe McBride's book on Welles and *Hitchcock/Truffaut*. Welles and Hitchcock were giants of the movies with contrasting styles, and you can't miss when you teach a course on them. That course was very successful.

Other undergrad courses I enjoyed included the Warner Bros. class I've mentioned, plus survey courses on American Film History. I also taught courses on film noir (without using my book), women and melodrama, and Hollywood movies about Hollywood. For graduate courses, in addition to the seminar on *Casablanca*, I did a class on adaptations and remakes and several surveys of film theory. I'm no doubt forgetting things.

One of the most successful grad courses was not a pure film offering but a two-semester class I taught with my colleague Patrick Brantlinger on modernity and culture. Pat's semester was about Victorian cultural arguments, beginning with Matthew Arnold and including such figures as Morris, Gissing, and Wilde; my semester was centered on 20th-century critics such as Walter Benjamin and Raymond Williams, together with the manifestos of avant-garde movements and various debates over the rise of mass culture. I included film sequences by Dziga Vertov

(*Man With a Movie Camera* [1929]), Joseph Cornell (*Rose Hobart* [1936]), and Busby Berkeley (the Broadway Lullaby number from *Gold Diggers of 1935*). I think no other course I taught had such a strong impact for both me and the students. It inspired a critical anthology that Pat and I co-edited for IU Press, and was the foundation for what became the university's Cultural Studies Program.

*Joe McBride and I were once discussing auteurism, and he thought it was interesting that although other theoretical underpinnings have arisen in academia over the years, many courses are still organized around directors. Did you find that to be the case at IU?*

There was a course in Comparative Literature called "Authorship in the Cinema." I'm not sure if that course still exists and if directors are taught in the curriculum of the new Media School at IU. In the old days, Peter Bondanella regularly taught courses on Italian directors for the IU department of French and Italian, and maybe Claudia Gorbman taught a course on Godard.

It's not surprising that directors are still studied in courses at many schools. Why not? Most good films depend chiefly on the artistic instinct of the director rather than the ideas of producers or a team of contributors. Directors can be fascinating objects for a semester's study, and students can learn a good deal about things besides the director—film styles, for example, or production methods. But *pace* Andrew Sarris, auteurism and authorship have never been theories, nor do they have theoretical underpinning. Auteurism was simply a policy of treating some directors as the authors of certain films. The rise of leftist film theory in the Sixties and Seventies was predicated to a degree on a critique of the common but un-theorized idea of authorship, whether in literature or film. The point was to apply theory in order to de-romanticize the artist-hero. But the High Theorists and their followers didn't stop talking about authors and auteurs. See Roland Barthes on Balzac and the famous, or should I say infamous, *Cahiers du Cinéma* study of John Ford's *Young Mr. Lincoln* (1939).

Having said this, I should add that teaching or writing about directors can sometimes be questionable. Several of the house directors of major films in the classic Hollywood studio system did little more than watch performances and decide if a scene went well. They didn't determine the visual style or even the camera angles, leaving that work to the DP. I've always been a bit suspicious of Raoul Walsh, who was highly regarded by the auteurists and has his name on many excellent films; Walsh lost an eye when he was acting in silent movies, and according to some of his actors, he would rub his other eye while a scene was being shot. For me, the best directors—among them Ford, Hawks, Welles, Hitchcock, Sternberg, Ophüls, Minnelli and Kubrick—have a distinctive visual style. I also think writer-directors are worth study, especially Joseph L. Mankiewicz and Preston Sturges. I greatly admire Ida Lupino, who doesn't seem to have a distinct visual style but who has consistent thematic interests. Of course it's also true that sometimes a writer or producer can have more influence on a good film than the director.

*You've said you are happy to be retired from teaching, but if you were still doing it would you enjoy teaching a course on a topic you haven't done before?*

I sometimes think it would be interesting to do a course with mostly grad students on film comedy. It would be a hard thing to do but it might be productive. There are some good writings on the topic having to do with both theater and film. But the choice of movies would be a problem. It would have to be very eclectic because comedy is a broad category that includes such a variety of things as *Sherlock, Jr.* (1924), *Trouble in Paradise* (1932), and *Airplane!* (1980). Probably I would need to limit the course to a certain kind of comedy. If I weren't so old and could live forever, there are many old and new directors that would be worth featuring in a class. I would probably pick older directors such as Lupino, Vidor, Wellman, or Wyler.

## Classroom Technology and Educational Film

*What was teaching like for you in the days before digital technology?*

Digital technology has made it vastly easier to teach film courses. For many years I lugged 16mm Pageant projectors to classrooms and loaded them to a spot so that I could "quote" something. At my own expense, I had lots of 35mm slides made of film frames, which I projected as visual aids during lectures. At one point the IU Film Studies program had an analytical projector, which enabled you to isolate frames or sequences from 16mm reels and play them at slow or fast speeds. All this technology was bulky and needed to be transported from a storage room to the different classrooms. When I projected silent features for my classes in fully equipped auditoria, I usually improvised a music score with records or tape recordings. For Keaton I used Scott Joplin, for *Metropolis* (1927) I used Tangerine Dream, and for *Man with a Movie Camera* I used Philip Glass.

But once the classrooms were outfitted for digital projection, the teaching of film was vastly improved. It was almost a revolution. The one downside is that unlike 16mm and VHS tapes, video discs have a relatively short shelf life. If film study survives the next fifty years, somebody will need to remaster a mountain of movies on CD. I fear this is going to be a problem for movies in general, because nowadays when you see a film in a theater, you're viewing not celluloid but a Digital Cinema Package. Nobody in the industry seems to be thinking about the survival of film history. It's potentially worse than the old days, when the industry thought its product didn't need to be saved; at least then there was a chance that celluloid could last and be rescued.

In the category of teaching, I suppose I should mention that in 1984, during the pre-digital years, I wrote and co-directed a 16mm educational film titled *A Nickel for the Movies*. I was able to do this under the auspices of the IU audio-visual department, which had been producing educational films since World War II and was once a major distributor of films for schools. My film was a twenty-minute 16mm color picture based on what I still believe was a good idea. I adapted the opening part of it from a small episode in Scott Fitzgerald's *The Last Tycoon*, in which a Hollywood producer explains to a famous British novelist how to write a film. I eliminated the producer and dramatized the scene he described, showing a frustrated movie writer in his office who is surprised by a series of strange incidents. I then had the film replay parts of the scene, using it to explain movie techniques to students (eyeline matches, jump cuts, the 180-degree rule, narrative construction, etc.).

Unfortunately, every time this film is shown I want to hide under a table. Although it was professionally done, I knew too little about the full process of making a film. I wanted it to be in black and white, but that had become too expensive because the 16mm labs that made workprints were mostly devoted to color—a reverse of what had once been the case. I had to yield to the experienced unit on some things, and I didn't agree with some of what they did. I wince at certain mistakes I made. It's far from what I hoped to achieve—too brightly lit, for example, with an original but overly upbeat music score. Nevertheless it couldn't have been made without the help of the professionals. I learned a great deal, especially about editing and post-production of the soundtrack. I probably learned more than students who saw it. It convinced me that anyone who teaches film would profit from taking a production course.

# MOVIE-GOING
# EXPERIENCES

*What have been some of your favorite movie theaters— regionally, nationally, or internationally?*

The *Kommunalen Kino* in Hamburg was impressive. In that theater I saw the two parts of Fritz Lang's *Die Nibelungen* (1924) with full orchestral accompaniment. Another of my memorable experiences was at the McMahon repertory theater in Paris, which had the biggest screen and best projection I had seen up to that point. The film they were showing was a revival of King Vidor's *Beyond the Forest* (1949), an excellent picture, long underrated, which is often described as pure camp—maybe because Bette Davis utters the immortal line, "What a dump!"

But hands down the best equipped and most spectacular cinemas were in Los Angeles. The sound and image in the Egyptian Theater were superb, like nothing I had experienced before, although I can't remember what they were showing. There was an almost equally impressive theater in Century City, where Darlene and I saw *Addams Family Values* (1993). It was all the more spectacular because we went to a matinee and were almost the only people in the place. I've also been fond of art theaters: the Orson Welles in Boston, MoMA in New York, the Music Box and the Siskel Center in Chicago, etc. But too many theaters of all kinds are dying off, just like newspapers and bookstores. When Darlene and I first lived in Chicago, there were at least seven movie screens in walking distance of our apartment. All are gone, replaced by distant multiplexes.

*The Indiana University Cinema is still fairly young. I was lucky enough to have just started at IU when it officially opened in January 2011. How did it come into being?*

I lobbied for years in hopes of having a dedicated university cinema in Bloomington, and when Michael McRobbie became IU president my dream came true. At his inauguration, he announced that he wanted to create a cinema at the site of the old university drama theater, which was no longer in use. I had recently retired, but he made me the chair of the planning committee and approved everything I suggested. The results were beyond my expectations. The theater was completely remodeled, preserving only its impressive Thomas Hart Benton murals, which date back to the WPA in the 1930s. A state-of-the-art projection and sound system was installed, supervised by a noted specialist from Chicago whose name, if you can believe it, is James Bond. An orchestra pit was constructed where musicians from IU's distinguished music school provided music for silent film and sometimes composed new scores.

Most important, the faculty committee chose Jon Vickers as the cinema's founding director and programmer. Jon had operated the Vickers Theater in Michigan and done film programming for Notre Dame. His work in Bloomington was jaw dropping. With help from donors, he invited an array of important film people to campus, where they were interviewed on stage. I've already mentioned some of these. They also included Roger Corman, Pedro Costa, Claire Denis, Bette Gordon, Jim Jarmusch, Abbas Kiarostami, Kleber Mendonça Filho, Nelson Pereira dos Santos, Kelly Reichardt, Walter Salles, Paul Schrader, Frederick Wiseman, and Meryl Streep and Kevin Kline—there were more celebrated figures than I can list here. Under Jon's guidance, IU Cinema was the best university movie theater in the country. He moved on after ten years of exhausting work and the place has never been quite the same. We miss him a great deal.

*You got to program some films and film series there, correct? How did you go about selecting films? Were you interested in tying them into the curriculum, or was it a simpler matter of selecting films that you yourself liked and hoped that audiences would like too?*

I didn't program many films and was retired from teaching. The programming job was left mostly to Jon. He got some suggestions from a faculty committee representing film, fine arts, and the various languages. We established a rule that if a department wanted a particular film, it would pay for it. But I stayed away from governance of the cinema because with Jon in charge, I didn't want to try and influence anything. The showings weren't often tied to curriculum; I thought the cinema should never be used as a daytime classroom, but I lost that argument to a degree.

The only times I remember selecting films were when Jon asked three of the film specialists—Barbara Klinger, Greg Waller, and me—to pick a single film and talk about it. I picked an oddity: Anthony Mann's collaboration with the great noir photographer John Alton on *Reign of Terror* (1949), a costume picture about the French revolution. The audience was sparse and probably didn't care for it as much as I do—it's little known and has never been a popular film. Later, Jon did me the honor of asking me to program a series. I chose films by Renoir and Ophüls: *Boudu Saved from Drowning* (1932), *The River* (1951), *Letter from an*

*Unknown Woman*, and *The Earrings of Madame de...*
(1953). The series wasn't a big hit, maybe because I chose
older films. I would never have been a great programmer;
I mostly just sat back and enjoyed Jon's work

The biggest crowd I can remember at the cinema, an
overflow, was at a pre-release showing of Nicolas Winding
Refn's *Drive* (2011), with Refn as a guest. He drew lots
of young people. (My grandson got his autograph.) I also
much enjoyed seeing Jim Jarmusch, who showed his wild
and crazy short films, one of them involving throwing a
camera down a hill while it was running. Jon had long tried
to get Jarmusch for an appearance at the theater. Jarmusch is
a very likable fellow, and he brought his band with him for
onstage music to accompany the shorts.

*A highlight for me was creating the Orson Welles Centenary
Symposium with Jon, you, and others. What were some of
your favorite IU Cinema experiences, in terms of films,
programs, or guests?*

You and others probably did more for that symposium than
I did. My contribution was a keynote address on Welles.
I think I also did an introduction for a showing of *Macbeth*
(1948), and I later wrote a brief introduction to a collection
of symposium essays published as *Orson Welles in Focus*.
In any event, the symposium was a memorable occasion.
It attracted several Welles aficionados as guests, including
Joseph McBride, Jonathan Rosenbaum, Patrick McGilligan,
Catherine Benamou, Marguerite Rippy, Josh Karp, and
my old friend François Thomas, who is the preeminent
French historian of Welles. Your Lilly Library exhibition
was a highlight. My only disappointment was the visit of
Filip Jan Rymsza, who was at work on the yet to be released
*The Other Side of the Wind*. There was an interesting panel
discussion with him, but I had hoped he would show us
a bit of the film in progress. Instead he showed a short,
relatively well-known video clip that Welles had used for
his AFI award ceremony.

*Do you have any memories, good or bad, of watching movies
with audiences at IU Cinema or elsewhere?*

I've already mentioned the audiences at *Psycho* and *Jaws*.
I don't remember anything special at IU Cinema other than
the high quality of the movies and guests. There were many
times at other venues when people drove me nuts by talking
during the movie. I thought this was due to watching

pictures at home on TV, but it turns out it was nothing new; Manny Farber had complained of it back in the 1940s. I remember that some theaters in Europe allowed people to smoke during the film—I was a smoker, but smoking in a movie theater was annoying to me. In France and Portugal, there were theaters that stopped projection for an interval, when staff went round the auditorium selling ice cream or candy.

One of the most interesting experiences was when Darlene and I attended the Cuban Film Festival in Havana. Fidel Castro briefly mingled with the delegates at a party—a memorable celebrity sighting, equaled only by our seeing Muhammad Ali holding a baby in the Los Angeles airport. The theaters in Havana were vintage, well-preserved buildings from the 1950s, with big lighted marquees. We enjoyed watching films in them, but the screenings were open to the general public, which reacted in unexpected ways. Whenever there was any hint of homosexuality on the screen, as there was when we saw Nelson Pereira dos Santos' *Memories of Prison* (1984) the audience booed and hissed.

Another memorable movie event was in Chicago at the old Fine Arts Theater, across the street from the Chicago Art Museum. They had two screens. Darlene and I went there one day to watch two new movies back to back: *Sid and Nancy* (1986) and *Blue Velvet* (1986). Imagine seeing those two as a double feature! We came out gobsmacked by what we'd seen, looking at one another with stunned, astonished expressions. We had been witnessing perversely weird things for four hours and were speechless.

*Preceding the IU Cinema by at least three decades was the Ryder Series on campus. Peter LoPilato, who could be called the face of that series of film programming, passed away in March of 2024. What are your memories of the Ryder?*

The death of Peter LoPilato was a major blow, largely because he and I had long been friends. Peter always seemed to me to be a real New Yorker of the kind who read *The Village Voice* regularly. He published and edited a local culture journal called *The Ryder*, which was about music, books, film, and important upcoming events. I always thought he should publish a volume of essays from that very hip journal, but unfortunately he never got around to it. Every bit as important was The Ryder film series, supported by local businesses and audiences. Peter had exceptional talent as a programmer of independent and foreign films. He was very aware of the new films from the various festivals, and after Jon left the IU Cinema he became my primary source for seeing pictures that would never make it to the local multiplex. For only one example, because of Peter I got to see Radu Jude's *Bad Luck Banging or Loony Porn* (2021), a revelatory political satire—it's a bit like Godard, but much funnier. Peter is an irreplaceable loss, not only for me but also for the community.

*Bad Luck Banging, or Loony Porn*

*Did you ever go to drive-in movies?*

They're scarce today, but in my youth they were everywhere. Kids old enough to have a driver's license would go to them with a date in order to make out in relative privacy. I don't recall for sure what movies I saw in one, but I vaguely remember viewing *Singin' in the Rain* (1952) at a drive-in. Probably for the benefit of pot smokers, the drive-ins sometimes showed old exploitation pictures like *Reefer Madness* (1936). Drive-ins appear in some good movies: Kubrick's *Lolita*, Welles' *The Other Side of the Wind*, and most memorably in Bogdanovich's *Targets* (1968), where we see the concessions, the projection booth, and a sniper trying to pick off Boris Karloff at one of his B-movie personal appearances.

# ON ADAPTATION

*You edited an influential anthology,* Film Adaptation *(2000). Are movie adaptations as critically important to you as original pictures? Are they less cinematic?*

Adaptations are just as important as originals In the year when I wrote an introduction for that anthology, at least half of Hollywood's movies were based on books or plays. If you include sources like radio, TV, video games, operas, comic books, graphic novels, folk tales, and mythology, the adaptation totals in today's cinema would be a good deal more than half. Since even before *The Birth of a Nation* (1915), which is based on a play, commercial movies have relied primarily on adaptation. All but three of Orson Welles' movies were adaptations (not counting *Hearts of Age*) and all but two of Stanley Kubrick's. The major Hollywood studios were virtual factories of adaptation, with reader's departments for suggesting published material to producers. Independent filmmakers have relied on adaptation just as often as big Hollywood. As long as movies are a storytelling form, they'll adapt stories from other media.

I wouldn't say that adaptations are less cinematic than originals. Is *Kane* more cinematic than *Ambersons*? Nope. Both types rely on narrative and dialogue just as much as plays and novels do. Films that aspire to media-specific form— Michael Snow's *La Région centrale* (1971), for instance— are usually classed apart, as avant garde or "structuralist." Kubrick's *2001* gets close to a media-specific form, but it still has narrative (inspired by a short story) and dialogue.

Some writers, Dickens and Maugham, for example, have been adapted many times because their plots are melodramatic (in Maugham's case also sexy). But some modern literature is almost entirely medium-specific. Joyce's *Ulysses* and Woolf's *To the Lighthouse*, which have almost no plot in the conventional sense, are almost impossible to adapt because they depend so much on language, style, and what I suppose one could call mise-en-page. In his book *Joysprick*, Anthony Burgess rewrites the first chapter of *Ulysses* in the form of the average best-seller and shows how much is lost and how much it seems to aspire to the condition of a film. It becomes "closer to film… the referents ache to be free of their words."

One of my favorite contemporary novelists, Laurent Binet, would probably never have some of his novels adapted for film because they're a bit esoteric or unusual and the ordinary moviegoer might not get the jokes. I suspect that one of the easiest literary forms to adapt is the detective story or thriller. My favorite writer of tough thrillers is the great French novelist Jean-Patrick Manchette, whom I've already mentioned. He's the author of several novels, among them *3 to Kill*, *The Prone Gunman*, and *No Room at the Morgue*, all of which have been filmed, none of which I have actually seen. I'm also a fan of the Swedish married couple Maj Sjöwall and Per Wahlöö, who wrote ten novels about the career of Stockholm police inspector Martin Beck, all of them critical of the "Middle Way" politics that were governing Sweden. (The last word of the tenth novel is "Marx.") To my knowledge only one movie has been based on their work: *The Laughing Policeman* (1974), which changes the setting to San Francisco. There's also a Swedish TV series called *Beck* (1990–95), which is entertaining but not as good as the novels.

*I know the answer to this but I'll ask anyway. Should an adaptation be judged on the basis of fidelity to the source? And do you think movie audiences are less forgiving today than in the past for adaptations that stray too far from the source material, and if so, why? I don't mean only the* Harry Potter *fans, who seem to want an exact facsimile of every page (even though many of those books run far too long to include everything in even a two-and-a-half-hour feature film), but it seems like every movie adapted from a bestseller risks the wrath of the book's readers if it deviates, and movie marketers appear extremely eager to get endorsements from authors as a seal of approval, like David Gran's fulsome praise for Scorsese's* Killers of the Flower Moon *(2023), months before it was even released.*

Movie adaptations needn't always be faithful to the source, but I've already mentioned that Welles' version of *The Trial* bothers me because in some ways it isn't true to Kafka. There are, however, good films that try to be as close as possible to their literary models. One of the most faithful adaptations (in every sense) is Robert Bresson's *Diary of a Country Priest* (1950), based on a novel by Goerges Bernanos. And sometimes the author of a novel collaborates with the film's director on the adaptation, as when László Krasznahorkai co-wrote the screenplay for Béla Tarr's amazing, seven-hour *Sátántangó* (1994).

I guess everybody has had the experience of seeing a film based on a major work of literature and disliking it because it doesn't seem enough like the book. There are always exceptions to the rule—films that work precisely because they take liberties. Tony Richardson's *Tom Jones* isn't exactly like the source, but to me it's delightfully true to it (in its fashion, as Cole Porter would say). On the other hand I've never seen an adaptation of *The Great Gatsby*, no matter how faithful, that's nearly as good as the book—this is a puzzle, because the book seems so adaptable. Ditto for Nathaniel West. And except for the opening scenes of *The Killers* (1946), which use Hemingway's dialogue almost completely, no Hollywood adaptation of Hemingway has seemed to me to resemble him—this, too, is surprising, given his style. Or maybe it's because of his style.

The notion that an adaptation should always be true to its source derives mainly from older writings about movies based on canonical literature. A great many good films have been unfaithful to celebrated novels, and have also been made from bad books or books few people have read. I'm afraid I have no opinion about contemporary audiences, but it seems obvious that when a book is made into a movie it can also boost the book sales. Just go in a bookstore and notice the many covers advertising the fact that a book has become a movie. Ultimately, though, it comes down to whether the film is good, regardless of whether it resembles the source. Kubrick's *Lolita* and *Barry Lyndon* are based respectively on an important book and a flawed, nearly forgotten one. Both are unfaithful, but I like them.

# Henry James and the Movies: Wyler vs. Bogdanovich

*Can you talk a bit more about specific film adaptations? I think readers would be interested if you made a deeper dive into some films.*

Okay, but first I should say that adapting novels into films is always difficult because you have to omit things to fit the length of a feature film. Most of the good literary adaptations involve short novels, novellas, or short stories. I'll start with a couple of novelistic examples based on Henry James. One is unfaithful and the other close to the source, but they're both good.

James' plots were melodramatic and he believed in showing rather than telling. That should make him easily adaptable, but his style was mannered and ultra-subtle, spiced with witty, insightful judgements of character. When movies adapted him, they usually heightened the melodrama and made characterization less subtle. That's the case with William Wyler's *The Heiress* (1949), based on James' short 1880 novel *Washington Square*. For all its virtues, the picture virtually smacks you over the head with melodrama. (It's derived from a successful theater adaptation of the novel by Ruth and Augustus Goetz, who also wrote the screenplay.)

James himself was a bit disappointed with *Washington Square*, which is a less challenging novel than his later work. But *The Heiress* is dramatically impressive. It opens out the action of the Goetz play, occasionally taking us outside the stylish Washington Square home of a wealthy New Yorker, Dr. Sloper (Ralph Richardson), and in keeping with the "melos" of melodrama, it heightens emotion with music. There's a lovely non-diegetic score by Aaron Copland and a digetically performed song, "Plaisir d'amour" by 18th-century composer Jean-Paul Egide, which describes and predicts the plot. ("The joys of love last but a moment/the pains of love last a whole life long.")

The stars are Olivia de Havilland as Dr. Sloper's homely daughter Catherine, and Montgomery Clift as Morris Townsend, her handsome suitor. An aging Miriam Hopkins, one of the luminous women of 1930s Paramount, plays Aunt Penniman, an excitable, romantically obsessed relative who lives with the Slopers and serves as Catherine's companion. She's what James called a *ficelle*, a minor but important character who facilitates the plot.

The film centers on Catherine, an unaccomplished, unfashionable young woman who spends most of her time working on needlepoint. Her father and aunt are greatly responsible for sucking the life out of her—the father, whose beautiful wife died in giving childbirth to Catherine, is convinced she's plain and dimwitted, and the aunt is frustrated because she wants to use Catherine vicariously to fulfill romantic fantasies. (De Havilland, a great beauty of the previous decade who had often worked with Errol Flynn, was eager to play this role and won an Academy Award.)

Catherine has a kind heart, as we see when she attends a dance celebrating the marriage of a pretty cousin and looks on with pleasure rather than envy. She's used to sitting alone at dances, but she's approached by Townsend, the most glamorous young man at the party, who asks for a dance and isn't disappointed when she's clumsy. They sit together the rest of the evening. Townsend is gentle and unpretentiously charming, and a friendship develops.

When Townsend later visits Catherine at her home, their relationship deepens and we begin to see her latent beauty and passion. He soon wants to marry her. The impediment is Dr. Sloper, who is convinced that his daughter is unmarriageable and sure that Townsend is only interested in her money. We've come to dislike Sloper and root for Catherine. At roughly this point, Townsend arranges a

*The Heiress*

private meeting with Sloper to ask for Catherine's hand in marriage.

I once showed the film to a large class of undergraduates in an intro to film course and deliberately stopped it just before the meeting with Sloper and Townsend. I told the students we would see the rest of the picture next week and asked a question: did they think Morris Townsend was Prince Charming or a gold-digger? They were almost equally divided—some of the more cynical students voted in favor of Townsend because they assumed Hollywood movies back in the 1940s had happy endings. I told them I wasn't going to give them a grade based on who made the right choice. I only wanted to emphasize that by the end of the film the question would be answered. The Hollywood narrative is constructed so that certain questions keep us watching, and at the end nothing is left in doubt.

As the film continues, Sloper tells Townsend what he thinks of him and tries to dissuade Catherine by taking her on a tour of Europe so that she will come to her senses. When this doesn't work, he announces that if she marries he will disinherit her. Soon after, she and Townsend have a passionate moonlit meeting in which she seems almost radiantly beautiful. She says she has renounced her inheritance and wants to elope. Townsend eventually agrees, and with the help of Aunt Penniman, they establish a late-night hour for him to sweep Catherine away in a carriage. Catherine joyfully prepares for romantic escape, but when the hour arrives Townsend doesn't appear. Catherine has an agonizing wait and during the long night she's driven to the realization that she will have nothing in her life but isolation and needlepoint.

The remainder of the film further heightens melodramatic emotion. Dr. Sloper becomes ill and realizes that he's dying. Catherine stands over him and says he has never loved her, has made her insecure since childhood, and has destroyed her only chance for happiness; she's going to give him no comfort as he dies. As he expires, she goes outside to the square and sits on a park bench, ignoring a pretty servant who tells her that Dr. Sloper is crying out for her. Catherine then becomes a wealthy spinster, living in the Washington Square mansion with her needlepoint and her aunt.

Both James' novella and the film end years later when, with the help of Aunt Penniman, Townsend reappears and tries to reestablish his importance for Catherine. In James' ending, Catherine tells him calmly that she no longer has resentment but has changed irrevocably; he shouldn't have come. In the hallway, as he exits, he tells Aunt Penniman that he doubts she'll agree to see him again. "Drat," he says in mild frustration as he pops his top hat open and leaves. In the last line of the novel, James says that Catherine is returning to her needlepoint, "for life, as it were."

Again the movie version stresses melodrama. When Townsend meets with Catherine he looks less charming — Montgomery Clift is wearing cheap clothes and has a mustache. She somewhat reluctantly agrees to marry him if he returns to carry her off as they originally planned. But when he eagerly returns at the appointed hour, nobody comes to the door. Inside, Catherine is working on her needlepoint. Outside, as the music rises, we see Townsend dramatically pounding on the door and shouting in frustration. Catherine uses scissors to snip the last thread in her needlepoint, silently cutting the cord with Townsend. She may not be happy, but she's had her revenge on the man who jilted her. I would argue that this ending is over the top, but the picture as a whole is powerfully effective.

The other example of a movie based on Henry James is Peter Bogdanovich's *Daisy Miller* (1974), which is much closer to the source and in some ways a perfectly faithful adaptation of a canonical author. The 1878 novella was one of James' most successful creations — so popular he once unsuccessfully tried adapting it as a play (with a happy ending!). But *Daisy Miller* already has a strong dramatic structure and seems almost to be asking to become a film. Bogdanovich turned it into one of his most underrated pictures, an adaptation that fits his particular talents and honors James.

The project apparently began when Bogdanovich heard Orson Welles say how much he admired James' novella. Soon Bogdanovich pitched the idea of adapting it with Welles as director and himself and Cybill Shepherd as stars. Producers weren't interested and Welles may not have been, but Bogdanovich was riding high in Hollywood. When he, Francis Coppola, and William Friedkin joined forces to create The Producers Company, *Daisy Miller* was Bogdanovich's choice for his contribution to the organization. He directed Cybill Shepherd in the title role, paired with the young actor Barry Brown (who looks a bit like Bogdanovich). The completed film got some favorable reviews but was a commercial flop that affected the rest of his career. Hollywood insiders who resented his and Shepherd's fame as a celebrity couple wallowed in schadenfreude, insisting that it was nothing more than a vanity project.

*Daisy Miller*

The novella is a comedy of manners that turns into a tragedy of manners—an early exploration of James' favored theme of Americans abroad, emphasizing American naiveté and European hyper-cultivation. The story centers on innocent American Daisy Miller, an attractive, flirtatious ingénue from Schenectady, New York, who is visiting Europe for the first time. At a Swiss Grand Hotel, she meets an upper-class young Britisher named Winterborne (the names are pretty clearly symbolic), who is immediately attracted but also amused, secretly condescending, and bewildered by her youthful Americanness. They develop a friendship against the advice of Winterbourne's social circle, who view Daisy as déclassé, even disreputable. The gossip is that she spends too much time with the wrong kind of men. When Daisy travels to Rome, Winterbourn follows, conflicted by his mix of attraction, suspicion, and latent jealousy. One evening he spies on Daisy sitting in the Roman Colosseum with Giovanelli, an Italian whom the British regard as shockingly inappropriate. He intercedes, going to the couple and chiding Daisy, warning that the air in the Colosseum could give her "Roman Fever." He then leaves, deciding she hasn't been worthy. The next day, Daisy dies of fever.

Bogdanovich follows this pattern precisely, giving the ending a dramatic punch. The credit for screenwriting went to Frederic Raphael (who later complained about collaborating with Kubrick on *Eyes Wide Shut*), but Raphael did very little, contributing only one scene, a not very comic moment in the waters of a Swiss spa. The chief credit belongs to Bogdanovich, who respected James, but whose cinematic influences were always Welles, Hawks, and Ford (with an added soupçon of Lubitsch). Here the Wellesian element is apparent—a sophisticated treatment of a provincial America and 19th-century manners, plus an impressive, almost virtuoso use of long takes. The Hawksian element is equally apparent—a flair for fast-paced comedy and a fondness for unconventional women. Quentin Tarantino, who admires the film, has praised Bogdanovich's skill with non-improvised but speedy dialogue. To me the speed is a bit off-putting in the opening scenes but works beautifully elsewhere.

Cybill Shepherd's performance is one of the best aspects of the film. Sometimes she resembles Hepburn in a Hawks comedy, but her role is complex and challenging. Daisy is skillfully flirtatious but also socially insecure; she's assertive and independent but also a small-town chatterbox who keeps twirling her white umbrella and saying, "I declare!" However annoying she might sometimes seem, she's strong and admirable, and her death is a rebuke to Winterbourne, who doesn't know what to feel.

## Stage to Screen: Hitchcock vs. Lumet

*How do you feel about adaptation going in the other direction— e.g., films adapted from plays? It seems to be happening with increasing frequency. Do films based on plays involve special problems of adaptation? Could you talk about that?*

Three-act proscenium plays are a frequent source for movies, but some critics have claimed that they're uncinematic, probably, I suspect, because they hesitate to acknowledge that theater, of all the arts, is the one closest to cinema. Filmmakers often feel a need to open out the stage-bound action, inventing a flashback, moving an indoor scene to outdoors, or shooting scenes on locations that are only mentioned in the original dialogue. The French call this practice "ventilating" the play, and André Bazin was right when he opposed it. Good theater, he argued, is structurally designed for a limited space, and something is lost when film adaptations don't preserve the spatial dynamics.

Alfred Hitchcock had the same idea, maybe because he liked to make movies in confined spaces, such as a lifeboat. He had also been an avid theatergoer in his youth and often used theater scenes in his films. When he discussed *Dial M for Murder* (1954) with François Truffaut, he said, "I have a theory on the way they made pictures based on stage plays... the [old] idea was to do something that would take it away from the confined stage setting... The basic quality of any play is precisely its confinement within the proscenium."

*Dial M for Murder* is based on a successful West-End play by Frederick Knott, and Hitchcock is credited as co-screenwriter with Knott. It was shot in thirty-six days in 3D and completed in 1953, but not exhibited until 1954 because the Knott play hadn't finished its stage run. Warners Bros. had lost confidence in 3-D and released the film in flat form. Hitchcock seems to have thought lightly of it, explaining that he was "running for cover... coasting, playing it safe." But Truffaut defends the film: "This is one of the pictures I see over and over again. I enjoy it more every time I see it." I agree with him. The film almost completely preserves the dialogue of the play and its apartment-sized space, but I find it highly cinematic.

Nearly all of the action takes place in the tastefully appointed London apartment of Tony (Ray Milland) and Margo (Grace Kelly), who are suppressing the longstanding troubles in their marriage. The wealthy Margo is having an affair with a visiting American writer of detective fiction (Robert Cummings), and Tony, a retired tennis professional who has married Margo for her money, secretly plans to profit from murdering her. Hitchcock shows us all four walls of their apartment, at one point giving us an impossible shot—a view from the position of a wall where drink bottles stand on a cabinet. (In the 3-D version of the film, the bottles create a feeling of a separate dimension in the space of the room).

Occasionally we view action from the space where a proscenium would be, and Hitchcock had a trench built for the extremely large 3-D camera so that it could sometimes take a front-row center position, looking slightly upward past objects in the extreme foreground. At other times we view

*Dial M for Murder*

things from the position of Tony's desk near the left wall. There are no long takes, but at one point Hitchcock tours around the apartment in several shots, and at another he views the action from a high angle, looking down from the ceiling.

We leave the apartment briefly on three occasions. When Tony goes out to a stag party, we see him telephoning Margo—a signal for a hired killer to emerge from hiding and strangle her. (In the play, we only hear Tony's voice from the phone when she answers.) When she kills her attacker with a pair of scissors, Tony manipulates things so that she's tried and convicted of murder—a trial Hitchcock shows briefly in an expressionist montage of Grace Kelly's face as she hears the voices of lawyers and a judge. (In the play, we learn about the trial from a radio in the apartment.) Later, when a detective (John Williams) becomes suspicious of Tony, there's climactic action involving a key to the apartment which Tony has given to the hired killer. We see Tony in the hallway outside the apartment doorway, searching for the key. (In the play, the audience hears his footsteps from inside the apartment— the actor wore special shoes to make the sound audible.)

Truffaut makes an important point about the film: "It isn't easy to command the audience's undivided attention for a continuous dialogue... the real achievement is that something very difficult has been carried out in a way that makes it seem quite easy." As an example, I would pick the lengthy scene when Tony invites a ne'er-do-well named Lesgate to the apartment and with a combination of blackmail and blood money recruits him to kill Margot. The dialogue and stage business are much as they are in the play, and Hitchcock avoids closeups. But the combination of camera angles, cutting, and performance is fascinating. It's my favorite scene in the movie.

An opposite approach is taken in *Deathtrap* (1982), an adaptation of a hit 1978 play by Ira Levin, who wrote the screenplay with Jay Presson Allen. It's a black comedy about playwriting, directed by the versatile Sidney Lumet. The plot involves Sidney Bruhl (Michael Caine), a once-successful author of murder plays who is suffering from a series of disastrous flops. Clifford Anderson (Christopher Reeve), a student from one of his creative writing classes, has sent him a perfect play, which only increases his frustration and rage. He tells his beautiful wife (Dyan Cannon) that he'd like to murder Clifford and steal the play. We can't be sure if he's serious, but his wife, a perpetually anxious smoker with a heart condition, becomes almost hysterical. Sidney then contacts Clifford and invites him to their home. He proposes that he and Clifford collaborate on the play, but then he apparently murders Clifford, enlisting the hysterical wife's help in hiding the body. When she goes to bed that night with lots of pills, a wall in her bedroom suddenly crashes open and Clifford, covered with cuts and bruises, rushes in like a violent ghost. The wife immediately dies of a heart attack.

It turns out that Sidney and Clifford have been planning this all along. Sidney inherits his rich wife's money and Clifford moves in under the guise of Sidney's resident apprentice and secretary. The two work facing one another on dual typewriters at Sidney's antique writer's desk, ostensibly revising their play. In reality they have a homosexual relationship, and Clifford, who is revealed as a sociopath, is secretly writing a play about the murder they've committed. Sidney discovers this betrayal, but things become complicated when Helga Ten Dorp (Irene Worth), a neighbor who claims to be a psychic, senses that murder is in the air. Tension rises. The two men, armed with various souvenir weapons from Sidney's previous plays, have a fight, and both of them die. Helga reveals to the police what has happened, takes charge of Clifford's secret play, writes its conclusion, and arranges to have it produced. It becomes a giant Broadway hit.

Lumet, Levin, and Allen "ventilated" the original play, finding ways to stage scenes outside the interior of Sidney's home. At the beginning we're at a Broadway theater, where we see the last moments of Sidney's latest disaster. He goes to a bar and gets stupefyingly drunk, watches brutal reviews of the play on the bar's TV, staggers to the train station, falls asleep on the journey to his East Hampton residence, misses his stop, and gets off at the end of the line.

*Deathtrap*

In East Hampton, he lives on spacious grounds in a spectacularly beautiful old windmill that has been converted into a modern home. A few scenes are staged on the grounds or on the home's veranda. At the end we return to the Broadway theater and see the last moments of the fight between Sidney and Clifford acted on the stage. But despite the ventilation, this is a very theatrical movie. It's a film about a man who writes a play, a student who writes another play, two male lovers who revise a play, a killer who writes still another play, and a female detective who writes a conclusion to that play. The clever production design by Tony Walton converts the ground floor of Sidney Bruhl's house into a kind of stage where most of the action occurs. In the foreground is a living area and work space, and on the raised background is an "upstage," where Sidney's collection of armory from his theatrical success—pistols, knives, a crossbow, spears, and what he claims to be Houdini's handcuffs—is arrayed on the wall. There's a moment when Sidney and Clifford act out one of the scenes they're writing to see if it works. As befits a comedy that turns violent, the actors project their dialogue in theatrical fashion, and there's a good deal of performance within performance—occasions when we can sense that the characters are lying to one another, putting on an act to conceal their true intentions. Lumet also has fun with various entrances and exits on the ground floor of the house.

Christoper Reeve gives a subtle and amusing hint of effeminacy to his role, and the moment when he and Sidney kiss was a shock to 1982 audiences. Reportedly, some of the viewers booed or shouted, "Oh no, Superman, don't do it!" The studio claimed this scene cost them ten million dollars in box office. Whatever the case, the movie hasn't lost its considerable wit and style.

# CINEMA
# IN THE AGE OF
# STREAMING

*How do you feel about streaming and its effects on traditional cinema?*

Let me repeat that unless we're talking about live shows, commercials, news broadcasts, sporting events, cooking shows, quiz contests, or how-to programs, I don't see a radical difference between the two forms of exhibition. But there is a difference, and it sometimes matters. In a theater you're given an extremely large, sometimes engulfing image and better sound. In a theater you have no opportunity to stop the image or rewind; the cinematic experience is unique in the sense that it's an appointment event, designed to be absorbing. Streaming is far more convenient, less of an appointment, and its convenience can have an impact on its quality. Nevertheless, at some point early in this century home viewing eclipsed theatrical viewing—the result is a transformation like the one Friedrich Engels described, in which quantity becomes quality.

In discussing this, we should be aware that people who live in Europe, Asia, Latin America, and Africa also have TV and streaming, but they don't have the same programming as North America. I should add that the digital era, which makes streaming possible, presents great dangers for representations of history and for the survival of cinema history in particular. But we can talk more about that later.

Like God and the author, movies in theaters aren't dead, despite the occasional pronouncements to the contrary. This past year at my local cineplex, where good films are rarely shown, I've seen *Anora*, the 2024 Palme d'or winner at Cannes. I liked the way that film mixes the erotic, the sleazy, the violent, and the screwball-comic; it's a very good film, in some ways vaguely reminiscent of the Safdie brothers. I've also just seen Jesse Eisenberg's unusual, quietly touching *A Real Pain*, in which Eisenberg wears an IU hat for most of the movie. (His wife is from Bloomington, and they live here much of the time.) I like the way he avoids especially dramatic moments and nicely individuates among a group of Jews on a guided tour of Poland. The film also has a moving performance by Kieran Culkin as Eisenberg's cousin—a real pain but a sadly lovable character.

And at a Bloomington pop-up theater called Cicada Cinema, I've also recently seen John Paizs' wonderfully zany *Crimewave* (1985), which has been digitally restored and is being released on Blu-ray. A superbly surreal picture about a would-be screenwriter who can invent the beginnings and endings of movies but has trouble with the middles, it has a cunningly amateurish quality that enhances its satiric comedy and wit. Paizs makes films in Winnipeg, Canada, the home of Guy Maddin and George Toles, and this film has the absurd but poetic qualities of their work—in fact, Toles is credited as story consultant. *Crimewave* is a little-known classic that you probably won't find on current TV or in ordinary theaters.

But there's some truth in Louis Menand's recent claim in *The New Yorker* that "People don't ask today, 'What are you reading?' They ask, 'What are you streaming?'" Almost everybody tends to watch TV between dinner and bed, and that's the same way people used to read Dickens and Balzac in the 19th century. Today's successful movies go to streaming very soon after their theatrical run, and many of the made-for-TV films and series are as artful as theatrical movies ever were. It's also worth noting, where adaptation is concerned, that TV is now the major place to see good films based on fairly recent books; consider *Slow Horses* (2022–) and *My Brilliant Friend* (2018–2024).

In this context, let me put in a good word for middlebrow art, which highbrow critics often disdain or compare unfavorably to the high and lowbrow. These terms, products of mid-20th-century sociology, obviously have social-class connotations and are grossly oversimplified. Some of the very best cinema—several of Orson Welles' films, for example—is in the middlebrow range. (For an intelligent commentary on the importance of certain kinds of middlebrow art, see Michael Denning's book, *Cultural Front*.) PBS' *Masterpiece*, a major source of what can be called middlebrow or "prestige" TV, has aired an adaptation of Hilary Mantel's *Wolf Hall* (2015–25), which deals with England in the age of Henry VIII. I found the two-part series dramatically riveting and thought-provoking.

For me, another great thing about streaming is that one can watch far more foreign series and films than ever before. I'm a big consumer of subtitled shows and movies from Germany, Italy, Scandinavia, Poland, etc. If one can afford to subscribe not only to Netflix and Amazon, but also to places like Apple, Mubi, and Criterion, it's a cornucopia. I've recently watched the Belgian show *Chantale* (2022–5), about a woman who gets a job as chief detective in a small town police department. Basically a comedy, it has a laid-back humor somewhat reminiscent of Jarmusch. Even better is the Swedish mini-series *R.I.P. Henry* (2023), about a gifted surgeon in a small town who discovers he has brain cancer. This might sound grim, but it's often amusing and the surprise ending is profound about life and death.

Some movies are of course best seen on the big screen: *Lawrence of Arabia, 2001, Oppenheimer*, and *The Brutalist* aren't the same experience on TV, because they're among increasingly rare, theater-specific pictures. But in the long history of TV's challenge to theatrical movies, beginning with the invention of color TV, the two forms of exhibition have grown closer together and the feature film has suffered at the box office. As more and more old movies became available for home viewing from the 1960s on, some of the black and white classics were garishly colorized, and the widescreen pictures were adjusted so that their aspect ratio conformed to TV screens. But colorizing, which began in the 1980s, soon died and letterboxing triumphed. Today, most people have wide-screen TV sets, where they see a great variety of aspect ratios, although not always the original ones—there are sometimes reformatted films and minor differences determined by the streaming platforms. To its credit, Turner Classic Movies has shown *How the West Was Won* (1962) in the curved Cinerama format, which on TV makes it look narrow in the middle and very broad at either end. It isn't the real thing, but at least it gives you a sense of the entire aspect ratio.

My feeling is that streaming has had no important formal effect on movies made for theatrical runs, which tend to use far more CGI and have much bigger budgets, but it's had an effect on movies and series made for TV, which at the level of style can be quite artful and interesting. (Of course, the TV shows can also have big budgets and ambitious themes; the Steven Spielberg-produced *Masters of the Air* [2024], about the U.S. Army Air Force bombing of Germany in World War II, has some of the best uses of CGI I've ever seen.) At the same time there are drawbacks to streaming, especially for scholarly study. DVDs and Blu-rays (which unlike celluloid won't last forever) no longer have the large market they briefly had, and when they're shown on streaming platforms it's rare to have access to their extras (though the Criterion Channel often has them). Films on Netflix and Amazon aren't permanently available—*The Other Side of the Wind* was shown for a while but it seems to have been dropped. The digital world has made it impossible to count frames, and today's critics or historians have never touched a 35mm print. If only in the service of preservation, it should be the duty of university cinemas like the one here in Bloomington to show more films on celluloid rather than in a digital system.

# Style and Technology
# in Contemporary Films and Series

*You've remarked on style. Can you give some examples?*

Yes, let me start with some technical innovations in movies since the 1950s that have an impact on style in both theatrical and TV film. Most of today's series TV, especially on the networks, use at least three cameras rather than the single camera of old studio movies. Some of the old movies had multiple cameras (Chaplin shot *The Gold Rush* with two cameras placed side by side), but today's cameras have variable lenses and focus pullers who can adjust the depth of field and change easily from wide-angle to telephoto. At least one of the three or four cameras regularly on the set is a Steadicam, which results in much more camera movement or reframing. I've seen a perhaps rare episode of the still popular TV series *Law and Order* (1990–) that uses a moving camera in almost every shot, not only for walk-and-talk scenes but also for sequences in which three or four characters are standing, sitting in a room, or talking out on the street. The camera swings left or right when a character moves, sometimes reframing for a closeup, or it pans right or left between two characters as they speak. Sometimes it executes complicated, almost balletic movements between and around two or three characters who are talking and moving. The effect is as invisible as traditional Hollywood editing, but it involves complicated timing between an actor hitting a mark and the camera stopping its movement.

Another development is the drone camera, which has greatly increased the number of overhead shots of landscapes or automobiles travelling along roadways. Sometimes the drone starts at almost ground level and as a character walks away toward a house or building it smoothly rises higher than any crane shot in old Hollywood, revealing a distant land or seascape and the line of a horizon. In the elaborately produced but for me disappointing miniseries *The Agency* (2024), there's a drone shot of a drone in flight, something that's become a cliché.

Because cameras are smaller and more portable today, they can be easily positioned inside a car or on the hood looking at the driver through the windshield. Orson Welles put a heavy camera on the hood of a moving car in *Touch of Evil*, but by the 1960s it was easier to do this. Probably the most influential car chase in the movies is in *Bullitt* (1968), where the speed sometimes reached over 120mph. There's a camera car following at equally high speed and another camera that sometimes occupies the seat next to Steve McQueen. By the time of the big chase sequence in *The French Connection*, cameras could be positioned just outside the front window and at other spots inside the car.

All this is small potatoes compared to the big budget theater spectacles *Mad Max: Fury Road* (2015) and its prequel, *Furiosa: A Mad Max Saga* (2024), for which DPs John Seale and Simon Duggan not only used multiple cameras but also a towing rig, a tracking vehicle with a crane, and at least five smaller Red cameras for tight closeups. I suppose the state of the art for car chases (though not the best ones) is the *Fast and Furious* franchise (2001–21), which not only positions cameras inside and outside cars and trucks but also augments everything with drones, an army of stunt people and lots of digital post-production effects.

Because multiple cameras are in use for TV films, editing becomes busier than ever (and easier because of digital technology). Sometimes a driving scene, which in the old days would be shot with back projection, will show a view from the back seat of the car, then from the driver's door window, then from the passenger's door window, then from the hood, and then from the car's exterior mirrors.

In the old days, a sequence involving two or three characters sitting across from one another or standing in a room would involve somewhere between three and five camera setups: an establishing shot, shot/reverse shot closeups, and maybe a couple of bigger, more intense closeups on key reactions or lines of dialogue. Today, sequences of this type typically involve seven to nine camera views, and the sequences can sometimes be played through by the actors because there's less need to stop and reposition a camera. The Irish TV series *Suspects* (2014–16), for example, is shot in neorealist style with lots of hand-held camera work, but every episode also contains scenes in which a suspect is interviewed by cops and lawyers in a small, windowless interrogation room; we're given shots from the viewpoint of all four walls and the ceiling, plus multiple closeups of the characters from constantly shifting vantage points, resulting in a dozen or more changes of view.

In the Joe Penhall and David Fincher series *Mindhunter* (2017–19), there's a scene in which a crime psychologist sits at her desk and two FBI agents sit across from her to have a conversation. I counted twelve camera setups during the sequence, some of which may have involved nothing more than a change of camera lens. This technique not only involves busier editing but also, as I've said, allows the actors to play much of the scene straight through. With more than two characters, it also enables more frequent cuts to subtle reactions of someone who is relatively silent.

Long takes are relatively rare, but the Steadicam sometimes gives us beauties, as in *The Studio* (2025). In *The Agency*, there's a shot in which the camera tours a large, open-plan government office, picking up workers as they pass, then zeroing in on two characters who walk and talk toward us. It goes on following them around the office to a long hallway leading to an elevator, goes inside the elevator with them, rides up a few floors and gets out with the two actors, following them down another long hallway to a big conference room, which it enters. But interesting as this is, it's nowhere near the grace, beauty, and meaningful movements in the films of Max Ophüls, who did wonders with heavy cranes and big cameras.

The most remarkable Steadicam shot I've seen in recent movies or on TV is in the outstanding Montreal-based series *19-2*, which has two very similar versions, one in French (2011), the other in English (2014). Both of these I highly recommend. It's a great cop show about a couple of patrolmen who ride around the city responding to calls. Both versions have an astonishing episode about a shooter in a high school who is armed with a repeating rifle. In the English version (season 2, episode 1) it takes almost thirty minutes for the police to neutralize this killer by shooting him (turns out he is a fifteen-year-old kid). At least fifteen minutes of that action consists of an elaborate, wonderfully choreographed Steadicam shot. It roams the entire high school with the police as they dodge bullets, moving through the classrooms, stairways, and auditoria, encountering dead students on the floors, live students hiding or running for cover, and students being held hostage by the shooter. It's almost excruciatingly suspenseful.

*19-2*

The opening of the 2018 British series *Collateral*, written by David Hare and directed by S. J. Clarkson, has a long sequence shot of police arriving to investigate the strange shooting of a pizza delivery man. The camera travels toward the body, back to the nearby pizza delivery site, and 360 degrees around the entire area as a police investigator (Cary Mulligan) questions people. This series also does interesting things with over-the-shoulder shots of conversations. It's in widescreen, and often during a conversation we see an actor's face speaking from the far left or right side of the frame, while out-of-focus objects in the foreground obscure the rest of the image.

In other TV shows that use widescreen, I've seen a decentering technique that would have been forbidden in the old days. Sometimes a shot of an actor facing more or less toward us is positioned so that the figure is at the right or left side of the screen, leaving the rest of the space empty. This sort of deliberate imbalance can also be seen in dialogue scenes. Imagine a closeup profile of an actor looking to the left, speaking to someone offscreen. The normal way of shooting the closeup would be to have the actor's profile either at the center or at the right side of the image. In the latter case, the left half of the image is empty but the actor's gaze toward the offscreen space keeps the composition in balance. But I've seen several instances when the profile is at the *left* of the screen with the actor looking left. The empty space is behind the actor rather than in front, and the image is deliberately out of balance.

*Do you enjoy flamboyant style, such as the visual flourishes occasionally rolled out on* Breaking Bad *and* Better Call Saul? *Hitchcock used to joke that whenever he saw a scene in a motion picture with an angle from a fireplace, he would ask, "Who's in the fireplace?" I love Vince Gilligan's shows, but when there's a POV shot looking up at Saul Goodman grinding coffee, for example, I think of Hitch wondering, "Who's in the coffee grinder?"*

I've got nothing against coffee-grinder POVs or the style in *Breaking Bad* and *Better Call Saul*, but as Hitchcock's remarks indicate, there's nothing new about flamboyant style, which I sometimes like. (I also like Ozu and Costa, whose styles are at the opposite extreme.) In the history of movies there have been lots of "impossible" shots, including one I've already mentioned in *Dial M for Murder*. In *Period of Adjustment* (1962), the camera is inside a fireplace, looking out into a room through burning logs. An earlier example that comes to mind is Michael Curtiz's *The Kennel Murder Case* (1933), a standard locked-room mystery, brilliantly staged and shot in an advanced style by Curtiz, in which Philo Vance (William Powell) looks for clues in a small clothes closet and the camera looks out at him from within the closet.

A more extravagant kind of flourish is in the opening scenes of Curtiz's *The Unsuspected* (1947), when a camera apparently pans from a closeup of man in a train compartment to his reflection in the compartment window, moves through the window, glides down a city street to the neon-lit window of a flophouse, and moves through that window into a room, where it circles around and looks out the window to show four letters of the blinking neon outside the flophouse: KILL. All this was done with imperceptible dissolves or smooth cuts from one shot to another. Curtiz was a very flamboyant fellow (he was especially fond of implausibly cast shadows) and I like both of those movies.

*Matt Zoller Seitz and Chris Wade were cited in a 2017 article by Siobhan Lyons regarding the term "cinematic television," and how it's been overused and frequently misunderstood. Lyons states that Seitz and Wade "argue that the term 'Cinematic TV' is thrown around quite often, usually attributed to shows that are 'big' and 'expensive,' such as* Game of Thrones *(2011–19). Camerawork and cinematography play a role, but, they argue, there is more to cinematic television than simply good camerawork: 'Cinematic value doesn't automatically equate to scale or expense [...] sometimes great cinematic direction is a matter of tone and rhythm.'" Would you agree with that assessment?*

I guess I agree. I don't think I've heard of "cinematic television" but I've just been implicitly talking about it. I certainly don't think a film viewed in a theater or on TV needs to be big budget to be called cinematic. For some of the people you quote, cinematic seems to be an adjective meaning "good," or maybe elaborately showy. But for me cinematic"isn't a normative but a descriptive term. Tone and rhythm may have something to do with effective films, but one needs to be specific about what creates tone and rhythm. Rhythm is an especially tricky concept; I know what rhythm is in poetry, prose, music, and dance, and maybe it can describe performance style. But it isn't the same thing as pace or tempo and I'm not sure how to analyze it. I suppose it has to do with actor movement, but also with the pace of shots, sequences, and events that follow one another in a narrative. Cinema in theaters or on TV is above all a temporal medium.

In place of the writings you describe, I would try to answer Bazin's question: What is cinema? For me it's simply moving pictures recorded on celluloid or by digital reproduction. The essence of the cinematic is the movement of images, which can be enhanced by framing, camera movement, and editing. Andy Warhol's *Empire* (1964) and *Sleep* (1964) challenge this idea, but you can still sense movement or change in those basically static films, which are all the more "cinematic" because of their sly transgressions. Chris Marker's great *La Jetée* (1963) is a succession of still photographs and one brief, powerful image of a woman's eyelids blinking. Today, it's also possible to film an entire feature in one take, as in *Russian Ark* (2002), where the camera and the players are in constant movement through a giant museum. But good cinema can depend on a lot of things besides camera movement and shot selection. It can also have to do with sound, writing, acting, etc.

I can describe one example of what I think of as minimally cinematic with an experience I had years ago when I took a film production course at Indiana as preparation for making *A Nickel for the Movies*. The first assignment in the class was to shoot one hundred feet of film and edit your footage in the camera—in other words, there was no actual cutting and the shots were filmed in sequence. A short film could have been made in a single long take and still be cinematic, but the assignment was about the art of shot selection. I don't recall exactly what I did (maybe it was so bad I've repressed it, or maybe my pants are on fire), but let's say you've decided to make a short movie about a woman putting money in a parking meter. Shot one is a ground-level closeup of high-heeled shoes walking forward a few steps and stopping near a post or a pole of some kind. Shot two is a view of a woman from the waist up, revealing that she's at a parking meter and is looking in her purse for change. Shot three is a closeup of her hand trying to put coins in the meter but dropping most of them. Shot four shows the coins rolling off the sidewalk into an open grate at the curb. Shot five shows the woman's face, clearly frustrated. She turns her head and looks left. Shot six shows an empty street from her POV. In shot seven, she looks right. Shot eight is another POV of an empty street. In shot nine, she decides to go on her errand without paying. That's not much of a movie but I would say it's cinematic.

Given all this, let me add that there are many contemporary TV films which, because of their budgets and production values, seem to me more like what one might expect in a movie theater. I'm not talking about *Game of*

*Thrones,* which is filled with female nudity, violence, and over-the-top spectacle, but about more realistic, movie-length productions with performers who don't often appear on TV. A recent example is the miniseries *Disclaimer* (2024), written and directed by Alfonso Cuarón, which is based on a novel by Renée Knight. It was originally shown at several international film festivals, then moved to Apple TV. A complicated, sometimes unreliable narrative, it jumps back and forth in time, changes narrative point of view from one character to another, and uses the voices of two offscreen narrators. Its cast includes Cate Blanchett, an almost unrecognizable Kevin Kline, and, amazingly, Sacha Baron Cohen in a straight role.

This series got mixed reviews but I mostly liked it. I especially admire the way Cuarón uses the widescreen, sometimes augmenting its depth with a wide-angle lens (the DPs are Emmanuel Lubezki and Bruno Delbonnel). Blanchett plays a wealthy, celebrated Londoner whose life is destroyed when Klein self-publishes a novel exposing a scandalous misdeed from her past. When her husband and son discover this, she's banished from her home. Cuarón shows her on crowded busses, pressed together with working-class people of color. Throughout, the extras are very skillfully chosen and played, especially in a closing scene when Blanchett and Cohen (the estranged wife and husband) are seated in a hospital waiting room; it's a wide shot and a long take in which the various other characters in the room make a significant point.

*Have you seen* Say Nothing, *the new limited series on Hulu about The Troubles in Northern Ireland? You mentioned drone shots earlier, and I confess to be growing weary of them (especially in documentaries). But in the second episode, directed by Michael Lennox, there's an overhead drone shot of one of the IRA members fleeing British authorities by running through a neighborhood where all the doors are open to him. The gimmick is put to good use in this case, because it tells us something about the culture that a more conventional set-up would not have.*

Yes, I've seen that, and it's a good example. I haven't felt that the drone shot is overused, but you've made me think about it—there are certainly lots of drone shots looking straight down at a road or pathway bordered by trees, which is an unusual angle and not always necessary to the action. But if you're shooting a film on the Faro islands, as in the 2022 TV series *Trom,* it helps to have a drone. The same is true if you're in the far outback of Australia. The Australian film *Goldstone* (2016) was shot in the tiny town of Middleton, Queensland, which is the backend of nowhere, with dry, red-clay land that's as flat as a pool table and a single, two-lane highway running straight to the horizon. The drone shots give a powerful sense of the vast, lonely space. There's also a brief drone shot of a gunfight amid a bunch of trailer-sized offices of a mining company. You see five or six guys with rifles maneuvering through a sort of maze. All the drone shots I can think of in this and other films provide at least minimal narrative information. But I guess I also like landscape.

*Goldstone*

*Do you think that contemporary TV has been liberating for some filmmakers in terms of style? I'm thinking offhand of Steven Zaillian, who has been an A-list screenwriter for thirty years and has directed at least one good feature film* (Searching for Bobby Fischer [1993]), *but at the age of 70, directed the eight-part* Ripley *series (2024) for Netflix, which in terms of form and content is nothing like anything he's ever done before (nor looks anything like the previous iterations of Patricia Highsmith's novels).*

I completely agree with you about *Ripley*, which I've already mentioned because of its widescreen, black and white photography. Everything about that series—the music, the casting, the off-beat, unexpected adaptation of *The Talented Mr. Ripley*—is impressive. I'm afraid I can't think of other examples in that category, but you know more about TV than I.

I wouldn't say that Carl Franklin, a director I admire, was liberated by the episodes he did for *Mindhunter*, but I could feel his presence. A departure from the usual format of the show, which is mostly about a pair of FBI agents interviewing convicted serial killers, Franklin's episodes involve an ongoing police investigation of the serial killing of Black children in Atlanta. Most of the characters are Black, and the leading players are looking for a killer, not simply doing research by interviewing convicted monsters.

*This example isn't contemporary, but Budd Boetticher directed the 1957 pilot episode of* Maverick, *and he moves the camera more (and in one scene even includes an axial cut) in that episode more than in all five of his Ranown Westerns combined. He then directed the next two episodes in a more perfunctory manner, which suggests he got the memo to be less stylish.*

Directors seem to have more wiggle room to be stylish and inventive in the pilot episodes for series TV. Sam Peckinpah started out by directing some stylish TV. But once the general pattern of story, characters, and photographic style in the hit shows is set, other directors are brought on as hired guns and things tend to become conventional.

# ON GENRES

*We haven't yet discussed film genres, except arguably film noir (if it is a genre) and indirectly through your writings on specific filmmakers. Are genre studies prominent in scholarly and critical writings on film, or have they ever been?*

There's a very large and mostly excellent literature on film genres, and the topic has often been part of university courses. Because I'm no longer teaching, I can't say whether this is still the case in schools. The contemporary cinema doesn't often produce classic genres such as Westerns and musicals, and that may have resulted in a fall off of writing and teaching.

As I said earlier, writing about genre, while necessary, is always problematic because it's impossible to precisely define any generic category. There are always anomalous or hybrid members. There are also categories that aren't usually thought of as full-fledged genres but have generic attributes—the bio-pic, for instance, which includes the 1930s Warner Bros. cycle of pictures about such figures as Zola and Madame Curie; *Citizen Kane*, which could be described as a faux bio-pic; and the 2024 Timothée Chalamet movie about Bob Dylan. The gangster film is a similar, near-generic category.

One way of thinking about genre is in terms of the cycle. In the commercial film industry, a major hit often spawns imitations that also make money. In the 1940s, hits like *The Maltese Falcon* and *Double Indemnity* led to other, roughly similar movies, and the cycle eventually grew large enough to be called noir. In contemporary TV, *Game of Thrones* quickly spawned imitations.

Whatever the case, an idea of genre has always been fundamental to Western poetics. The distinction between tragedy, comedy, and epic is as old as classical Greece and it persists despite the great difficulty of pinning down the meaning of the centuries-old terms. I suppose you could describe the three descriptors as forms of affect: tragedy makes you sad, comedy makes you laugh, and epic makes you feel awe. But in Aristotle, comedy and tragedy are *dramatic* forms and epic is a *narrative* form, such as *The Odyssey*. (Brecht described his "epic theater" as a semi-narrative form, not because he was writing vast adventures but because he wanted the audience to keep a certain emotional distance from the drama.) You could complicate the distinctions in modern America: there are tragic cowboy movies, comic cowboy movies, and epic cowboy movies. Maybe we should call them modes rather than genres.

*Are films that do mash-ups (i.e., amalgams) of different genres relatively new to cinema, or do we just tend to be more conscious of them, perhaps because many of those films are themselves self-conscious (scholars connecting David Lynch's oft-unclassifiable films to postmodernism, for instance)?*

Again there's nothing new about what some people today call mash-ups. As I mentioned earlier, genres have always mingled with one another. I'm also a bit skeptical about the term postmodernism, unless we want to call the 21st century post-postmodern. But you're right about a visible self-consciousness in filmmakers like Lynch. It sometimes tends to become camp or pastiche, which aren't new either, but typical of what's called postmodern art. The point I would emphasize, though, is that a great many movies can't be easily slotted into a simple category. Are the first two parts of *The Godfather* (1972–74) a gangster movie, a family epic, a tragedy, or all three?

## Westerns

*Have you ever written about Westerns? Do you like them?*

I haven't written about Westerns but like most people I like them. Among my favorites are *Red River* (1948), *Rio Bravo* (1959), *My Darling Clementine* (1946), *She Wore a Yellow Ribbon* (1949), *The Big Country* (1958), and *One-Eyed Jacks*. Darlene is a much bigger fan of Westerns (and of Tarzan movies), and we both love William Wellman's *Westward the Women* (1951).

The Western is quintessentially American. (Sergio Leone's spaghetti Westerns were of course made in Italy or Spain, but their landscapes look American, and they made Clint Eastwood a star.) And because it serves as a ground for national myths or allegories, the Western is especially fascinating from an ideological perspective. The best thing written on that important topic is Jim Kitses' *Horizons West*, a fine study of individual films and directors, but also a smart analysis of how Hollywood negotiated the contradictions of American nationalism.

Kitses points out that the "shifting ideological play" of Westerns can be described with a series of antinomies growing out of an opposition between wilderness and civilization. Wilderness is West and civilization East, and this opposition forms a subcategory of nature versus culture. On the Western side is individuality, freedom, honor, self-interest, purity, pragmatism, brutalization, and savagery; on the Eastern side is restriction, institutions, social responsibility, democracy, corruption, knowledge, idealism, and refinement. Other binaries are America vs. Europe, equality vs. class, agrarianism vs. industrialism, tradition vs. change, and past vs. future. Notice that there are positive and negative aspects on either side. The classic Western had the impossible job of resolving a dialectic by reconciling or smoothing over ideological contradictions.

The movies weren't alone in this. James Fennimore Cooper's *The Last of the Mohicans* and Mark Twain's *Huckleberry Finn* struggled with the same oppositions. But from the time of *The Great Train Robbery* (1903), the Western movie became the chief way of dramatizing the battle between nature and culture. The genre was at first associated with movies about the post-civil war decades, when "Go West, young man" was something of a national motto and the Turner Thesis valorized a continual Westward expansion of America in the name of progress. The prototypical prestige Western was *Stagecoach* (1939), which put all the ideological contradictions in play. Here was Eastern and Southern civilization vs. the Indians of the West; the puritanical and repressive town vs. the free range; the outlaw vs. the sheriff; the corrupt banker vs. the community.

*Stagecoach*

In *Stagecoach*, Claire Trevor plays a dance-hall girl (classic Hollywood's substitute for a prostitute) who is thrown out of town by puritanical church ladies, and John Wayne plays Johnny Ringo, a supposed outlaw who is also ostracized by the town. These two are more likeable and admirable than the more civilized passengers on the stagecoach, and at the end they become a couple. In the closing scene they board a buggy heading further west. Thomas Mitchell, a likeable Irish doctor and drunkard who has also been shunned by the town, smiles and says that they are "free of the blessings of civilization." It's a criticism of the town, but in fact Trevor and Wayne are heading west to have children and establish more civilization.

Certain directors treated Western themes differently. Peter Wollen has pointed out that women, who were key elements of the Western representing civilization and nurture, were put on a pedestal by John Ford and treated as one of the boys by Howard Hawks. (William Wellman made them as tough and rugged as any male pioneer.) But as decades passed, American society changed, leading to bigger changes in the Western. The westward expansion had long ended, and nostalgia for the old west was tempered by critical or revisionist films. In *The Wild Bunch* (1969), the West is no longer associated with freedom. Kids in the town torture insects, and the cowboy outlaw has become an aging relic; Mexico offers an escape to nature and freedom, but is also a site of modern violence and corruption. *Little Big Man* (1970) and other films of the period critique White treatment of Indians, expose the racism and brutality of America's westward expansion, and de-mythologize characters like Buffalo Bill. Blacks were virtually invisible in the classic Western until Ford's *Sergeant Rutledge* (1960), and later came Mel Brooks' *Blazing Saddles* (1974). But despite all this, the old antinomies could be partly reinstated in an urban setting, as in *Coogan's Bluff* (1968), which later inspired a TV series.

I've made it sound as though the Western is a fairly uniform generic category. To complicate things, I recommend another book: Peter Stanfield's impressively researched *Horse Opera*. People tend to forget that in the 1930s and 40s one of the most popular characters in the Western was the singing cowboy, epitomized by Gene Autry, Roy Rogers, and Tex Ritter, who were the stars of B pictures aimed at rural, working-class audiences and their children. (We also tend to forget that the young John Wayne starred in many of these at Republic, once or twice as a singing cowboy.) Stanfield reminds us that the pictures weren't always about the 19th century, and were often at least partly musical, with a comic side-kick for the star.

Besides the Saturday matinee singing cowboys, there was also big-budget fare like the Bob Hope musical comedy *The Paleface* (1948), in which a timid easterner travels west and sings the hit song "Buttons and Bows," with lyrics declaring, "East is East and West is West, and the wrong one I have chose." Even earlier, there was *Way Out West* (1937), with Laurel and Hardy doing a sublime soft-shoe number.

The singing cowboy shows up in an A-list movie in *Rio Bravo* (1959), when Ricky Nelson and Dean Martin sing a duet of "My Rifle, My Pony, and Me." There's a charming French film, not a Western but a comedy, called *My Donkey, My Lover & I* (2020) directed by Caroline Vignal and starring Laure Calamy, which alludes to *Rio Bravo* and ends with the song.

*Rio Bravo*

*In thinking about your analysis of film acting: does the Western genre benefit particular types of actors more than others? At one end of the spectrum, there are John Wayne and Clint Eastwood and Randolph Scott, who have been said to play more or less the same character every time. I don't agree with that, but their styles are admittedly different from James Stewart in the Westerns he made with Anthony Mann.*

The B-movie cowboys of the pre-and-post WWII era were usually dandies, with big white hats, fancy boots, tight pants, and glittering belts holstering pearl-handled six-guns. They also had showy horses like Roy Rogers' Trigger, adorned with silver-studded saddles. The stars of the prestige Westerns, on the other hand, rode ordinary-looking horses and wore plausible costumes (Ford, however, was something of a costume fetishist). They all played the cowboy type—an expert horseman who was heroic, taciturn, and tough. Some, however, occasionally went against type, as the big stars of almost every genre did. Wayne was a near anti-hero in his best films, *Red River* and *The Searchers* (1956), perfecting a glowering, angry, scary determination. Scott played a sometimes untrustworthy character in *Ride the High Country* (1962); Henry Fonda could be menacing and played a bad guy for Leone; and Gary Cooper, the "yep" and "nope" cowboy, was often folksy and comic. The major surprise, as you indicate, was Stewart. He had a lean, lanky, fragile-looking body, a drawling wit, and hands that sometimes looked awkward or fluttery. He was also the most emotionally intense leading man in classic Hollywood—vulnerable, troubled, occasionally cranky, and able to cry onscreen without losing his masculinity. ("There is a vulnerability in everything I do," he once told an interviewer.) Despite all this, he became one of the major stars of the Western. In the pictures with Anthony Mann he was both heroic and neurotic, the sweat stains around his cowboy hat signifying heat and anxiety, and he almost fainted outright when he was shot in the hand in *The Man from Laramie* (1955).

*Is the Western a dead genre, as some have claimed? Kevin Costner's* Horizon: An American Saga, Chapter 1 *(2024) would seem to indicate that. On the other hand, I did enjoy* The English *(2022), an unconventional British Western series on* Prime; *and to a point* The Harder They Fall *(2021) on Netflix, directed by Jeymes Samuel as kind of an overheated homage to spaghetti Westerns and Blaxploitation-era Westerns like Sidney Poitier's* Buck and the Preacher *(1972), or a mash-up such as* Take a Hard Ride *(1975), starring Jim Brown and Fred Williamson, directed by Antonio Margheriti (a Tarantino favorite).*

I would say that the Western is virtually dead in theaters. The last one with lots of critical praise was New Zealand filmmaker Jane Campion's *The Power of the Dog* (2021), which is something of an art film. I agree with you about *The English*, which has one of the scariest villains I've ever seen. I think the Western today is mainly to be found on TV, but in a modernized form. One of the most popular shows in America for the past few years is *Yellowstone* (2018–24) about a rich modern-day rancher who inhabits a world reminiscent of the old *Dallas* prime-time soap opera. I much prefer the *Longmire* series (2012–17), about a modern sheriff in Arizona; it's one of the best Westerns I've seen in a long time. I also like the Australian series *Mystery Road* (2018–20). Critics can't seem to decide what genre it belongs to, but I would say it's Western-like. It's set in the outback, and it features Aaron Pedersen as an Aboriginal police officer in a cowboy hat and boots. He sometimes looks like John Wayne. And there's also the excellent *Dark Winds* (2022–), about a Navajo sheriff.

# Musicals

*Besides the advent of the Sound Era, what are the origins of the movie musical?*

When most people talk about the musical, they're referring to films produced by the Hollywood studios during the 1930s, 40s, and 50s. Those films aren't the only musicals, but all of them originate in one way or another from the Broadway musical theater and wouldn't have existed without it.

In 1930s New York, there were lots of musical comedies—chiefly boy-meets-girl stories involving such themes as college life, gangsters, show business, etc. There were also operettas set in Ruritanian locales, with slower paced songs and quasi-fairy tale narratives. Another popular form was the revue, a loosely connected series of songs, comic sketches, and dances organized by a theme such as a round-the-world trip. Roughly parallel with these shows were a separate category of all-Black musicals, which were less thematically unified. There was also a sort of modernist opera: Gertrude Stein's *4 Saints in 3 Acts*, George Gershwin's *Porgy and Bess*, Marc Blitzstein's *The Cradle Will Rock*, and the American production of Brecht and Weil's *Threepenny Opera*.

Most of the composers, writers, and performers of New York theater went to Hollywood and created what we think of as the classic-era musical. Of these films, the least directly indebted to Broadway were the Warner Bros. cycle of mostly "putting on a show" movies, beginning with *42nd Street* (1933) and featuring Busby Berkeley's increasingly elaborate production numbers. Some of the Astaire-Rogers pictures at Universal were adapted from Broadway, but the seminal one, *Flying Down to Rio* (1933), was an original. (The "Carioca" number in that film is one of my favorites, even though the Astaire-Rogers team has only a minor moment—the real charm is the choreography of the dancing ensemble.) Beginning in the 1940s, the Freed unit at MGM became the leading producer of musicals, and many of their pictures were adaptations of Broadway hits: *Annie Get Your Gun* (1950), *Show Boat* (1951), *Kiss Me, Kate* (1953), *South Pacific* (1958), etc. *The Band Wagon* was MGM's tribute to the old Broadway revue musicals, with a variety of numbers ranging from ballet to pop. Minnelli's *Meet Me in St. Louis* (1944) was an original and contributed along with Broadway itself to the development of the integrated musical, in which talking melted into singing and walking into dancing. (This at the moment when Brecht was going in the opposite direction, arguing for a "radical separation of elements.")

*Along with Minnelli, whom do you consider to be some of the masters of the form?*

Where Hollywood is concerned, I'm a big fan of the Paramount musicals produced and mainly directed by Ernst Lubitsch: *The Love Parade* (1929), *Monte Carlo* (1930), *The Smiling Lieutenant* (1931), and *One Hour With You* (1932). These were modernized descendants of Broadway's Ruritanian operettas, and they starred Maurice Chevalier. They have all of Lubitsch's charm and wit, and are, like most of his work, inimitable. Also at Paramount was Rouben Mamoulian, whose *Love Me Tonight* (1932) is admired by almost everybody. Mamoulian also directed the CinemaScope *Silk Stockings* (1957), a musical remake of *Ninotchka* (1939), one of Lubitsch's most famous pictures. The other major director of Hollywood musicals was George Cukor. The reconstructed version of *A Star is Born*, a rare example of a non-comic Hollywood musical, is far better than the other versions of that story and one of the best musical films ever made.

*A Star is Born*

We should remember, though, that important musical films were made outside of Hollywood. In Britain, Michael Powell and Emeric Pressburger made *The Red Shoes* (1948) and *The Tales of Hoffmann* (1951), two non-comic, vividly colorful, almost surreal tributes to ballet and opera. And in France, Jacques Demy made *The Umbrellas of Cherbourg* (1964) and *The Young Girls of Rochefort* (1967), two of the world's most melodic and cinematically graceful movies, in both of which, courtesy of Michel Legrand, all speech becomes musical lyricism.

*Regarding musicals associated with Old Hollywood, one significant difference I've noticed is that song and dance numbers in more contemporary musicals tend to be edited sometimes to the point of incomprehension compared to musical numbers in the classical era. (I'm thinking of Richard Gere's tap-dance in* Chicago *[2002], but there are plenty of other examples.) Is there a reason for this, aside from (to be blunt) some film actors can't sing or dance, and directors need to cover for them?*

It's partly that some people can't dance, but it also seems to me directors have forgotten how to film dance effectively. Maybe it's because the music-video craze on MTV changed film culture. I dimly recall that one of those videos featured Cyd Charisse dancing, and the number was cut to ribbons. Jennifer Beals had an expert double for her big audition number in the awful *Flashdance* (1983); the double performed stunningly acrobatic leaps, spins, and dance moves, but the whole thing was splintered into fragments. Fred Astaire had a rule that his dances had to show the whole body and be covered in only one or two shots. For me, the beginning of the end of good dance sequences was probably *West Side Story* (1961), in which Robert Wise had the best dancers in the world but heavily edited their work. The Spielberg remake wasn't any better.

*The Western, as you indicated, is pretty much DOA as a cinematic form, though it still exists on television. But would you say movie musicals are undergoing something of a revival? There was* The Greatest Showman (2017) *a few years ago, and* Wicked  *(2025) had boffo box office. Musicals have never really taken to TV (remember* Cop Rock *[1990]?) with one notable exception: Rachel Bloom's* Crazy Ex-Girlfriend (2015-2019), *which I really enjoyed, and Jonathan Rosenbaum loved, not least because its choreography and compositions were frequently throwbacks or affectionate pastiches of the classics.*

I like *Crazy Ex-Girlfriend*, too, but for me *The Greatest Showman* and *Wicked* are very far from a revival. It seems to me that the decline of the musical has a lot to do with changes in popular music. The Gershwin-Porter-Berlin-Rogers and Hart generations, who created the great American Song Book, survive today mainly in jazz, and it would probably be impossible to create a musical today that has the feeling of the mid-20th century. As the nadir of the form, I would pick *Xanadu* (1980), which has horrible music and photography, plus Olivia Newton John and the aging Gene Kelly on roller skates.

One example of a modern film that gives me that old feeling is John Carney's *Once* (2006), a low-budget picture from Ireland about a street singer and a Czech flower seller. It doesn't involve drugs, booze, and the corrosive effects of fame, which are the usual tropes of contemporary show-biz movies, and some of its simple tunes, such as "Broken Hearted Hoover Fixer-Upper Guy," are charming. A duet on guitar and piano in a music store was performed live rather than using playback, and in its own modest way, it's as good as MGM in its heyday. At some points you could even call the film neorealist Minnelli. But where splashy production is concerned, I also very much like Damien Chazelle's *La La Land* (2016) and his TV series *The Eddy* (2020), which is about a jazz band. (I wish someone could make a good musical based on the songs of Leonard Cohen.)

*There's also a subgenre of jukebox musical, which, according to infallible Wikipedia, employs pre-existing popular music, and began onstage like every other type of musical. That's probably correct in this case. It's likely more debatable that* Yankee Doodle Dandy *(1942) was the first motion-picture jukebox musical, according to that definition. The most recent was* Joker: Folie à Deux *(2024), about which the less said the better. Do you prefer musicals that have original music?* Emelia Pérez *(2024) is a polarizing example of one.*

I should first say that new music didn't completely destroy musicals. Depends on the music. Many films in the heyday of the Hollywood musical had original scores, but many others were adapted from stage hits or were bio-pics like *Words and Music* (1948), which is about Rodgers and Hart — it's a bad movie with wonderful songs. I'm personally very fond of *The Buddy Holly Story* (1978), which I guess you could call a jukebox musical. Gary Busey gives an amazing performance and did all the songs live. Should the Elvis pictures be considered jukebox? Their songs were issued as records at the same time the films were released. I would say that *A Hard Day's Night* is a jukebox musical. And what about *Saturday Night Fever* (1977)?

*Do you like musicals that deconstruct the form? There haven't been many, but a few are celebrated. Dennis Potter's* Pennies from Heaven *(1978) and* The Singing Detective *(1986) aired originally as BBC serials (the former starring Bob Hoskins, the latter Michael Gambon) before the former was adapted as a feature film: Herbert Ross'* Pennies from Heaven *(1981), starring Steve Martin, was a box-office bomb but it has its admirers, and features a bravura dance number by Christopher Walken that was praised by Gene Kelly and Fred Astaire. There's also Bob Fosse's* All That Jazz *(1979), which takes Fellini's* 8½ *and converts it into Fosse's personal autocritique.*

I dislike all the titles you mention, except perhaps *The Singing Detective* (a pastiche of musical and noir), though I like watching Walken dance or do anything else. One reason I dislike those films has to do with my respect for the old musicals, which, as Richard Dyer has pointed out, have a utopian quality, an imagery of energy, abundance, intensity, transparency, and community—a vision of how things ought to be, or of something we want deeply that our day-to-day lives don't provide. I don't think the musical improves by being what you call deconstructive, except maybe in the case of *Threepenny Opera* (which respects the form it makes Brechtian), or sometimes in Fosse's *Cabaret* (1972), which isn't very deconstructive. Another reason I dislike the ones you name is that, Walken aside, I'm not impressed with their songs or dances.

# Horror

*Unlike musicals and Westerns, the horror genre has proven not only durable, but seems to be a viable point of entry into the movie business for aspiring filmmakers, given that it doesn't have to be based on any pre-existing IP (intellectual property). Any thoughts as to why this is?*

I can't figure out why people voted for Trump (though I have some dark suspicions), so how can I explain the ubiquity and apparent popularity of many contemporary horror movies? At my local cineplex it often seems that half the features are horror (horror in every respect, including art). From the previews alone, I can tell they're overusing jump scares. I suppose a certain kind of horror doesn't need good writing and is easier to do on a relatively lower budget. I should add, though, that John Lithgow and Geoffrey

*Vampyr*

Rush recently performed in a horror movie, *The Rule of Jenny Pen* (2024), and Steven Soderbergh has made *Presence* (2024).

*I'm curious as to what your favorite horror movies are, but I'm also curious about what you would consider to be the most significant or pivotal horror movies throughout cinema history, for good or ill?*

First let me deal with the problem of defining the horror movie. It's a genre that's mostly defined by its affect, but horror movies aren't always scary or horrific—they can have a range of emotional qualities. Furthermore, as with other genres, some films fit the category better than others. Is *The Thing from Another World* horror or sci-fi? (Horror seems related to dystopian sci-fi, as in *Alien* [1979] and *Blade Runner* [1982].) And what do we make of monster movies in general. Does *King Kong* count?

Personally, I've never been fond of *Halloween*-style slashers, but some of the greatest filmmakers in history have done horror pictures. Carl Dreyer's *Vampyr* (1932) is a powerful expression of subtle psychological horror, done with brilliant lighting and real settings. For me, it's better than any of the scores of vampire movies since then.

F. W. Murnau's *Nosferatu* (1922) is a landmark of otherworldly sexual monstrosity. (It was remade by Werner Herzog in 1979—naturally, because Herzog had Klaus Kinski—and remade less impressively in 2024 by Robert Eggers.) Hitchcock's *Psycho* is a horror movie, and so is *The Birds* (1963). Hitchcock was of course the major influence on Brian De Palma's experiments with horror.

Roman Polanski's *Repulsion* (1965), *Rosemary's Baby* (1968), and *The Tenant* (1976) are stories of perversion and madness so skillfully done that they give me the creeps. And I should include one of my favorite movies of any kind, Charles Laughton's *Night of the Hunter* (1955), which is expressionist horror mixed with Griffith-like pastoral. (I always weep at the beautiful end of that movie.) To this list I would add the low-budget Val Lewton pictures at RKO, especially the two directed by Jacques Tourneur: *Cat People* (1942) and *I Walked with a Zombie*. These were never high on the fright meter, but they were outstanding examples of poetic, psychological horror. In terms of landmark horror films, one would have to include James Whale's *Frankenstein* (1931), which set off Universal's cycle of horror-movie monsters and literally saved that studio from the Depression.

I can recommend two books about horror movies. My colleague Joan Hawkins has written *Cutting Edge: Art-Horror and the Horrific Avant-Garde*, an intriguing argument for the relationship between the outsider status of both vanguard horrific art and midnight-movie horror in the 1970s and 80s. As a cultural argument, I think that's exactly right. (The more respectable avant garde has long been interested in horror: see French Impressionist Jean Epstein's *The Fall of the House of Usher* [1928] and German Expressionist Carl Mayer and Robert Weine's *The Cabinet of Dr. Caligari* [1919].)

The second book I recommend is William Paul's *Laughing/Screaming*, a wonderfully smart discussion of mostly low-brow comedy and horror, covering such phenomena as *Nightmare on Elm Street* (1984). Paul makes the surprising and convincing argument that the most influential horror film of the mid-20th century was *The Bad Seed* (1956), a not very good movie starring Patty McCormick as a murderous child. It established a pattern for subsequent horrific children movies, most of which featured a malignantly evil child who is pubescent or pre-pubescent and who exhibits a disturbing combination of precociousness and regression. The most significant of the latter of these films—maybe more of a landmark than even *Psycho* had been—was *The Exorcist* (1973), a blockbuster hit that set off national news stories of audience members fainting or vomiting. "People either loved it or hated it," Paul writes, "sometimes loving it *and* hating it." The Catholic church provided it with advisors and embraced it, but later withdrew support. *The Exorcist* had upped the ante of the devil worship in *Rosemary's Baby* by giving us a prepubescent child who is possessed by the devil and given exorcism by art-movie icon Max von Sydow.

Equally important, Paul shows that one result of that film was the birth of gross-out horror, as in *Carrie* (1976). I've never liked *The Exorcist*, but I admit that when Linda Blair vomits or gives an evil grin while her head spins around on her shoulders, it scares the hell out of me. I would say the next development in horror was set off by the popularity of Jonathan Demme's *The Silence of the Lambs* (1991), a new and more explicit treatment of sexual sadism and serial killing. But I think the better adaptation of Thomas Harris' Hannibal Lecter novels was Michael Mann's *Manhunter* (1986).

Most of these trends—especially art-horror, body horror, and gross-out—come to an apex in Coralie Fargeat's *The Substance* (2024), a satiric movie about an aging star of a Jane Fonda-style exercise show who injects a "substance" to stay young. This picture got a screenplay award from Cannes (WTF!?), a Golden Globe award for Best Actress in a Musical or Comedy (WTF!!?), and nominations for Oscars (WTF!!!?). I sympathize with the fact that it's trying to make a feminist statement, but I find it overstated, overlong, and seldom scary or funny. It's shot with a fish-eye lens that makes all its closeups look hideously grotesque, its design is based on a primary-colored dream version of L.A. (much of it shot in France), and it has a motif of revolting food. The food thing has something to do with the cultural pressure on women to stay slender, but eating is never established as a concern of the central character. The film oscillates between nude or spandex-clad cheesecake of a beautiful young woman, horrific views of birth from a spinal cord, a doppelganger's bloody revenge, and monstrous images of age and deformity. Yuck. I hope I'm not being male chauvinist piggy by suggesting that Aaron Schimberg's *A Different Man* (2024), the story of an actor with a horribly disfigured face who can get work only in low-budget horror movies and off-Broadway theater, is a far better picture.

Obviously I'm not a fan of most recent horror films, but I did enjoy Mark Mylod's *The Menu* (2022), a movie about the horrors of fine dining and wealthy foodies, which made me ravenous for a cheeseburger. Let me also take the opportunity to mention two recent films that are not only excellent but also show how flexible and various horror movies are. First is *As Boas maneiras* (*Good Manners*) (2017), an offbeat, memorable film with a domestic setting, directed by the Brazilians Juliana Rojas and Marco Dutra. And second is Jordan Peele's *Get Out* (2017), a satiric horror story that shows just how scary white people can be.

*I confess to being afraid to watch certain types of horror movies—Giallo, for example, and body horror, some examples of which have been made by revered artists like Dario Argento or David Cronenberg. (I have even less use for slasher movies or torture porn.) I'm averse to gore unless it's comedic, like* Shaun of the Dead *(2004). Do any horror movies fill you with that degree of dread, or am I just a wimp?*

If you're a wimp so am I. I recoil from violence and torture, although I do admire Cronenberg, who sometimes makes me squint or turn away but seems a legitimate artist, not just a purveyor of body horror. The films that frighten me the most aren't violent, gross, or sadistic. I'm genuinely frightened by Jennifer Kent's *The Babadook* (2014), which evokes a child's fears and a mother's madness. I'm also unsettled by Jack Clayton's *The Innocents* (1961), which is by far the best adaptation of Henry James' *Turn of the Screw*. For some reason, I get more disturbed by a mysterious face at a window than by somebody jumping out with a knife. Both of those movies scared me so much I haven't been able to rewatch them.

*Do you see political subtext in many horror movies?* Get Out *certainly has it, as does Coralie Fargeat's* The Substance *(I'm hardly the first to suggest that there's a terrific 90-minute shocker inside its bloated 140-minute running time). But George Romero's original* Night of the Living Dead *(1968), with its Black protagonist (played by Duane Jones), and a twist ending that packs quite a wallop, has earned quite a bit of political analysis, as have his sequels in the series, notably* Dawn of the Dead *(1978), with its satirical portrait of zombies staggering through a shopping mall.*

I think you've partly answered your question, and I agree that *The Substance*, which has a political message, would be somewhat (but only somewhat) improved if a half-hour were lopped off. Horror, like most genres, always has ideological and political implications. It can be racist or anti-racist, satiric or self-critical, left wing or right wing. (I woul call *Night of the Living Dead* left wing and *The Exorcist* right wing.) But these aren't intrinsic qualities of the genre.

## Screwball comedy vs. romantic comedy

*If you'll indulge me another thought experiment about genre (or subgenre) boundaries, there's an argument that posits that the screwball comedy, which peaked in the 1930s and 1940s, was eventually replaced by the romantic comedy (or romcom) as we more or less know it today. Arbitrariness of labels and fluidity of formats notwithstanding, do you see differences between examples of the romcom and the, er, screwcom?*

Comedy is such a capacious category that I'm glad you offered up subcategories. But I wouldn't say that romantic comedy replaced screwball. That would mean *What's Up, Doc?* (1972) and *Hit Man* (2023), along with a slew of others in the past fifty or so years, aren't screwball. I would say the two forms are difficult to separate neatly and have tended to co-exist, with screwball dominating the contest once the censorship rules changed.

As William Paul has pointed out, screwball and romantic are roughly comparable to what classical Greece referred to as Old Comedy, which was bawdy, satiric, loosely structured slapstick, and "New Comedy," which had a unified plot and ended happily with marriage or restoration of love between a heterosexual couple. In my view, the greatest romantic comedy ever made (and one of the greatest films period) is Lubitsch's *Trouble in Paradise*. Sara Kosloff, in her fine book on dialogue in Hollywood pictures, calls it a screwball comedy, but it seems to me much more romantically plotted than screwball. The irony is that *Trouble in Paradise* is sexy, funny, and romantic precisely because it overturns romantic clichés (beginning with the very first shot—a garbage-collecting gondolier on Venice's Grand Canal singing *O Solo Mio* in a fine voice). Nobody has come close to the stylish perfection, sophisticated glamour, and witty charm of this film. Later romantic comedy, with the notable exception of Lubitsch's own *Ninotchka* (1939), *The Shop Around the Corner* and *Heaven Can Wait* (1943), is tepid by comparison.

But in movies, the two forms mingle or appear alongside one another in every period. Most film historians agree that screwball has something in common with silent slapstick comedy, especially with silent short films; but Chaplin, Keaton, and Lloyd gave a boy/girl love plot to all their pictures. If anything, romantic comedy was in movies in advance of screwball, because the boy-meets-girl formula has long been used in every kind of Hollywood movie. Some of the most profitable of the romantic comedies of post-classical Hollywood (which Andrew Sarris described as "sex comedies without the sex") were remakes of earlier models: Nora Ephron's *Sleepless in Seattle* (1993) is a remake of Leo McCarey's superior *An Affair to Remember* (1957), which itself was a remake of McCarey's *Love Affair* (1939), and Ephron's *You've Got Mail* (1998) is a remake of Lubitsch's vastly superior *The Shop Around the Corner*.

The term "screwball" originates in the 1930s with such films as *Twentieth Century* (1934), *My Man Godfrey* (1936), *Bringing Up Baby*, and *I Love you Again* (1940). These films have romantic plots but are filled with eccentric, crazy-comic characters, slapstick, rapid-fire repartee, farcical situations, and sexual innuendo. One of them also has a moment of comic cross-dressing. All of their traits were used to the limit in Wilder's *Some Like It Hot* (1959), which is set in the 1930s.

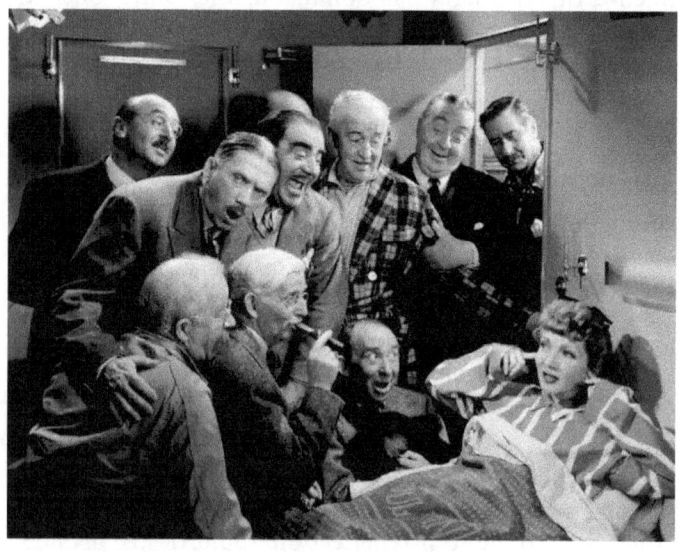

*The Palm Beach Story*

The screwball films, like some of the romantic comedies, tend to satirize the upper class or figures of authority. In Preston Sturges' great *The Palm Beach Story* (1942), Joel McCrea goes chasing after his wife, Claudette Colbert, who, after dealing with the aged, deaf, and rich "Weenie King," runs off in a train to Palm Beach, attracting the nutty Ale and Quail Club and eventually hooking up with the wealthy but stiff Rudy Vallee. McCrea finds a sleeping-car porter who was working on the train and asks, "Was she alone?" The porter replies, "Well, you might practically say she's alone. The gentleman who got off with her gave me ten cents from New York to Jacksonville. She's alone but she don't know it." (Sturges was among the finest comic dialogue writers, and he also loved slapstick—not only that, but your late cat was named for him.)

There can be screwball elements in a variety of films. As I've mentioned and as several critics have said, the recent *Anora* turns into screwball for quite a while, but it's no romantic comedy. In an interview for *Cineaste*, director Sean Baker says, "it is a love story for perhaps the first hour, but then it goes haywire." He also acknowledges a debt to films like *Bringing Up Baby*. When I looked up recent examples of screwball comedy on Wikipedia, they claimed *The Big Lebowski* (1998) is screwball. I don't think I would call it that, but a lot of the Coen Brothers films have screwball qualities. One of them, *O Brother Where Art Thou?* (2000), is in many ways derived from Sturges.

## Documentary

*Should we describe documentary films as a genre?*

I'm not sure. They're obviously a category, but so baggy that contemporary historians have invented the term "non-fiction film." There is now an academic society called Visible Evidence that deals with it, and here at Indiana there's a lively Center for Documentary Research, headed by my colleague Joshua Malitsky.

Godard once said, "All great fiction films tend toward documentary, just as all great documentaries tend toward fiction." I tend to agree, although the great animated films prove an exception. It's certainly not unusual for fiction films to have documentary elements. A recent example is Brian Helgeland's *Finestkind* (2023), which has extended footage of scallop fishing in the waters near New Bedford, Massachusetts. During World War II, Hollywood often used stock newsreel footage in battle scenes of ships at sea, as in the Bogart vehicle, *Action in the North Atlantic* (1943). And it's also not unusual for great documentaries to have staged moments. This is true as early as Robert Flaherty's *Nanook of the North* (1922), which takes liberties with its depiction of the Inuit people. Flaherty once defended himself by saying, "one often has to distort a thing in order to catch its true spirit."

There are also semi-faux or ironic documentaries with a genuine documentary impact. The greatest of these, to my mind, is Luis Buñuel's *Land Without Bread* (1933), which was filmed as if it were an ordinary travelogue about Las Hurdes, Spain. It's a shattering depiction of poverty, backed with the music of Brahms and a flat, bland narration that describes horrific conditions. "I didn't find a single drawing, nor a song, nor a firearm," Buñuel once said. "It was almost neolithic culture, without folklore." At one point he wanted to film a Las Hurdes donkey being stung by bees, a not uncommon event in the area, and to make it more realistic he spread honey on the animal.

My wife, Darlene Sadlier, is the author of *A Century of Brazilian Documentary Film: From Nationalism to Protest*. Doubtless I will be accused of bias, but her book is not only a fine critical study but also a great source for demonstrating how amazingly various the category of documentary can be. She begins with two feature-length pictures: *In the Country of the Amazons* (1922), an ethnographic, travelogue-style documentary shot by Silvino Santos, who had studied with the Lumière brothers; and *São Paulo: Symphony of the Metropolis* (1929) by Adalberto Kemeny and Rodolfo Rex Lustig, one of several important city-symphony films that were made in countries around the world during the 1920s.

Among the many other films she discusses are short educational/scientific movies; films about Brazilian art history; the Cinema Novo classic *Arraial do Cabo* (1959), which uses industrial sounds to document a seaside area blighted by factories; *Viramundo* (1964), about a migrant community that was being filmed for the first time; *Public Opinion* (1967), consisting of impromptu interviews with everyday Brazilians; documentary bio-pics of Carmen Miranda and other famed individuals; *Isle of Flowers* (1989), a partly animated, ironically narrated film about the life of a tomato, which ends at a massive, disease-ridden dump site; *Where the Land Ends* (2001), a making-of documentary about the rarely seen avant-garde feature *Limit* (1931), which is regarded by many as the greatest of all Brazilian films (Orson Welles, whom the Brazilians adored because of his aborted *It's All True*, was one of the early American viewers of *Limit*); and Petra Costa's *The Edge of Democracy* (2019), a montage of TV news, home movies, and other material about the impeachment of President Dilma Rousseff, the imprisonment of Worker's Party leader Lula da Silva, and the rise of Bolsonaro's right-wing forces.

She also includes a very amusing faux documentary, *Recife Frio (Frozen Recife)* (2009) by the talented Kléber Mendonça Filho, one of Brazil's best filmmakers. Kléber lives in Recife, which is an almost tropically warm city by the sea, and he has fun imagining a meteor that crashes on the beach and alters the climate. He documents the city but also shows penguins wandering the beach. The only citizen who is happy is the guy who plays Santa Claus at Christmas; for once he's comfortable in his thick coat and fake beard.

*Your comments on Darlene's book remind me that documentaries have gone through lots of historical changes, not only in political aims but in style.*

Yes, I think one of the big changes has to do with the fact that for most of their history documentaries have relied on narration. (Riefenstahl's *Triumph of the Will* (1935) is something of an exception because there are only a few minutes of narration at the opening.) The presence of a narrator raises political/ideological issues because it seems like a voice of god, interpreting and judging the evidence for us.

One of the best illustrations I can give of how narration affects documentary is my experience with the two versions of John Huston's *The Battle of San Pietro* (1945), which Huston and his unit filmed during one of the bloodiest battles of World War II. The completed film troubled the War Department and was suppressed for some years. I first saw it (or thought I saw it) when I was a freshman at LSU, where all the first-year males had to take an ROTC course. (This requirement was a vestige of the university's early history as a military school.) You were issued a uniform to keep starched and brass to keep polished, you learned to salute, and you had regular marching drills with a heavy M-1 rifle. There were also classes on things like map reading. During one of those classes, my instructor (no doubt to kill time) showed us *The Battle of San Pietro*. I was amazed because I had heard about the film and thought it was forbidden by the Army.

Years later, I discovered I had seen a doctored version, strategically reduced in length and narrated portentously by Walter Huston. The original, consisting mostly of newsreel-style battle scenes, was written and narrated by John Huston in a dry, factual, Hemingwayesque style that sometimes has ironic force. Bill Nichols has given us a fine analysis of this narration in his book *Ideology and the Image*. For me, the two versions of *San Pietro* vividly show the difference between a documentary that's mostly truth (Huston's version) and a documentary that's mostly propaganda (the Army's version). And this difference has a good deal to do with narration.

*The cinema-vérité movement got rid of narration.*

Yes. This was partly due to developments in technology—portable cameras and NAGRA recording equipment that could be used in many different locations. But it was chiefly initiated, at least in America, during the Sixties by Robert Drew of Drew Associates, who made *Primary* (1960), about the Wisconsin Democratic primary contest between JFK and Hubert Humphrey. That picture influenced a generation of documentary filmmakers, among them Richard Leacock, D. A. Pennebaker, the Maysles brothers, Shirley Clarke, Barbara Kopple, and Frederick Wiseman. The movement was influenced by Jean Rouch in France—hence it was sometimes given the French title, although Rouch's films were more participatory, involving contributions from people who were the subjects. The more accurate American term is "direct cinema." It mostly dispensed with narration, interviews, and music, giving us the information straight, no chaser, though of course the filmmakers could make points through the choice of shots and the editing.

Editing was especially important because direct cinema directors shot miles of film with no script and had to shape it into a rudimentary form of narrative or argument. In a recent issue of *The New Yorker* (January 2025), Michael Schulman has written an essay about the relatively unsung Charlotte Zwerin, who edited several of the Maysles films and who could be described as an auteur. She was responsible, to give only two examples, for giving shape to *Salesman* (1969), about a group of travelling Bible salesmen, and also to *Gimme Shelter* (1970), about a Rolling Stones concert, which became one of the most controversial documentaries in history. For both of those, she got credit as director alongside the Maysles. (I recommend Joe McElhaney's excellent book about Albert Maysles, published in the *Contemporary Film Directors* series.)

Direct cinema soon became an object of criticism because of its implicit claims of unmediated objectivity. It had ignored the Heisenberg principle, which reminds us that no matter how objective, the act of viewing has an effect on our sense of the thing viewed. Eventually, documentaries that used portable equipment and only rudimentary scripts abandoned the pretense of neutrality and became openly political. Peter Davis' Vietnam war film, *Hearts and Minds* (1974), which is filled with on-the-spot footage and interviews with the military, is one example, and so is two-time Academy-Award winner Barbara Kopple's film about a Kentucky miner's strike, *Harlan County, USA*

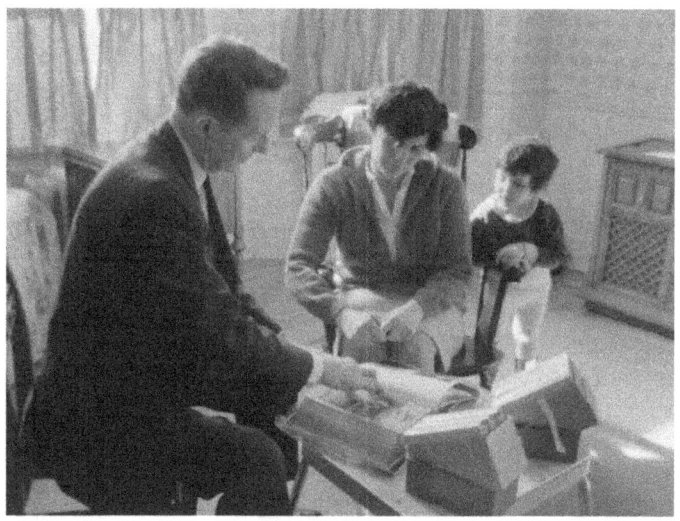

*Salesman*

(1976). The Kopple film is an instance of the filmmaker herself becoming part of the action; she shows herself being threatened by the coal-company's strike breakers.

During this period, the L.A. rebellion film-makers, among them Charles Burnett, Billy Woodberry, and Haile Gerima, had strong documentary underpinnings; they've often been compared to the Italian neorealists, but one of the important differences is that the Black directors had lived the experiences of the things they fictionalized, and they knew first-hand the neighborhoods they filmed — theirs was a personalized, intensified realism. Of this L.A. group, Billy Woodberry, who now lives in Portugal, became the most important documentarian. His *And When I Die, I Won't Stay Dead* (2015) is a portrait of the Beat poet Bob Kaufman, and a fine commentary on the art and importance of poetry. More recently, Woodberry's *Mário* (2024), a biographical account of pan-African activist and intellectual Mário de Andrade, is a fascinating account of the success and failings of the Pan-African movement in post-colonial Africa. Both of these films have interviews and stock news footage, and both are educational in the best sense.

The death of direct cinema or the transformation of it into Reality TV was Craig Gilbert's *An American Family* (1973), a highly successful PBS series about the upper middle-class Loud family in Santa Barbara, California. This show, which was created from over three hundred hours of 16mm footage, encountered the same criticism that the creators of direct cinema had experienced — it ignored the rule that the "objective" observer changes the nature of the thing observed.

Soon *An American Family* resulted in a satiric film, Albert Brooks' *Real Life* (1979), about an ambitious documentary filmmaker who hopes to win the Nobel Prize.

It's sometimes said that Orson Welles' *F for Fake* (1973) is the origin of a species of documentary nowadays called the essay film. It's certainly an absorbing, essay-style picture, in which Welles becomes a guide to various kinds of fakery, especially the "lies" of movie editing. He performs a magic trick, comments on art forgery, appropriates footage from another film and changes its original meaning, and quotes Picasso to the effect that "Art is a lie that makes us recognize the truth." He promises that for an hour everything in the film will be the truth, but at the end he sneaks in a fictional story without saying so and without reminding us that an hour has passed. Reality—the very foundation of documentary practice—he describes as mundane, "the toothbrush waiting for you in the glass, a bus ticket, or the grave."

I wouldn't pick *F for Fake* as the first essay film— it's dangerous to say anything is the first. Alain Resnais and Jean Cayrol's *Night and Fog* (1955) might count as an earlier example of the form; it's devoted to the truth of what happened at Auschwitz and to the ultimate truth of death. Welles' film, on the other hand, is a sort of meta documentary that wittily, sometimes poignantly reveals the almost inevitable fakery of documentary practice. Today, documentaries come in all imaginable forms and many are brilliant, but their principle home seems to be TV. Both PBS and HBO, for example, frequently screen documentaries.

*What's your opinion on the use of reenactments in documentaries, e.g., Errol Morris'* The Thin Blue Line *(1988)? Or, also pertaining to Morris, any thoughts about his technique, such as his use of the Interrotron camera, for example* The Fog of War *(2003)?*

Thanks for reminding me. I should have mentioned Morris, who added a new wrinkle to documentary. For me, *The Thin Blue Line* counts as an essay as much as a documentary, and though some thought of it as a radical breakthrough, it was actually confirmation of how documentary and drama often blend. The Interrotron makes me a bit uncomfortable because it seems a strategy (in the guise of objectivity) to make the interviewee look bad. It's interesting that a recent fiction film, Paul Schrader's *Oh, Canada* (2024) is about a famous documentary filmmaker who is nearing death and who becomes the subject of a Morris-like documentary. He tries to turn it to his own ends.

*Any thoughts on Werner Herzog's documentaries, which seem to be a good example of the use of staged scenes that you mentioned? At his Q&A at IU Auditorium, he mentioned reading reviews that raved about the scene near the end of* Grizzly Man, *when a helicopter pilot sings a moving song about Tim Treadwell, and Herzog practically boasted, "I told him to sing it."*

Good example. Several of Herzog's non-fiction films could be called essays. Maybe I should also mention a species of film called docu-drama. One of the best examples is Peter Watkins' made-for-TV *Culloden* (1964), about a 16th-century peasant rebellion in Scotland, in which most of the rebels were slaughtered by British troops. It's shot in newsreel-style black and white and has the uncanny effect of centuries-old history preserved on film.

*Matt Zoller Seitz recently published a piece on rogerebert. com that's critical of contemporary documentaries, and touches on a few of the same topics that you did above. Do current documentaries borrow too much from the narrative structure of commercial films?*

I haven't kept count of recent documentaries, but what Seitz says is probably true. It seems to me it's unusual to find any documentary, whether old or new, that doesn't have at least a rudimentary narrative form. Documentary is almost always trying to tell a story. But I suppose you could say Fredrick Wiseman's important films, many of them recent, aren't narrative; they usually document some kind of basic process within an institution and therefore give us only a slight sense of beginning and end. Pedro Costa's two documentaries are also about process—in his case artistic process—and have very little narrative structure. That kind of documentary is rare. I would say that in recent years there's been a big increase in talking heads, offscreen narration, and story-telling form, which contribute to the effect Seitz describes.

# ON CRITICISM

*You've written lots of criticism. Do you think criticism is necessary for movies or art in general? Could we get along without it? What value does it have?*

Criticism obviously isn't as necessary as food, shelter, and clothing, but I don't think we could get along fine without it. There were no critics around when somebody composed (or recited) *Beowulf*, but the Greek society that produced Sophocles' *Oedipus* and Homer's *Odyssey* also produced Aristotle and Plato. Classical Greece, Oscar Wilde has pointed out, was an inherently critical society. Critics have long been with us, and for good reason.

I assume that people who read books, essays, and reviews about films start with *a priori* interest in the subject. Borrowing from what W. H. Auden writes about literary critics in *The Dyer's Hand*, I would say that at minimum a good film critic can provide me with six important services: 1) Introduce me to films or filmmakers I know little about. 2) Persuade me that I've undervalued or overestimated a film. 3) Show the styles or relationship of films from different cultures about which I'm relatively ignorant. 4) Give me a reading of a film that enhances my appreciation. 5) Show the relation between a film and a larger realm of art, society, ideology, ethics, religion, etc. 6) Give me a better understanding of how films are made and the conditions under which a particular film was produced.

Numbers 1, 3, 5, and 6 require learning and scholarship. Readers, especially in America, need to be informed about little-known or foreign filmmakers who aren't publicized by the Hollywood marketing system. It's an important service to let them know about Radu Jude or Agnès Varda, which means the good critic should know about other cultures, and should have a broad knowledge of film history. It helps as well if the critic has read about politics, psychology, and art history in general. Several of these services mean that the critic needs to know not only about the film industry but also about the technology of filmmaking. Nobody could be a good critic of poetry if they were ignorant of versification, and by the same token a good critic of film needs to know something about cameras, lenses, lighting, sound recording, etc.

# Critics and Artists

*Is good criticism a craft or an art?*

The *OED* defines one use of "critic" as a person who specializes in "the art of exercising judgement." I don't consider myself an artist, but any craft or activity, whether writing, carpentry, or marching bands, can become an art. Furthermore, as Oscar Wilde says in *The Critic as Artist*, "Without the critical faculty, there is no artistic creation at all."

Novelists, poets, and filmmakers use the critical faculty every time they make something, just as you or I evaluate and revise when we write academic books and essays. Jackson Pollock must have occasionally paused from throwing paints at a canvas to judge and modify the effects he created. I suspect the surrealists were critically selective when they published samples of their automatic writing, and anyone who thinks that Buñuel's *Un Chien Andalou* (1928) and *L'Age d'Or* (1930) were just slapped together by free association knows nothing about making movies. There is probably no form of artistic expression that requires the critical faculty more than directing a movie. A movie director is faced with dozens of critical decisions every day, not only the set but also during pre- and post-production.

Many artists have written criticism that's almost indistinguishable from their art. T. S. Eliot not only wrote *The Waste Land* (with critical help from Ezra Pound) but also some of the most important criticism of the 20th century. Virginia Woolf was a superb critic (see *The Common Reader*) and so was W. H. Auden. I'm not a great admirer of D. H. Lawrence's novels (his poetry is another matter), but his *Studies in Classic American Literature* is full of thought-provoking insight that can also be applied to American movies. Vladimir Nabokov, who pretended he didn't like movies and once said that calling films cinema was equivalent to calling undertakers morticians, wrote lectures on English and Russian literature that are as impressive and enjoyable as his novels. Besides these figures, there are critics who didn't make art but seem to me exceptional writers. In the literary field, my short list would include Edmund Wilson, Hugh Kenner, Helen Vendler, Frank Kermode, and Terry Eagleton. Among art critics, I've learned from my friend David Anfam's writings about abstract expressionism. He died recently. I miss him, but I have his books and often return to them.

I sometimes enjoy re-reading the great critics more than re-reading canonical novelists and poets. (I haven't given up my addiction to crime fiction.) There are of course also many film critics who could be called great practitioners of their craft. The primary qualification for the honor is a broad knowledge of not only film but of the other arts, and the ability to write good prose.

*I can't resist an opening like that: who among film critics should be considered great?*

I fear this question because I might forget to mention one or more people I personally know. I'll start with critics who were also filmmakers. The obvious examples are Godard, Truffaut, Rohmer, and Chabrol—directors of the French New Wave who began their careers as writers for *Cahiers*, *Arts*, and other journals. Truffaut later published critical books and Godard never stopped being an intensely engaged critic, even in his films. In America, Peter Bogdanovich qualifies. There are others from almost every country in Europe. Pedro Costa hasn't written enough to be known as a critic, but he has a brilliant essay on Howard Hawks' *Land of the Pharaohs* (1955) and his lectures on film for students in Tokyo, together with the lengthy program on major directors he mounted at the Lisbon cinematheque, can count as types of criticism. Writers such as these have a major influence on the formation of canons and artistic values. Some are also important writers on film theory and esthetics—Sergei Eisenstein, for example, and most of the Soviet avant garde.

Especially where film is concerned, we need to distinguish between journalists and academics. Journalistic critics have the job of evaluating new films, and they usually write short pieces on a deadline. I've always thought of the ones I admire as real writers, as opposed to academics like me, whose income comes largely from university jobs. But it's difficult to make exact distinctions between journalists and academics because their work sometimes overlaps.

The work of film reviewers is so evaluative that some readers will inevitably disagree with them, and their writings for newspapers and magazines can become yesterday's news. But the best of the reviewers overcome objections and are worthy of reprinting. In *An Invention Without a Future*, I've written about four journalist-critics who are important to film literature and were significant for me personally: James Agee, who was also a novelist, poet, and screenwriter; Manny Farber, who was also a painter; Jonathan Rosenbaum, who has written enough books and taught at enough schools to qualify as at least a part-time academic; and Andrew Sarris, who was also a university teacher. I would call these great practitioners of their craft because they know so much and write so well that I enjoy re-reading them.

Among today's journalistic critics in America, my favorites are Manohla Dargis and Richard Brody, and I hope someday they'll publish books of their reviews. There are also film critics who seem to occupy a liminal space between journalism and the academy. Robin Wood, who was always highly evaluative, had academic appointments and for me was one of the very best writers on film. (His acknowledged model was the Cambridge literary critic F. R. Leavis.) Raymond Durgnat, who also wrote poetry and taught in an art school, was a big influence on me when I began publishing about film. Molly Haskell's *From Reverence to Rape* is a major feminist argument about Hollywood, as intelligent and important today as it was when it first appeared. And even though I often disagree with David Thomson, he's also been an academic and is an exceptionally talented writer.

Academic critics usually depend more on research and their evaluations are implicit, conveyed through analysis and appreciation. Their writing helps get them secure academic jobs, but the best among them don't write just to acquire tenure; they can have a fairly large readership, and their work endures. I respect so many of them that I won't try to list them for fear of forgetting someone I know personally. I'll limit names and just say that for me and many others, the late David Bordwell was important, not only because of the quality of his writing and research, but also because he achieved a full-scale poetics of cinema. My favorites of his many books are *On the History of Film Style*, *Reinventing Hollywood*, and *Perplexing Plots*. He didn't write about politics or ideology and was skeptical of zeitgeist arguments, and because he was so closely focused on narrative, photography, editing, and other purely cinematic practices, he had little to say about how ethnicity, sexuality, or subcultures affect film. But he was always implicitly evaluative and extremely wide ranging; it's clear that he liked Sturges and Tarantino as much as Mizoguchi and Angelopoulos. Because of his skill at analyzing style, he taught me more than anyone else about how to look closely at film form.

George Toles, an academic who is also a screenwriter for Guy Maddin, has a collection of essays entitled *A House Made of Light*, which I think is as important as any film criticism ever written. I would say the same thing about the late Gilberto Perez's *The Material Ghost*. Among the biographer/critics, most of whom are academics but who seem to me to belong to a special category, I would list Joseph McBride. His *Searching for John Ford* is definitive, and he has written impressive critical biographies of Lubitsch and Wilder. His recent book on Cukor has many biographical elements but is primarily an excellent study of the many actors and performances Cukor oversaw. I can't imagine how much is involved in writing a biography and I've always been afraid to attempt one. McBride's books are big, deeply researched, and have a critical edge, so that biographical information is always accompanied by intelligent evaluation of films. He writes well, and because he's not only an academic but also experienced Hollywood first-hand as an actor and screenwriter, he's exceptionally good at commenting on what goes on behind the scenes in movies. I would also list Patrick McGilligan, the author of a fascinating biography of Fritz Lang, and of *Young Orson*, which is by far the best book about Welles' origins and early work. His most recent biography, *Woody Allen: A Travesty of a Mockery of a Sham*, is devoted to a challenging subject, which he treats intelligently and thoroughly. I could go on at length with names from around the world and I hope the many academics I admire will forgive me for not mentioning them.

## Critics and Evaluation

*To what degree should the critic evaluate rather than explain or interpret?*

There's a kind of useful scholarly writing on film that avoids evaluation—I'm thinking, for example, of Barry Salt's empirical study of the history of film style (the first closeups, the first camera movements, etc.). But when I published my collection of essays, one of my aims was to counter a growing tendency in academic cultural studies, which had turned away from evaluation and become interested in populist forms of reception. I'm obviously not a populist, and I believe academics who write about film ought to implicitly or explicitly evaluate art. Without evaluation, there's less art and no useful politics. (I nevertheless dread the prospect of having my books reviewed and at the same time hope they will be reviewed. I'm sure artists feel the same way about their work.)

Nietzsche famously said, "We have art in order not to die of truth," but we couldn't have worthwhile art without some form of criticism. I would despair if there were no art, and I believe good criticism has a useful symbiotic relation with artists; it both feeds off them and facilitates them, in part by showing us how art is done and in part by constructing a canon and a sense of art history. In fact, criticism and scholarship is the chief means by which an artist's work survives over long periods. Botticelli was once considered a minor Renaissance artist (even Vasari gave him only muted praise) but 19th-century critics made him canonical.

The canons and histories aren't fixed in stone. Where movies are concerned, they're created by critics, festivals, museums, and award ceremonies, and they change over time as movie technology changes, new artists appear, new voices emerge, and histories are revised or challenged. I've already mentioned David Bordwell's *On the History of Film Style*, which nicely illustrates this process. Early writing about film, as Bordwell shows, was eager to establish film as the "Seventh Art," and the films it valorized were from the silent era. When the Seventh Art became a valid subject for art history, the Museum of Modern Art, where Iris Barry was in charge of motion picture acquisition, established a canon of 16mm prints that were circulated to schools. Eisenstein and Pudovkin were made essential, but Vertov and Kuleshov were virtually ignored (Chaplin was considered too theatrical). When sound arrived, the Seventh Art critics thought cinema had been dealt a death blow and was reduced to nothing more than canned theater. Everything changed fundamentally in postwar France, where André Bazin dethroned montage and praised dialogue films by Welles, Wyler, and Renoir. Soon a new canon was formed. Then a younger generation of French cinephiles admired American cinema and used it to promote an auteurist agenda. This made icons of certain Hollywood directors who hadn't been taken seriously, and further reshaped the canon.

With all this in mind, we should recognize our unfortunate tendency to read film history in presentist fashion, shaping the canon in the light of our current interests. All critical writing is historically situated and its awareness of history is crucial, but we shouldn't live in a world where old films, old canons, or old theories are tossed aside like dilapidated cars. At the same time, people like me rely on good journalistic critics who discuss new pictures. In all this I'm of course talking about the best criticism. Like most everything, a great deal of criticism is as unnecessary and unreliable as the book ratings on Amazon. The trick is to discern what's useful and reliable—to criticize the critic. Nowadays everybody's a critic, and we're going to have to live with that, whether we like it or not.

*Do you think one has to agree with a critic (more often than not) to find that critic worth reading?*

No. I've had occasional strong disagreements with all the film critics I've mentioned, but that doesn't make me stop reading them. The critic I've most often disagreed with was Pauline Kael, but she determined how a great many movies were received and I sometimes re-read her, occasionally threatening to throw her books at the wall.

*Have you ever had personal experience of journalistic criticism or film reviewing? I think you were once a reviewer for* Film Quarterly.

Yes, but only to a degree. From 2008 until 2011, while Rob White was editing *Film Quarterly*, I had the opportunity to do an annual column celebrating what I thought were the ten best films of the year. It was a good deal of work. I attended film festivals and Rob got me screeners—but I enjoyed it, in part because it enabled me to show my admiration for foreign films and write about things other than Hollywood.

Unlike an ordinary reviewer, I didn't have to write about bad films. I think writing attacks on bad movies becomes bad for one's character (I say this despite having attacked *The Substance*), and I think the best service reviewers can provide is to champion the films people may not know about. That was what I tried to do.

It immediately became obvious that no critic can see every film made in a given year, and that festival and art theater programmers shape film history every bit as much as critics. My number one pictures for those four years were Pedro Costa's *Colossal Youth*, Jia Zhangke's *24 City*, Corneliu Porumboiu's *Police, Adjective* (2009), and Apichatpong Weerasethakul's *Uncle Boonmee Who Can Recall His Past Lives*. Among the many films high on the lists were Sarah Polley's *Away from Her* (2006), Sergey Dvortsevoy's *Tulpan* (2008), Richard Linklater's *Me and Orson Welles* (2008), Abderrahmane Sissako's *Bamako* (2006), Guy Maddin's *My Winnipeg* (2007), Kelly Reichardt's *Wendy and Lucy* (2008), Abbas Kiarostami's *Shirin* (2008), Raúl Ruiz's *Mysteries of Lisbon* (2010), Eran Kolirin's *The Band's Visit* (2007), Olivier Assayas' *Carlos* (2010), Tomas Alfredson's *Let the Right One In* (2008), Mike Leigh's *Happy-Go-Lucky* (2008), and Maren Ade's *Everyone Else* (2009). I tossed in two animated features, Brad Bird and Jan Pinkava's *Ratatouille* (2007) and Nina Paley's *Sita Sings the Blues* (2008); two revivals, Pere Portabella's *Cuadecuc-Vampir* (1970) and Kent Mackenzie's *The Exiles* (1961); and one TV show, the first season of *Mad Men* (2007). I obviously can't know if those films will be remembered, but I would still recommend them.

*Those films are excellent. But I have to kid you about* Mad Men. *This has nothing to do with the show's quality, but rather because I raise this question in another book I'm working on: How is a TV series a movie? I ask because, generally, critics have thought so little of television that they gave the TV work of Hitchcock, Welles, and other filmmakers scant attention at best. A notable exception: Andrew Sarris ranked George Cukor's* Love Among the Ruins *(1973) one of the best films of the 1970s. But that was at least a made-for-TV-movie, not a season of episodic television like* Twin Peaks: The Return, *which the critics at* Cahiers du Cinéma *in 2019 nonetheless deemed the best film of the decade. There has clearly been a shift, and I have a few ideas on how to account for it, but I'm curious about your thoughts on this subject. It fascinates me.*

I'm happy to discover I beat *Cahiers du Cinéma* by eleven years, although unlike them I didn't pick the first season of *Mad Men* as the best film of the decade. It was my number ten pick in 2008. It's as well made as any theatrical film of that year (the credits are worthy of, and clearly influenced by, Saul Bass) and far more interesting than most. If I had been doing the same sort of thing back in 1955, when Andrew Sarris listed Roberto Rossellini's *Journey to Italy* (1954) as number one and Sam Fuller's *House of Bamboo* (1955) as number ten, I would certainly have listed the first season of *Alfred Hitchcock Presents* (1955). If I had been doing it in 2001, Lynch's *Mulholland Drive*, which was originally supposed to be a TV series, would have been my number one. If I were doing it today, a TV series on a streaming channel would almost certainly be on my list. As far as I'm concerned, a film doesn't have to be projected in a theater or be non-episodic TV to be called a film. But I would be interested to know your ideas about a shift.

*The shift among film critics is a matter of going from a general dismissal of television altogether to defining good TV as a movie. TV critics like Alan Sepinwall, Kathryn VanArendonk, and even Matt Zoller Seitz (who also writes about film) object strongly to that because they feel that there's a step missing: defining good television as good television. I actually like your* Mad Men *choice because it doesn't hinge on an auteur director (maybe an auteur showrunner in Matthew Weiner), though it was a well-*

*directed series from episode to episode. Auteur directors like Lynch are fond of statements like "I've made an eighteen-hour movie," but have they really? Television has become a more acceptable venue for film directors (and writers and actors) over the last 20 or so years for multiple reasons, but one is that the film industry is no longer hospitable for many of them to make the movies they want to make. (There's another development in recent years—streaming—that blurs and complicates the dividing line further.) I guess what I'm getting at is: Are there attributes that distinguish* Twin Peaks *(1990-91) the series from* Twin Peaks: Fire Walk With Me *(1992) (released as a feature film)? Or* Mulholland Drive *as a pilot episode of an unmade series from the great film we know as* Mulholland Drive?

I strongly agree with most of what you say, although I suspect the advent of the showrunner has made many talented and famous directors reluctant to do series TV except as director of pilot episodes or as a hired gun. Julie Dash, an important member of the L.A. Rebellion group, once visited Bloomington and told me that working under a showrunner was valuable mainly because it enabled her to play with new equipment.

You can correct me on this, but I think that starting in the 1970s, shows like Masterpiece Theater began to appear regularly and networks began producing feature-length versions of *Moby Dick* (1998 & 2011) and *The Count of Monte Cristo* (1975 and 2024)—a conscious strategy based on literary adaptations and aimed at "quality" middlebrow programming. It made TV seem more like movies and reinforced the idea that regular TV had been inferior.

When I was young I thought movies in theaters were always different from TV, but now I think the difference is far less, and sometimes none at all. Anything photographed on celluloid or a digital medium is a film, whether it's episodic or not, and whether it's projected on a bed sheet or viewed on TV. One marginal exception might be a sitcom like, *I Love Lucy* (1951-57), which had a brightly lit stage, three cameras, and a laugh track. *The Jack Benny Program* (1950-65) was similar, but was photographed by Nicolas Musuraca, who was responsible for *Out of the Past* at RKO. The Jackie Gleason comedy series *The Honeymooners* (1955-56) is in my view a masterpiece of short-form cinema, almost as good as the old Laurel and Hardy shorts. (As I write this, Turner Classic Movies is showing old episodes of *The Carol Burnett Show* [1967-76].) People who wrestle over what counts as a movie and what counts as TV seem to me to be similar to people who try to define what counts as a film noir.

*Even if we need criticism, why do most other forms of art not have ten-best lists?*

Maybe because certain kinds of movies, like certain kinds of music, are a form of popular art and their fans are interested in ratings. You don't see this kind of thing with new forms of classical music, fine art, sculpture, and architecture, but in recent years there have been a great many book-prize competitions that give short and long lists of the year's contenders. (*The New York Times* already has a list of the hundred best books of the 21st century.) James Agee and Manny Farber occasionally gave year's-end rankings of films, which I find especially interesting. When Godard was a critic at *Cahiers*, he contributed a ten-best list every year and his choices were predictably unorthodox. In 1955, for example, his number one film was *Mr. Arkadin*. I don't think we have to have ten-best lists, but they can be informative, especially if they're backed up by critical discussion.

Where movies are concerned, I suppose the top of the lists would be the one that's made by a collective of critics and filmmakers: the *Sight and Sound* poll, which appears every decade and makes international news.

*You've participated in the* Sight and Sound *poll.*

Yes, I've done it twice. It was an honor to be asked but very tough to pick just ten films, as contributors are asked to do. Every film you list counts the same. You don't rank the films. If *Citizen Kane* turns out to be number one on the published list, that's because it was mentioned by most of the contributors. It's number three in the latest poll.

I won't list all the films I listed for *Sight and Sound*, but the choices of the individual contributors are published online and in issues of the online journal. I found myself wanting to give historical range to my choices, so that at least one silent movie (*Sherlock, Jr., Man with a Movie Camera*, or *L'Age d'Or*) and a few movies from different countries (*The Wind Will Carry Us* [1999]) would be mentioned. I think I also listed Barbara Loden's *Wanda* (1970) and Charles Burnett's *To Sleep with Anger* (1990) not only because I greatly admire those films but because I didn't want everything to be by white men. Maybe the best strategy would have been to list unorthodox, unexpected titles. Some people have simply listed their ten favorite movies, but I find that just as difficult as listing ten historically and artistically important films. No matter what you do, great movies are going to be left out. I agonized because I didn't list anything by Bresson or Ozu. I told *Sight and Sound* that because movies have been around so long, they ought to let us list twenty instead of ten. They didn't change their policy, but the latest poll tried to expand participation so there would be more contributions from women, ethnic minorities, and foreign countries. That's probably why *Jeanne Dielman, 23 quai du Commerce, 1080 Bruxelles* (1975), undoubtedly an important film, ended up as the surprise number one.

*After the 2012 list, where* Vertigo *(1958) supplanted* Kane, *you told me that you were sort of happy that the latter got bumped down, because (to paraphrase) "maybe now people can enjoy it." Do you still feel that way?*

Yes. I think it's a burden for any film to be listed as the best. I always worried when I showed *Kane* to my students because I felt that its reputation made it difficult for them to appreciate it for the first time.

*Also building on your answer about the* Sight and Sound *poll, could and should critics be doing more to shine a light on marginalized filmmakers? Siskel and Ebert occasionally did that on their TV show, but there's nothing similar today.*

As I've said, one of the most important things a critic can do is call attention to little-known filmmakers and explain why they're of interest. When I did the *Sight and Sound* poll, I didn't consciously try to rehabilitate marginalized films, but I did aim to represent a variety of titles, some of which might have been relatively unknown. (One year I think I listed Renoir's *La Nuit de Carrefour* [1932].) But I'm basically an academic critic who writes books and not reviews. In my book on film noir, I mentioned many little-known or undiscussed movies, and for the *Sight and Sound* poll, I voted for Bette Gordon's *Variety* (1983), which I guess was marginalized in some quarters. When I wrote for *Film Quarterly*, my number one films were quite marginal in the sense that they had limited distribution and relatively little critical commentary.

If we're talking about reviewers who deal regularly with contemporary Hollywood, it's obvious that in today's media landscape there's nothing like *Siskel & Ebert* (1986-2010). Their show was sometimes imitated, but other than a recurring parody called "Men on Film" in the comic TV show *In Living Color* (1990-94), nothing was as enjoyable. I think Ebert was the better critic by far of the two, but they usually picked interesting films for discussion. The possibility for such reviewing is very slim today because the theatrical marketplace has been geared toward comic-book heroes, fantasy, and animation. These movies have colossal budgets and several are quite well made, but I can seldom remember the names of their directors. Where smaller films are concerned, I'm pleased that in 2024, Guy Madden's *Rumours* is getting more attention from the press than anything he's done, maybe because it stars Cate Blanchett (a smart actor who knows a good director when she sees one) but also because it has a good distributor.

It's usually easy to infer a potential audience for all varieties of new films, but theatrical exhibition of many pictures is sadly limited. I don't know enough about social media or podcasts, but the death of newspapers has contributed to under-reviewed films, and in America there are very few serious film journals that review new films. *Cineaste* and *Film Quarterly* are the major ones.

*Do you think writers like yourself, who produce book-length critical studies, should valorize art cinema over popular cinema?*

No, I don't think that distinction is easy to maintain. Critics and historians should write about whatever interests them and whatever they find significant. In America, however, there's too little interest in important foreign-language films, and academics today have trouble finding publishers for research on foreign topics. I would like to see more writing about world art cinema. That was one reason why I edited the *Contemporary Film Directors* book series.

*Should the critic interpret films? Is it important to view them in the light of the artist's intentions rather than the critic's interests?*

Criticism always involves a degree of interpretation, even if it just describes the features of a plot. It's not a matter of explaining moral lessons, themes, symbols, or secret codes; it has more to do with pointing out motives, motifs, ambiguities, narrative techniques, visual or auditory details, and ideological or political implications. Every good film deserves a critical  reading, and some of the more puzzling films require interpretation. Readings that differ from one another sometimes make the film interesting.

But critics should never assume their chief job is to explain an artist's intention The idea that criticism and art history should describe intentions is derived from the expressive-realist ideas of the romantic period, which argued that the artist's aim was to observe the world closely and, with superior vision and intelligence, reveal its emotional, spiritual, or social effects. But artists often don't know their intentions, even when they believe they do. Warnings against the intentional fallacy have long been basic in modern theories of criticism. As D. H. Lawrence once said, always trust the tale, not the teller. Or as the noir novelist Dennis Lehane has put it, "the writer is about the last person you should trust when it comes to interpreting his work. If we truly knew what we were doing, we probably wouldn't do it; it would feel too much like a straight job."

Of course filmmakers can and do have political and ideological intentions. Welles' work on the stage and in film had obvious political aims for most of his career, at least up through *Touch of Evil*. His work in Europe had less to do with societal/political matters. At the same time, his films also had a kind of unconscious undertow, a tension or contradiction between his politics and his personal style. There was a neo-Gothic, potentially reactionary romanticism in his theatricality, and an only partly intentional feeling that he identified with characters like Charles Foster Kane. Kubrick, as I've indicated, had a relatively low regard for human nature and a fascination with warfare and violence. He was intentionally critical of these things, but his work also suggests that he was drawn to them in a less conscious degree. Filmmakers like Charles Burnett and Pedro Costa are a different matter. Burnett's entire career is consciously dedicated to the idea that Black lives matter. Costa has a low regard for *cinéma engagé*, which he thinks has been futile, but he has a clear love and commitment to the lives of the Cape Verdean underclass. Burnett and Costa are chroniclers of two distinct social formations, and that is certainly part of their intentions.

*Do you have any guilty pleasures as a critic, movies that you like but think of as bad?*

No. I've always disapproved of that term. I understand why people might be guilty about cigarettes, alcohol, candy, or pornography, but why feel guilty about liking a movie? I guess the people who do have snobbish friends and are embarrassed to admit enjoying certain things.

On the other hand, I have a personal category of films I call "irrational" or more accurately "comfort food" cinema. These are films that nobody would describe as immortal classics, but that I find myself re-watching every few years. I suppose most cinephiles have such pleasures. Among the numerous pictures I have in the category, in no particular order, are *The Transporter* (2002), starring Jason Statham, which I enjoy for the action scenes; George Seaton's *Teacher's Pet* (1958), which is a Doris Day-Clark Gable-Gig Young romantic comedy about newspapers and the need for education; the first half of John Sturges' *Ice Station Zebra* (1968), which is a picture Howard Hughes reportedly watched over and over as he lay dying (I don't like the second half because the snow looks like papier mâché rocks on a movie set); J. Lee Thompson's *The Guns of Navarone* (1961), which is a much better guys-on-a-mission movie that wastes no time getting started and has cliff-hanging moments; Fred Zinnemann's *Day of the Jackal* (1973), which has a superb cast that includes Delphine Seyrig, who acted in more good and great movies than anybody of her day; and John Farrow's *His Kind of Woman*, which is a delightful mix of noir, music, and comedy that I've written about on my website and elsewhere.

I have to see *Bullitt* at least once a year. I also like to re-watch Arthur Ripley's *The Chase* (1946), a bizarro noir that Guy Maddin and I discussed in a video for IU Cinema. It has the most unpredictable and unusual ending I've ever seen. I should also mention Herbert Ross' *The Last of Sheila* (1973), written by Stephen Sondheim and Anthony Perkins. (*the* Anthony Perkins?). It's a wonderfully cast murder mystery about people in the movie industry, and I've seen it four or five times. Even when you know who did it, it remains fun. I could go on in this vein, but will stop here.

*Perkins and Sondheim hosted murder mystery parties together, and they thought it would be fun to write a movie about one. Earlier, you mentioned that you thought some movies were evil. Not* Psycho, *of course. But I'll bet you were thinking of Griffith's* Birth of a Nation *and the Leni Riefenstahl films.*

Thanks for solving the mystery of Perkins for me! And yes, I wouldn't advocate burning or banning *Birth of a Nation* or *Triumph of the Will*, but they both need to be exhibited with care. The Griffith film has fine moments—especially the Civil War battle scenes and the assassination of Lincoln—but it's also lumbering, pretentious, sentimental, and racist to the core, especially in the way it portrays Reconstruction and feeds the typical Southern good-ole-boy fantasy of sex-craving Black men who want to rape white womanhood. It greatly stimulated the resurgence of the Klan in the 1920s, notably in Martinsville, Indiana, about thirty miles from where I'm writing to you. It also helped create Hollywood and is almost unavoidable in university film history courses. I taught it a couple of times, and said exactly what I thought about its racism and distortion of history. If I ever did that again I would hope I could get a Black student or professor to give the class their insights.

Riefenstahl's documentary of the 1936 Nuremberg rally is more artful and compelling, but it's also a dangerous piece of kitsch. I don't know what people in America today, some of whom are ignorant of even recent history, would make of this film if they were shown it without contextual information. It's great propaganda for Nazi power, so good cinematically that it's depressing. I can't see it now without comparing the 1936 Hitler rally to the typical Trump rally — they're both showbusiness spectacles designed to whip up the crowd of race haters and nationalists. Trump is more tacky and less military, and so are his on-stage participants, who aren't (at least not so far) asked to march in rhythm. But I'll bet he's watched Riefenstahl and has read *Mein Kampf*. (He said his favorite movie is *Citizen Kane*, maybe because it has a news headline reading FRAUD AT POLLS.)

# ON COLLABORATION

*You've centered most of your work on film directors, and you've said that your taste in movies was influenced by the auteurist movement. What do you think of the argument that movies are a "collaborative art"?*

It's obvious that most movies involve collaboration. My books about actors make that point, at least implicitly, but in my opinion most of the best movies are guided by their directors. Now and then, however, they're products of a writer like Paddy Chayefsky or a producer like Selznick or Zanuck. Chayefsky is the prime example of the writer as auteur, largely because of the success of *Marty* (1955), which led to a string of hit screenplays he authored. (Kubrick was offered the chance to direct *Network* [1976] but turned it down because he knew Chayefsky would be in control.) *Marty* was an adaptation of a TV drama, and in the mid-1950s the phenomenon of TV writer as auteur gained traction in the movies—the screenplay had become the thing. The other major figure was Rod Serling, producer/writer of *The Twilight Zone* (1959–64), a show that was enormously influential on other television and many films. Serling was more overtly political and left-wing than Chayefsky, and was famous for such films as *Requiem for a Heavyweight* (1962).

But it seems to me that directors are most often auteurs because they have has the job of overseeing the production process and are the meeting point of all the arts and crafts involved. There are directors who know too little about writing, photography, and other arts and crafts, but they seldom if ever make important films. On the other hand, some of the best directors have depended on the contributions of others, usually people they worked with regularly.

*Can you give some examples?*

Okay. I'll try to give a few examples at length having to do with screenwriting, photography, production design, editing, music, and graphics. Where screenplays are concerned, I'll avoid the tiresome controversy about who wrote *Citizen Kane* except to say that Welles wrote as much as Mankiewicz.

# Screenwriting

Movies that give us narrative fiction usually need good screenplays more than anything else because it's difficult to make a good fiction film without a good script, no matter how good the direction and photography. (A film like Herzog's *Aguirre, Wrath of God* [1972], which is loosely based on a 16th-century chronicle, is perhaps an exception because the story is so elemental—the performances, the location, the photography, and the purely cinematic elements have greater importance.)

Many of the best screenplays have been good enough to be published, but not in the somewhat unreadable style in which they were written. Most directors, especially today, don't want the writer to insert stage directions or instructions for the camera into the script. One writer who ignored that rule to an absurd degree was James Agee, some of whose scripts are published in *Agee on Film, Vol. II*. He obviously wanted to direct—he not only gave detailed instructions for blocking, but also elaborate descriptions of lighting effects, as when a candle illuminates a glint in a character's eye.

In the classic studio era, movies were often written by various hands, some of them uncredited. One of the lesser-known but talented writers was Frank Fenton, who wrote great uncredited dialogue for *Out of the Past*. (Jane Greer: "Is there any way to win?" Robert Mitchum: "There's a way to lose more slowly.") In 1938, Fenton wrote an article for *The American Mercury* titled "The Hollywood Literary Life," in which he warned aspirants that unless you were a famous author like Fitzgerald or Faulkner, the pay would be similar to the average schoolteacher. Your work would also be meddled with by producers, directors, and other writers, resulting in convoluted rewrites. Fenton was a respected novelist who avoided Hollywood when he could. The situation he described was somewhat ameliorated when the Writers Guild got tough on producers, as it did at several junctures, especially in the recent Hollywood writer's strike against A.I.

Ben Hecht, on the other hand, was one of the most famous, prolific, and successful writers of the studio era, and was also a valued script-doctor, doing uncredited work on scores of movies. He sometimes exaggerated his contributions, as when he claimed to have saved *Gone With the Wind*, but the big producers relied on him again and again. He repeatedly worked for Howard Hawks, with whom he seems to have had a strong rapport, but he also wrote screenplays, revisions, or scenes for such different directors as Sternberg, Lubitsch, Wellman, and Hitchcock. His personal style is most recognizable in his fast, cynical, ace-reporter dialogue, often written in collaboration with Charles MacArthur, Charles Lederer, or Gene Fowler, who were pals from his newspaper days. But his name is attached to an amazing variety of movies, among them *Scarface* (1932), *Design for Living* (1933), *Viva Villa!* (1934), *Nothing Sacred* (1937), *Gunga Din* (1939), *Wuthering Heights* (1939), *Spellbound* (1945), and *Kiss of Death* (1947). Some of these were excellent, others were so-so or worse. In *Talking Pictures: Screenwriters in Hollywood*, Richard Corliss points out that Lubitsch's *Design for Living*, an adaptation of a Noël Coward play, "is not only bad Coward, it is even bad Hecht—and, as a result, bad Lubitsch."

With Hecht's range of credits and the variable quality of the films, it's difficult to pin him down. It's much easier to assess the importance of Samson Raphaelson, who was the screenwriter for Hitchcock's *Suspicion*, but whose work with Lubitsch was what Corliss describes as "the most highly polished and perfectly sustained comedy style of any Hollywood writer." Raphaelson, like Hecht, was originally a playwright—one of his most successful plays was filmed as *The Jazz Singer* in 1927 and 1952—and in interviews he often said his work in theater was more important than his writing for movies. But nobody is likely to agree with him. He's the immortal Samson because of what he did with the immortal Ernst.

Lubitsch, a producer/director who specialized in urbane sex comedy tinged with an air of melancholy, always worked closely with his screenwriters. He would discuss a film in progress scene by scene, often saying things like, "This scene must be hilarious!" At the same time, he was very good at construction and the invention of jokes and turns of plot that required no dialogue. (He made a great silent film from Oscar Wilde's verbally rich *Lady Windermere's Fan* [1925].) Joseph McBride's biography of Lubitsch quotes Billy Wilder, one of the writers on *Ninotchka*, who said that Lubitsch "was the best writer who ever lived." Raphaelson gave roughly similar praise: "Lubitsch wrote some of my best lines and I supplied some typical Lubitsch touches." Whatever the case, the two were a perfect marriage, never more so than in *Trouble in Paradise*.

Everybody remembers Herbert Marshall's first line in that film: "Beginnings are always difficult," he says, elegantly dressed in evening clothes and smoking a cigarette on the moonlit balcony of a hotel overlooking the Grand Canal. He's anticipating a dinner *à deux* with a beautiful and wealthy lady (Miriam Hopkins), who is arriving by gondola. He decides to begin the evening with cocktails followed by champagne, and gives a series of instructions to a waiter who is standing behind him, taking notes. "Waiter," he says, "do you see that moon?" "Yes, Baron," the waiter says. Marshall says, "I want to see that moon in the champagne." "Yes,

Baron," the obsequious waiter says, and writes on his pad: "moon in champagne." "And as for you, waiter...," Gaston says. "Yes, Baron?" asks the waiter." "I don't want to see you at all." "Yes, Baron," the waiter says.

Herbert Marshall speaks every line in such dreamy, rhythmic fashion that we might be in a musical like the ones Lubitsch had recently made. But it soon turns out that he's no Baron and we're in a satire about a couple of self-made jewel thieves who are coping with the Great Depression, hoping they can find a way to survive "in times like these." Lilly, his glamourous dinner guest, is also an imposter. During dinner, she tells him, "Baron, I have a confession to make. You are a crook. You robbed the gentleman in rooms 253, -5, -7, and -9. Would you please pass the salt?" A bond is immediately formed; they're in love, and they begin returning various items they've just stolen from one another. Hopkins hands over Marshall's watch, explaining that she's corrected the time, and he returns her garter.

*Trouble in Paradise*

In Paris, Gaston robs the beautiful, extremely wealthy Mme. Colet (Kay Francis), who owns a perfume company. He also manages to become her private secretary, and hires Lilly, who masquerades as a working-class type, as *his* secretary. Soon a triangle develops. We grow very fond of both women, and every scene is buoyed by wit, sexiness, and understated suspense. Will the thieves be discovered? Will Gaston choose Mme. Colet or Lilly? Everything is resolved in the last, wordless scene, which repeats the gag we saw in the opening and manages to top it.

Raphaelson would go on to do similarly brilliant work with Lubitsch on *The Shop Around the Corner* and *Heaven Can Wait*, two pictures that I find not only amusing but profound. I smile with a feeling of wistful sadness whenever I think of those films.

## Photography

One of the most impressive and easily identifiable photographers in the 1940s and early 1950s was John Alton, about whom I've written in my book on noir. The best directors usually work closely with their photographers, but I sometimes think Alton was given more leeway and independence. His pictures with Anthony Mann (among them *T-Men* [1948] and *Border Incident* [1949]) or with John Sturges (*Mystery Street* [1950]) are visually quite unlike the other genre movies Mann and Sturges directed—they have Alton's signature low-level, wide-angle compositions and an unorthodox lighting that calls attention to itself in artful ways. He made every low-budget film he worked on better than it would have been without him, and he finally got an Academy Award for the climactic dance number in Minnelli's *An American in Paris* (1951), which was his first big-budget color picture (His pre-wedding nightmare in Minnelli's *Father of the Bride* is a black and white masterpiece.) Apparently he was often at war with lighting technicians and the unions. In some ways his style is reminiscent of Gregg Toland's trademark wide-angle, depth of field imagery, but Toland's work with Wyler, Ford, and Welles is varied in its effects, showing the influence of the three directors rather than the dominating personality of a DP.

In the 1950s and early 60s, I was especially impressed with Robert Burks' work with Hitchcock. Burks had begun as a special-effects photographer, and because of that background he was important to *The Birds*. (His contributions to that film not only gave us the great shots of birds in flight over an exploded gas station but also saved Hitchcock money on the budget.) There was no specific Burks style, but to me he was the best of all the VistaVision photographers, and his work on *Vertigo*, *North by Northwest*, and other films with Hitchcock was outstanding. He probably created the simultaneous tracking-back-zooming-in shot in *Vertigo*, and I've always admired his opening shot in *Rear Window*, which pans slowly around the giant set of a Greenwich Village courtyard, singling out various apartment-dwellers in the distance and ending with a big closeup of a bead of sweat on James Stewart's forehead. Tragically, he died in a fire, and Hitchcock's subsequent pictures were never quite as good.

John Bailey, who often worked with Paul Schrader, told interviewers Dennis Schaefer and Larry Salvato that he liked to do preparation with a director because "the director is really the key to whether the film works or not and if the director's vision isn't realized somehow, the film really doesn't have a chance at all." When he prepared to photograph *American Gigolo* (1980), he and Schrader repeatedly watched *The Conformist* (1970) and *Touch of Evil*, sometimes back to back: "I realized that Bertolucci's sense of movement, that particular kind of crane movement he has that totally surprises you and takes your breath away, comes from Welles... Filmmakers do watch films a lot." Some of the directors he worked with, however, were only concerned with the actors, which meant that they were "not going to come up with very inspired blocking. The blocking is what you key off of for your sense of camera movement and the kind of visual dynamics you have... Really exciting directors see actors as [visual] elements inside the film."

The most admired and influential DP of the late 20th century was Gordon Willis, who worked often with Woody Allen (*Manhattan* [1979]) and Alan Pakula (*Klute* [1971], *The Parallax View* [1974], and *All the President's Men* [1976]). He's probably most remembered for working with Francis Coppola on *The Godfather* trilogy. As David Thomson has pointed out, the first two *Godfather* films are a breakthrough in color film noir. They were innovative by virtue of their extremely low light levels and slight underexposure, which was entirely Willis' idea and earned him the sobriquet "The Prince of Darkness." He told Schaefer and Salvato that the technique was based on "evil," which was "the soul of the picture." The dominant period color of the film was amber, created by adding yellow to the footage during the lab work. Unlike traditional noir, *The Godfather* didn't have radical angles or obvious cast-shadow effects, but some early viewers complained because they often couldn't see the shaded eyes of the characters. You see those eyes whenever the drama needs you to.

I was reminded of Willis when I saw Edward Berger's *Conclave* (2024). I don't know much about the technology of digital-era cameras, but I'm sure Berger worked closely with his excellent DP Stéphane Fontaine, and probably also with the production designers. (The Sistine Chapel was a constructed set.) As with Willis, the light levels are low and often seem to come from a single overhead illumination combined with available light from lamps or open windows. The characters' eyes are relatively shaded except for crucial closeups, such as the important ones in the closing scenes. The dominant colors are from the blue end of the spectrum, although there are red highlights and moments of amber. It's one of the most visually mesmerizing films I've seen recently, its style appropriate for the film's mildly sinister, detective-story elements.

*The Godfather*

## Production Design

The work of production designers is difficult to describe because the job requires jacks-of-all-trades and can have a variable influence on film style. Most definitions of production designer say that it's a person who works closely with the director, cameraman, and art director to determine the visual look of the film and oversee important budgetary decisions involving locations, art work, and sets. But the distinction between production designer and art director has never been clear, probably because the term "art director" was used in Hollywood long before "production designer" became a regular part of the credits.

The first production designer credit in movies seems to be for William Cameron Menzies' work on *Gone With the Wind*. David Selznick put Menzies in charge of every visual aspect of the film, apparently giving him the power to overrule director, cameraman, costumer, the Technicolor lab, credit designer, etc. The film had two directors, Cukor and Fleming, but Menzies was chiefly responsible for its visual style.

Before that, Menzies had always been credited as art director, and had unusual influence over monumental settings in silent pictures such as *The Thief of Baghdad* (1924). Convinced that every shot of a film should be visually preplanned for both camera angle and actor movement, he created proto-storyboards for many films. He ultimately directed and completely controlled *Things to Come* (1936), the British sci-fi picture that repeatedly uses monumental settings, futuristic costume, canted angles, and extreme low or high-level shots that pose the characters against sky or ground. This movie is clearly influenced by Eisenstein, but Menzies' graphic compositions, spatial dynamics, and subject matter are less powerful than Eisenstein's more dynamic films. As David Bordwell has said, he's more like the Busby Berkeley of production design.

The best analysis of Menzies' career as a production designer is a 2010 entry of Bordwell's blog (www.davidbordwell.net/essays/menzies.php). The influence of the German expressionist *Caligari* and the Soviet montage films of the Twenties is apparent in all of Menzies' sound pictures, but the most interesting examples have to do with his work in the 1940s with director Sam Wood, especially on *Our Town* (1940) and *King's Row* (1942). According to James Wong Howe, who photographed the second of these, Wood knew nothing about the camera and he and Howe followed the instructions of Menzies, even to the point of camera angles and lenses for each shot. *King's Row* gets almost all its effectiveness from the photographic compositions, which resemble Welles minus long takes.

In *Our Town*, ostensibly photographed by Bert Glennon, there are repeated low-angle shots of characters viewed against the corner of a ceiling, creating sharp diagonal lines and a sense of tension; there are also many instances in both films of forced perspective and extreme depth of field, plus a kind of intensified composition that crowds two or more figures tightly together in the frame, surrounded by décor. In this period Menzies also experimented with extremely large, tight closeups showing only part of a character's face, sometimes at an angle, and he did this while avoiding any transitional editing from medium and close to intense view. The cut went straight from medium to huge. On other occasions he composed closeups in which the diagonal line of a window frame or some other object obscured part of a face. Hollywood in general produced a number of films in the 1940s using sets with hard ceilings, low angles, and depth of field, but the Menzies films have striking affinities with Welles and Toland on *Citizen Kane*. In the same period, Menzies also used unorthodox shots in which the characters occupy only the bottom third of the frame, with a room visible above and around them.

One of the most admired production designers of the late 20th century was Polly Platt, who was married to Peter Bogdanovich and had an important influence on his early films. After her divorce from Bogdanovich, she was an influence on Cameron Crowe, Wes Anderson, and especially James L. Brooks. Platt not only created the idea for and co-wrote Bogdanovich's *Targets* (1968), but also contributed to the color design and sets of the film. She recommended Larry McMurtry's *The Last Picture Show* to Bogdanovich and also discovered the young Cybill Shepherd. Her work on that film—finding locations, giving character to various rooms and spaces, assisting with the general look—and also on the very different, in some ways more challenging *What's Up, Doc?* and *Paper Moon* (1973), seems to have been crucial, especially because so many of Bogdanovich's subsequent pictures were disappointing.

*Paper Moon*

Platt became the first female member of Hollywood's Art Directors Guild, and her life with Bogdanovich was the basis for a *film à clef*: Charles Shyer's enjoyable comedy, *Irreconcilable Differences* (1984), which Platt said had gotten most things right. Bogdanovich said of her, "She worked on important pictures [and] knew all the departments on a workmanlike basis, as opposed to most producers who just know things in theory." James L. Brooks, with whom she worked on *Terms of Endearment* (1983), said, "Movies are a team sport, and she made teams function." Unfortunately, she never became a director—partly, one suspects, because of sexism in the industry.

## Editing

*Your previous statement compels me to ask about film editors, as historically more women in Hollywood have been editors than directors. How do you regard the collaborations between, for example, Martin Scorsese and Thelma Schoonmaker? Do you feel that Quentin Tarantino's movies have become less interesting or impressive since the tragic death of Sally Menke? (The last film she cut for him was* Inglourious Basterds *[2009].) And do you think an editor can be an auteur? One film critic has posited that Dede Allen after* Bonnie and Clyde *was an auteur, and I confess that the first time I saw* Slap Shot *(1977), I guessed that she edited it right before her name came up in the opening credits. Was that because she had a signature? I don't know, but I could say the same thing about Anne V. Coates in many of the movies she edited.*

Yes, women worked as editors almost from the beginning of movies, and some of the most honored editors have been women, although I've read that roughly eighty percent of editors in today's industry are men. You might be better at answering this question than I am. I have problems deciding if the signature belongs to the director or the editor, although having edited film on a couple of occasions I'm well aware of how much even small editorial decisions can alter and improve the final product.

The aesthetics of cinema are founded on editing— Griffith's cross-cutting and closeups, the montages of Eisenstein, Pudovkin, Kuleshov, Vertov, Yelizaveta Svilova, etc. Some documentary films, especially the direct cinema pictures of the 1960s, were composed from miles of footage that an editor shaped into feature length, thus becoming the virtual director. (I've already called Charlotte Zwerin an auteur.) And the style of certain directors, Hitchcock in particular, makes editing the most important element of their work.

But the Hollywood continuity style, from the beginning of the talkies until the 21st century, is a simplified, almost cookie-cutter method: the wide shots, medium shots, closeups, fades, and dissolves melt together invisibly. In the 1930s and 40s, the editing was emphasized only in what were once called "lighting mixes," in which one character's speech is cut off only to be completed by another character in a different time and place. (Examples can be seen in *Trouble in Paradise* and *Citizen Kane*—as Bazin pointed out, the latter film seems constructed so that long takes alternate with obvious cutting.) There were also Vorkapitch-style montages (calendar leaves falling as something undergoes construction, rapid shots of a stage show being rehearsed until it's ready, etc.) The really innovative moments were in Hitchcock's manipulation of point of view and Welles' avoidance of editing in favor of sequence shots.

This doesn't mean that the invisible style of editing is utterly formulaic and unimportant. Imagine a scene like the ones that happen fairly often in Robert Benton's low-key film *Nobody's Fool* (1994) or in a police-procedural TV series like *Prime Suspect* (1991–2006). We're shown three or more characters in a room, and least two of them are speaking. The conversation is shot mostly in closeups. Character A has a fairly long speech addressed to character B, who sometimes emotionally reacts or asks a question that gets an answer from A. Character C is mostly silent. The editor has a choice of exactly when to cut from A's speech to B's reverse-angle questions or reactions, and when to cut to C, who is off to the side, listening and subtly reacting. These small decisions and their timing can be very important to how well the scene plays.

The editor also has the choice, which might be determined by the director, of how to make transitions from one sequence to the next—a direct cut, a dissolve, or a long fade to black, sometimes with overlapping sound. In general, the art of editing is a bit like writing prose; the shots, like words or phrases, are put in an order that establishes sequences, marks temporal or spatial change, and determines the narrative development, tempo, and emotional effects. And of course chase scenes or fight scenes usually involve a great deal of cutting. But when it comes to evaluating the specific contribution of editors, I usually find it impossible to know just how much they have done to improve the finished film, just as I find it impossible to know how much revision a writer has done for a published text. Who knows what the original footage was, or what wound up on the cutting room floor?

I know Thema Schoonmaker has been important to Scorsese. Just look at a few of the episodes in *The Aviator* (2004), the sequences illustrating Howard Hughes making *Hell's Angels*; Hughes at a crowded Coconut Grove party talking with several people as we keep cutting to a bandstand where a weird singer performs "Stairway to Paradise"; Hughes breaking a speed record with a new single-engine plane; Hughes at a Hollywood premiere with Katharine Hepburn (played by Cate Blanchett, who had obviously studied *Bringing Up Baby*); and Hughes visiting the Hepburn family, who grill him over a lunch table. All these scenes are very rapidly and dazzlingly edited; they all have multiple characters, and they all make the virtuosity of editing apparent. I'm also aware that Sally Menke was important to Tarantino. He made a habit of having actors end a shot by saying "Hi, Sally!" and his book of essays, *Cinema Speculation*, contains what appears to be a photo of Steve McQueen conferring with Sam Peckinpah on the set of *The Getaway* (1972), crouched down next to a box labeled "Katie's Personal Box." This might be an in-joke because Sally Menke had a similar box, although the film was actually edited by Robert Wolfe.

But it's unclear to me exactly to what degree Schoonmaker and Menke are stylistically important, since Scorsese and Tarantino established the setups and the footage. (And I don't see a marked difference in the post-Menke Tarantino.) Anne V. Coates is said to have pioneered the sonic overlap, and she often used jump cuts, so maybe that counts as a signature. Is that what you mean about her films?

When the Motion Picture Academy hands out Oscars to editors, I never know how the voters made their decision. Some films have more cutting than others, and some have bravura sequences that call attention to cutting. Is that the criterion for good editing, and even if it is, how much credit is due the editor rather than the director or writer who shot or conceived the sequence? In the last analysis, the editor always determines how well a scene plays on screen, but it seems to me the evaluation of editing choices can be done only by people with inside knowledge.

*To answer your question about Anne V. Coates: Yes, jump cuts and sonic overlap. (I didn't know what the name was for the latter but now I do.) With Dede Allen there's often a distinctive slashing rhythm to the cutting—most famously in* Bonnie and Clyde, *of course, but it really aligns with the slashing rhythm of the ice skating in* Slap Shot.

*To also reply to an earlier comment: I wouldn't call an editor an author, but, somewhat mischievously, maybe a creator? I think of the two different versions of Sergio Leone's* Once Upon a Time in America *(1984), the complex structure of Leone's original, followed by the initial American release that lopped more than ninety minutes off the running time and restructured the narrative in chronological order (which added even more confusion than what the editing was supposed to eliminate). They're two different movies, the former vastly superior to the latter. I also think of the studio release of Jonathan Demme's* Swing Shift *(1984), compared to the bootleg of Demme's original cut, which I've*

*seen. Steve Vineberg wrote about both versions in a 1990*
Sight and Sound *article, and his description was correct: both*
*versions are 100 minutes long, but Demme's cut moves faster*
*and is superior to the Goldie Hawn-sanctioned studio release*
*in every way. You once told me, correctly, that ten different*
*directors could make ten different movies with the same*
*screenplay. Ten different editors could do the same, yes? Or*
*even one editor could make ten, twenty, or an infinite number*
*of versions of the same movie. A friend of mine, who's an*
*editor in Hollywood, once told me: "I can make anyone say or*
*do anything." He was being tongue-in-cheek flamboyant, but*
*there was some truth to what he said.*

I agree, and those are fine examples. The double versions of
the Leone and Demme films are especially good instances
of how an editor can ruin or improve things. And there
are probably times when an editor can transform the
proverbial sow's ear into a silk purse. In response to your
friend, I would say an editor can *almost* make anyone do
or say *almost* anything. (That's one reason why the direct
cinema movement became problematic.) Hence the famous
experiment illustrating the Kuleshov effect, and the many
instances of obvious editing trickery that's been employed
for jokes: the TV commercial showing Detective Joe Friday
and his partner discussing the merits of a brand of potato
chips; the music video showing Ronald Reagan piloting
a dive bomber that attacks a rock band; and Steve Martin
acting alongside a gallery of 1940s movie stars in *Dead Men
Don't Wear Plaid* (1982).

On the other hand, I know of older Hollywood films
that were defaced by editors because their directors had an
unorthodox approach and the studio interfered. In response
to the new management at RKO, Robert Wise, Jack Moss,
and Mark Robson tried to save *The Magnificent Ambersons*,
but they managed only to damage it. Viola Lawrence, under
orders from Harry Cohn at Columbia Pictures, did a very
questionable job of cutting on *The Lady from Shanghai*,
removing almost twenty percent of the film and inserting
glossy, studio-shot closeups of the stars. Ernest Nims
damaged *The Stranger*, cutting out all of the film's opening
scenes. Nims also inserted unnecessary closeups in Ophüls'
*Letter from an Unknown Woman* because he disliked long
takes, claiming that "audiences won't sit for them."

The best film I've seen about the process of editing
(Godard said it was the best film about editing anyone has
done) is Pedro Costa's *Where Does Your Hidden Smile
Lie?* (2001), a documentary shot in an editing room at Le

Fresnoy in northern France, where Jean-Marie Straub and Danièle Huillet were re-editing their 1999 film, *Sicilia!* The result is a film edited by Costa about a film that Straub and Huillet had once edited and are now editing again.

Straub and Huillet were unorthodox Marxists who took a Brechtian approach to performance and worked on very low budgets, with Straub co-writing and taking charge of mise-en-scène and Huillet doing virtually everything else. On this occasion the two were appointed as visiting teachers in France and were taking the opportunity to create a new, revised print of *Sicilia!* We see Straub wandering in and out of the editing room, puffing a cigar and pontificating about cinema for the benefit of offscreen students, while Huillet works at what looks like a Steenbeck flat-bed editing table, viewing and recutting the film from start to finish. It's an older, pre-digital technology, but it enables us to observe the work more clearly.

Sometimes they discuss their editing decisions, wisecracking and bickering like an old married couple. The film is often amusing, and Costa has described it as his only love story. Here's one example of Straub offering advice while Huillet is working:

> Straub: It's…
> Huillet: Shut up.
> Straub: He already has his mouth open.
> Huillet: Better that way, just this once.
> Straub: You're serving stones in gravy… It's where to cut. I don't trust…
> Huillet: Fasten your seatbelt. It's better like this.
> Straub: A one frame difference. Don't spend one hundred years.
> Huillet: I only need seventy.

And here's a longer, more testy example:

> Huillet: There's a smile lighting up his eyes.
> Straub: It would be better if we could keep it.
> Huillet: Not easy.
> Straub: Go back to the clap. There.
> Huillet: Don't start "There-ing" me. Because you keep interrupting me it keeps fucking up. You still don't have the discipline.
> Straub (*humbly*): I have something to say but I'll wait for your permission. [*pause*] I'll say it anyway.
> Huillet: Spit it out.

Straub: I don't want him to say "Gia"
    immediately. I don't want it to be an
    enthusiastic gesture.
Huillet: Tough luck. It works perfectly.
    When you see a continuity error in
    a good film, it's amusing.
Straub: (*addressing the students in the room*)
    You can't turn your actors into statues…
    even if we have precisely defined positions,
    which they discover for themselves.
    [*he pauses and looks at the edit*]
    I'm afraid you've won.
Huillet: Men!

We frequently see closeups of the editing table's screen
and hear the voices of the two debating about exactly where
a cut should happen. The situation is unusual because Straub
and Huillet advocated direct sound for their films, eschewing
what Straub calls "the soup," or the standard practice of
using pre-recorded ambient sound or non-diegetic music
to smooth over any sonic discrepancy between shots. As a
result, they're editing their film without an accompanying
strip of soundtrack. Their revisions are minor, often involving
arguments over things as small as the proper syllable to cut
away from an actor's speech. But it's evident that even the
very small things can have an impact.

## Music

*Film music is important, too, isn't it? Who do you think are
the best composers?*

I can't read music or play an instrument, so I may not be the
best judge. Music is nevertheless one of the most important
elements in movies—obviously so in musicals, but also in
dramatic pictures. Movies have almost never been completely
silent—there was piano music in the days of the nickelodeon,
and silent pictures in big cities were accompanied by
orchestras. Sound movies that avoid what was once called
background music or what critics today call non-diegetic
music are somewhat rare. The boardroom melodrama
*Executive Suite* (1954), for example, has no music, nor has
another boardroom film, *Patterns* (1956). Straub and Huillet,
who advocated direct sound for their films, dispensed with
all non-diegetic music. But classic Hollywood dramas of all
kinds were heavily dependent on orchestras and on music

composers, several of whom are legendary. Max Steiner often did wall-to-wall music and indulged in "Mickey Mousing," the technique of having music imitate the movements of a character. It's said that Bette Davis objected to him because he tended to compose music for when she walked up the stairs and when she walked down the stairs.

There are many good composers in the classic era of Hollywood—Steiner, Korngold, Tiomkin, etc.—but one name stands out: Bernard Herrmann, who is remembered chiefly for his exceptional work with Welles and Hitchcock. He gets my vote as the best composer/orchestrator of them all.

Shortly after arriving at Indiana, I got a post-doctoral fellowship that enabled me to do literary research in London. While I was there, I discovered that Herrmann was giving a public interview for an audience at the BFI's National Film Theatre, and I hot-footed to the occasion. It was a sparsely attended event, but memorable. As I recall, Herrmann talked exclusively about working with Welles and Hitchcock. He began by showing us the opening images of *Citizen Kane*, but with the sound turned off. We saw the camera rise slowly up a chain link fence accompanied by a series of dissolves until it reached a giant K above the fence. Then it moved slowly forward toward a distant, fairy-tale castle with a single lighted window. As it approached the castle, another series of dissolves took us past a surreal collection of images: monkeys in a cage, a gondola in a stream, a golf course, etc.

Herrmann's reason for showing all this without sound was paradoxically a way to call attention to the music, which was familiar to everyone. He explained that unlike the other directors he worked for, and unlike the standard studio practice, Welles wanted him to compose music for finished sequences rather than waiting for the whole film to be completed. The somber, almost funereal music he wrote for the beginning of *Kane*, which Herrmann called the "power" theme, would become an important leitmotif in the finished product; but what he was illustrating with his experiment at the NFT was how music affects your sense of time. Try turning off the volume on a *Kane* Blu-ray, and you'll find that the opening sequence seems overly slow, almost lugubrious, and much less effective. Play it again with the slow, dramatic music and everything changes, especially your sense of time. Music not only creates mood, but also pace and tempo, regardless of the editing.

Herrmann had a strong friendship with Welles, who described him as "a member of the family" and who knew a great deal about music. For the NFT, Herrman also talked a bit about *The Magnificent Ambersons*, which was the greatest disappointment of his career. Roughly half the music he wrote for that film was cut by RKO, and some of what we now have was done by a house composer, Freddie Fleck. At one point Herrmann wanted to have his name taken off the credits. He had an especially painful memory of the original ending of the film, which is of course lost.

It seems to me that commentators haven't fully accounted for the unusual way music is used in *Kane* and *Ambersons*. We don't remember the theme music of those two films in the same way we remember Herrmann's music for Hitchcock, and the reason is Welles' decision to use a good deal of diegetic music, putting less emphasis on the usual non-diegetic orchestration. In *Kane*, there's a theme for *News on the March*, a "Good old Charlie Kane" dance number with chorus girls, Susan's amateurish piano playing, and a Nat King Cole jazz number called "This Can't be Love."

*Citizen Kane*

Herrmann composed most of this, but above all he did the opera pastiche, *Salammbô*. Welles sent him a telegram just before shooting began on the film and asked for a fully orchestrated track of the opera to facilitate staging. "I believe there is no opera of importance where soprano leads with chin like this... suggest it be original... by you... Suggest *Salammbô*, which gives us phony production scene of ancient Rome or Carthage... Here is a chance for you to do something witty and amusing... I love you dearly."

Herrmann also talked about his work with Hitchcock, who knew less about music but gave him freedom. The example he used was *Psycho*, for which he composed a "black and white" score consisting entirely of strings. The only instruction he got from Hitchcock was that the shower sequence should have no music. When the completed film was assembled, Hitchcock was disappointed and was almost at the point of having it turned into a re-edited, two-part show for his TV program. Herrmann said he wanted to try doing music for the shower, and he created the slashing music we now have, which sounds to me like furious, vengeful birds. It's hard to imagine that sequence working without the music. Our sense of time would be different, and I think the violence less scary and more protracted.

*What's your favorite of Herrmann's compositions?*

I don't have a favorite. Most people will pick *Vertigo*, but I'm also fond of the driving blend of adventure and suspense music in *North by Northwest*. Herrmann did a variety of scores for Hitchcock and sometimes quoted other composers: Beethoven's *Eroica*, for example, and the Liebestod from *Tristan and Isolde*. He also did a semi-jazz score for *The Wrong Man*. Because I'm relatively ignorant of musical technique, I'm not sure why I can always recognize a Herrmann arrangement, no matter if he's working with Hitchcock, Ray Harryhausen, Nicholas Ray, or somebody else.

Unfortunately, Herrmann's career suffered when Hollywood discovered it could profit from theme music sold on LP recordings. One very talented composer who succeeded with this development (though he had trouble in the Blacklist days) was Elmer Bernstein, sometimes known as "Bernstein West" to distinguish him from Leonard. His theme music for *The Magnificent Seven* (1960) was so popular that it was sold to Marlboro Cigarettes for their TV ads. Another important composer of that period was Ennio Morricone, a classically trained jazz performer who did Italian TV shows and ultimately wrote the memorable scores of the Spaghetti Westerns. Producers in that period began to prefer scores that were catchy in one way or another, and Herrmann's more complex, classically-influenced scores went out of fashion. Hitchcock, after giving Herrmann credit for the electronic-instrument sounds in *The Birds*, dropped him as a composer. (Hitchcock rejected a score Herrmann wrote for *Torn Curtain* [1966] and the few who've heard it claim it's good.) Meanwhile, Orson Welles, who never had the power of Hitchcock and who always wanted to use a good deal of diegetic music, had his plans foiled by the studios. He resented what Columbia did with the music in *The Lady from Shanghai* and also what Universal did with *Touch of Evil*. Even so, I confess I very much like the Henry Mancini score in *Touch of Evil*.

There was a return to the musical style of the classic studios when John Williams began writing for Spielberg.

He's the most awarded composer in the history of movies and seems to have specialized in what some call a "neoromantic" style. I like the fun he has in Altman's *The Long Goodbye* (1973), where the theme song of the picture keeps recurring diagetically, performed by everything from a Mariachi band to door chimes. But to me he isn't in the class of Herrmann.

*Since you said that you prefer classical musicals to the deconstructive ones, am I right to assume that you prefer classical compositions to contemporary scores that seem designed to have an alienating effect (e.g., Trent Reznor and and Atticus Ross for David Fincher, Jonny Greenwood for Paul Thomas Anderson)?*

I have no interesting opinion about Reznor, but I don't think jazz scores are alienating. I can't understand why some people dislike the Greenwood jazz piano score for Anderson's *Phantom Thread* (2016). I also like Duke Ellington's score for *Anatomy of a Murder* (1959); Dave Grusin's unorthodox, semi-jazzy score for *The Firm* (1993); Lalo Schifrin's jazz score for *Bullitt*; and David Holmes' unobtrusive, jazz-influenced score for *Black Bag* (2025). Elmer Bernstein's orchestral score for *Sweet Smell of Success* is more conventional, but was what the industry once called "crime jazz."

*What's the history of needle-drops in cinema (i.e., when an independently recorded song is incorporated into a film)? Are they overused today? Who are some of the better filmmakers who put needle-drops to effective use?*

The most famous use of needle drops is Kubrick's *2001*. Kubrick commissioned Alex North to write a score for that film, but he abandoned it during the editing and began using classical and avant-garde recordings of music by Richard Strauss, Johann Strauss, Aram Khachaturian, and György Ligeti. The Strauss *Also Sprach Zarathustra* became a pop hit, as big as Bernstein's *The Magnificent Seven* music had been, and was forever identified with *2001*. (It shows up most recently and amusingly in *Barbie* [2023]) Kubrick's early work had scores composed by the talented Gerald Fried, but after *2001* he used needle drops for all his films.

But we need to distinguish between films that use the independently recorded music non-digetically and those that use it digetically. One of the best uses of the latter that

I've ever seen is Wim Wenders' *Perfect Days* (2023), about a Japanese man who cleans Tokyo's public toilets. He's an old-school guy who does his work assiduously and well. In his humble home, he cultivates plants and before going to bed he reads William Faulkner, Patricia Highsmith, and the essayist Aya Kōda. He doesn't have a cell phone, TV, or record player, but he has a major collection of cassette recordings featuring pop musicians of the 1960s and '70s. Each day he picks out something to play in his small van en route to work. The Animals' "House of the Rising Sun" is heard twice, once in his car and once in a Japanese version sung by a woman in a cafe. (Its lyric has Japanese associations.) Late in the film the toilet cleaner has a moment of intense grief and anxiety, a revelation of his past. But at the end he smiles through tears as he drives to the sound of Nina Simone's "Feeling Good." This movie has a vague Zen feeling and is sometimes reminiscent of Ozu. I think it's superb, and its use of old recorded music is essential.

## Graphic Design

The designs of credits and posters for movies were pretty conventional and unremarkable through most of the 20th century, although the studios had house designs for credits, so you could tell the difference between MGM and Warners. Everything changed in the late 1950s, mainly due to one artist: Saul Bass, who had enormous influence. Otto Preminger often used his designs, and they were among the things that made Preminger's films special. He's probably most remembered because of the credit sequences he did for Hitchcock. My favorite is the one for *Vertigo*, which seems to project out of Kim Novak's eye but seems to me an allusion to an eyeball being sliced in *Un Chien Andalou*. Behind the scenes, he also did storyboards for the shower sequence and the attack on Arbogast in *Psycho*, but Hitchcock downplayed Bass' influence on that film.

Bass was so innovative that movie reviewers sometimes said his credits were better than the pictures they opened. The most obvious case was *A Walk on the Wild Side* (1962), for which Bass made a mini-movie of a black cat roaming an alleyway. I'm also fond of his less ostentatious credits for Wyler's *The Big Country*, which appear over a moving stagecoach. I can't be sure, but I often wonder if the opportunity for him to become a designer of credits was influenced by the vanguard designs of record albums in the 1960s. In any case, his brilliant credits spilled over into

*Vertigo*

his designs for posters, as in the case of *North by Northwest*, and this made Hollywood hip to graphics as a form of advertising.

The James Bond franchise became identified with elaborate credit sequences, the earliest designed by John Brownjohn. Another important designer was the self-taught Cuban émigré Pablo Ferro, who started out by working with Stan Lee on filmed commercials. Ferro worked for Kubrick on *Dr. Strangelove* and *A Clockwork Orange*. (He also did credits for the remake of *Psycho*, but Bass' work for the original was much better.) Among the best examples of his many credit designs are *Bullitt* and *Goodfellas* (1990). He did the credits for *Stop Making Sense*, and the poster he designed for that movie, a simple grouping of the words of the title, is superb.

The use of stunning or unusual graphics seems to have declined in the past decades, maybe because directors seem to prefer having the credits spill over into the opening scenes. But the credit sequences in today's TV movies and series on streaming platforms, especially the foreign pictures, are often excellent.

**THREATS TO FILM HISTORY**

*You've pointed out some problems with the digital era, especially where streaming is concerned. I gather you have other worries about the new technology.*

Yes, let me give you two examples of apparent technological improvements that concern me. I don't consider myself a Luddite, but I also think progress can be a disaster.

The first example is Peter Jackson's *They Shall Not Grow Old* (2018), a highly successful documentary about World War I, in which Jackson uses old documentary films that show the grim experience of British foot soldiers in trenches, in encampments, and on battlefields. The film is undeniably fascinating, but for me it's problematic because of the way it uses contemporary technology to modernize the original material. Jackson gathered documentary film that was preserved in the Imperial War Museum in London and impressively colorized it; there was no narration, but for the soundtrack he hired lip-readers to transcribe the speech of soldiers, and actors to speak the lines. "I wanted to reach through the fog of time and pull these men into the modern world," he said.

Jackson claimed to have restored the footage he colorized, but it turns out, according to curators at the Imperial War Museum, that the footage wasn't in disrepair. I have no doubt that Jackson had honorable motives and sincerely wanted to honor the soldiers (he took no profits from the showings of his film), but this sort of manipulation of the original material was both unnecessary and potentially dangerous. Filmed evidence has always been subject to falsification through editing, but we now live in a brave new world in which visible evidence can be tinkered with as never before and transformed by A.I. to create deepfakes. Jackson's film was the beginning of what could become a serious threat to historical truth. While I don't deny that *They Shall Not Grow Old* does give us some historical truths, I would feel better if it hadn't embellished the existing record.

A more troubling problem, as I've already suggested, has to do with DCPs, or Digital Cinema Packages, which are the means by which movies everywhere are now projected in theaters. Many people don't realize that the technology that generates DCPs is a potential threat to cinema archives around the world. The need to conserve, preserve, and restore movies has always been crucial—it's what makes research and writing about film history possible—but the digital age is making the work of archivists more difficult and costly. Rachael Stoeltje, who until very recently was in charge of Indiana's impressive Moving Image Archive, is now the leading archivist at the Library of Congress, and she tells me her chief concern, and that of her colleagues everywhere, is the preservation of Digital Cinema Distribution Masters, a technology which generates the DCPs.

Even before DCPs, cinema history was threatened on several fronts. The Hollywood industry long thought of its products as mostly disposable. Certain high-grossing films could be preserved for re-release, but everything else was neglected — at least until the popularity of the TV late show, which gradually made more of the old films commercially valuable. Only about ten percent of silent film production has survived, and the survivors were rescued largely because of individual collectors. Until about 1950, the film industry used silver nitrate stock (the reason why motion pictures are called "the silver screen"), which, because of its flammability, was eventually replaced by celluloid. The surviving nitrate material is somewhat rare (it's featured at Eastman House's annual Nitrate Picture Show) and because access to it is limited and its projection needs caution, most of the prints were converted to celluloid. But we don't have original negatives of a great many films. There's no original negative of *Citizen Kane*, for example; the LaserDisc, digital, and Blu-ray versions are copies of the best available celluloid print.

Celluloid is by far the best material for film preservation, especially if it has a slightly refrigerated environment. DVDs and Blu-rays, as I've already indicated, have an even shorter shelf life than VHS tape, and DCPs create a potentially bigger problem. For anyone who wants to learn more about this, I recommend the testimony assembled on David Bordwell's blog under the heading "Pandora's Digital Box" (www.davidbordwell.net/blog/2012/02/13/pandoras-digital-box-pics-and-pixels). At that site, conservators, preservationists, and restorers give us some troubling information.

In the current theatrical marketplace, films are generated from what are called Digital Distribution Masters. When the exhibitor gets the DCP from the master digital file, it comes in the form of an encrypted file with an alphanumeric password. This system is good at preventing piracy, but the DCPs themselves last less than ten years, and sometimes less than five. Lots of passwords get lost, and there are constant changes of digital hardware, software, and playback systems that make recovery of older material difficult. Hence the need to preserve the Digital Distribution Masters. There doesn't seem to be an assured way of doing this in the film industry — some Masters are preserved, but producers and filmmakers don't always make sure that happens.

It's been estimated that America produces six to nine hundred feature films a year. The world-wide total is around five thousand five hundred. Storing 4K Digital Masters of these films costs eleven times more than storing celluloid masters. Ten years ago, Europe spent almost three million euros on digital film preservation, and I doubt if the cost is any lower today. It may become an unsupportable burden. It looks as if the industry is sleepwalking through problems or once again regarding some of its products as disposable residue. Unfortunately, film, like almost all visual art is subject to decay or deterioration. Oil paintings, for example, slowly begin to lose their original colors. Van Gogh's sunflowers don't look quite the same as they did, and need careful preservation. The movies need similar care.

*I keep thinking back to less than two years ago, when the WGA and SAG-AFTRA each went on strike for several months, while the DGA settled almost immediately. It is fair to say that some of the issues (such as A.I.) that writers and actors consider existential threats to their professions, directors regard as just more tools in their toolbox?*

Maybe. I can't speak to the motives of the directors, but my example of what Jackson did with *They Shall Not Grow Old* gives a sense of what a director/producer can do with digital effects. (For many years there have been ways directors can manipulate visible evidence in undetectable ways through digital post-production.) What you're describing doesn't essentially concern the preservation of history, but clearly it's important. A.I. will be making just as big a change of our world as the Internet has, and obviously it has scary implications. Unless a director has wise control over its use, it could cause problems. My guess is that the studio executives will favor it more than the creative workers, for the same reason that robotics are favored by auto manufacturers—it can save the studios time and money. I doubt it will improve art.

*You have concerns about the preservation of film history. Do you have concerns about the future of film?*

No. I believe that if Hollywood were to expire tomorrow, good and great films will continue to be made. Styles will of course change, fashions and film cycles will have their moments, new modes of exhibition will perhaps appear, but whatever happens to the industry, filmmakers will continue to practice their art. I have far more concern about the future of the United States. Frightening people are now in charge of this country. They will do very bad things and I hope they won't be around forever.

In the past year or two I've seen many excellent theatrical and TV films from around the world, some of which I mentioned during our conversation. Most recently, I've seen Walter Salles' powerful *I'm Still Here* (2024), which is about the years when Brazil was under a military dictatorship. I met Salles when he visited the IU Cinema and found him an enormously likeable and interesting person. His new film is a brilliantly directed story of a family, and has a compelling performance by Fernanda Torres as a mother who survives the arrest and murder of her husband. As I watched it, I realized how the events it describes could happen here, and are already heading in that direction. In comparison, such American films as *Civil War* (2024) and *The Apprentice* (2024) are shamefully timid and unimaginative. But I know Salles will continue to make films, which is a blessing.

*Now that we're nearing the end of this interview, how does it feel to have a book about your life?*

Somewhat surreal. I don't think of this as a book about my life—if it were, it would have gone into many of the more personal aspects of my history. But it's certainly a book about me—my education, my career, my writings, my teaching, my viewings, and my critical opinions. I never imagined I would get this kind of attention, and I hope it doesn't sound like false modesty when I tell you that I've wondered if I'm worth it. I'm honored to have been asked to do the interview and to be connected with this interesting and innovative series of books. Even so, I've been unable to participate without feeling a kind of guilty narcissism mixed with the fun or pleasure in being asked my opinions of this or that. Thanks for asking me questions; thanks to Paul Cronin for making everything happen; thanks to Darlene Sadlier for proof reading a draft of our text, making occasional suggestions, and fixing my computer goof-ups; and thanks to Carmel Curtis of Indiana's Moving Image Archives for helping with the illustrations.

# BIBLIOGRAPHY

# Books

*The Haunted Cinema of Pedro Costa*, co-written with Darlene J. Sadlier (Indiana University Press, 2025).

*On Kubrick: revised and expanded edition* (London: Bloomsbury BFI, 2023).

*Some Versions of Cary Grant* (New York: Oxford University Press, 2022).

*Letter from an Unknown Woman* (London: Bloomsbury BFI, 2021).

*Film Noir: A Very Short Introduction* (Oxford: Oxford University Press, 2019).

*Charles Burnett: A Cinema of Symbolic Knowledge* (Berkeley: University of California Press, 2017).

*An Invention Without a Future: Essays on Cinema* (Berkeley: University of California Press, 2014).

*Sweet Smell of Success* (London: BFI, 2010).

*On Kubrick* (London: BFI, 2007).
Italian trans. Carla Capetta (Turin: Edizioni Kaplan, (2010); Russian trans. (Moscow: Rosebud Publishing, 2011); Korean trans. (Seoul: CultureLook Publishing, 2016); Chinese trans. Xu Zhanxiong (Peking University Press, forthcoming).

*More than Night: Film Noir in Its Contexts* (Berkeley: University of California Press, 1998, revised and expanded edition, 2008). Chinese trans. Xu Zhanxiong (Guanxi Normal University Press, 2009).

*The Films of Vincente Minnelli* (New York: Cambridge University Press, 1993).

*Acting in the Cinema* (Berkeley: University of California Press, 1988). French trans. Christian Viviani (University Press of Rennes, 2014); Chinese trans. Xu Zhanxiong (Peking University Press, 2018); Romanian trans. Teodora Lascu (Cinemag; Romania, 2018); Italian trans. Giulia Carluccio, Giovanna Maina, and Mariapaola Pierini (Rome: Cue Press, 2024).

*The Magic World of Orson Welles* (New York: Oxford
University Press, 1978). Revised centennial
edition (Champaign: University of Illinois Press,
2015). Finnish trans. Antti Alanen (Helsinki:
Valtion, 1987); Italian trans. Daniela Fink
(Venice: Marsillo Editori, 1993).

*Filmguide to Psycho* (Bloomington: Indiana University
Press, 1973).

*The World without a Self: Virginia Woolf and the Novel*
(New Haven: Yale University Press, 1973).

## Edited Books

*Orson Welles' Citizen Kane: A Casebook* (New York:
Oxford University Press, 2004).

Series Editor, *Contemporary Film Directors*, thirty-three
volumes (Champaign: University of Illinois Press,
2003-13).

*Film Adaptation* (New Brunswick: Rutgers University
Press, 2000).

*North by Northwest* (New Brunswick: Rutgers University
Press, 1993).

*Modernity and Mass Culture*, co-editor, with Patrick
Brantlinger, (Bloomington: Indiana University Press, 1991).

*The Treasure of the Sierra Madre*, screenplay by John
Huston (Madison: University of Wisconsin Press, 1979).

## DVD Commentaries and essays

*The Magnificent Ambersons*, Criterion, 2018
(audio commentary with Jonathan Rosenbaum).

*Chimes at Midnight*, Criterion, 2016 (audio commentary).

*Foreign Correspondent*, Criterion, 2014 (essay).

*Fear and Desire*, Masters of Cinema, UK, 2012 (essay).

*The Sweet Smell of Success*, Criterion, 2011 (audio commentary).

*Paths of Glory*, Criterion, 2011 (essay).

*Touch of Evil*, Universal Pictures 50th Anniversary Edition, 2008 (audio commentary with Jonathan Rosenbaum).

*The Complete Mr. Arkadin*, Criterion, 2006 (audio commentary, with Jonathan Rosenbaum).

## Selected essays and book chapters

"Laurence Olivier in *Hamlet*," "Orson Welles, Citizen of the World," "Cornell Woolrich in Noir Fiction and Film," "The Wayward Pleasures of *His Kind of Woman*" and "Kubrick and Cold Modernism" (https://jamesnaremore.net/articles).

"Afterword" to Richard Schickel, *Double Indemnity* (London: Bloomsbury BFI, 2025).

"*Killer of Sheep*," in *From Street to Screen*, ed. Michael T. Martin and David C. Wall (Bloomington: Indiana University Press, 2021).

"You Don't Win, You Survive: Charles Burnett's Shorter Films," Criterion Channel newsletter (May 2019).

"The Death of the Auteur: Orson Welles' *The Other Side of the Wind*," *Cineaste* (Vol. XLIV, No. 1): 8-12. (Italian trans. Alberto Anile, *Cabiria* [192], 7-19).

"Foreword," *Orson Welles in Focus*, ed. James N. Gilmore and Sidney Gottlieb (Bloomington: Indiana University Press, 2018).

"Minnelli, the Aesthete in the Factory," Dutch trans. Elias Grootars and Sis Matthe, *Sabzian*, www. sabzian.be/articles.

"Charles Burnett: A Cinema of Symbolic Knowledge," *Cineaste* (Vol XLII, No. 3), 20-23.

"Two Screenplays by Charles Burnett: *Bless Their Little Hearts* (1984) and *Man in a Basket* (2003)," *Black Camera* (Vol. 8, No. 2, Spring 2017), 7-24.

"Notes on Comedy and Humor in Charles Burnett," in *Charles Burnett, A Troublesome Filmmaker*, ed. Maria Migues and Victor Paz (Galicia, Spain: Play-doc Books), 108-116.

"Orson Welles: Director, Magician, Pedagogue," *New England Review* (Vol. 36, No. 2, 2015).

"Orson Welles at 100," *Revista de Occidente* (Madrid), trans. Hilario J. Rodriguez (April 2015).

"The Cinema According to James Agee," *New England Review* (Vol. 35, No. 2, 2014), 100-115.

"Clara Bow in *Mantrap*," *Cine-Files* (Vol. 6, Spring 2014) www. thecinefiles.com.

"Foreword," *A Companion to Film Noir*, ed. Andrew Spicer and Helen Hanson (Oxford, UK: Blackwell, 2013), xix-xx.

"Films of the Year." Writer at Large, Contributing Editor, *Film Quarterly*, 2007-2013.

"Film Acting and the Arts of Imitation," *Film Quarterly* (Summer 2012), 34-42. Spanish trans. Paula Saiz Hontangas, *L'Atalante, Revista de Estudios Cinematograficos* (Vol.19, January-June 2015).

"The Magician: Orson Welles and Film Style," *Wiley-Blackwell History of American Film*, Vol. II, 1929 to 1945, ed. Cynthia Lucia, Roy Grundmann, and Art Simon (Chichester, UK: Wiley-Blackwell, 2012), 339-57.

"Hearts of Darkness: Orson Welles and Joseph Conrad," *True to the Spirit*: *Film Adaptation and the Question of Fidelity*," ed. Colin MacCabe, Kathleen Murray, and Rick Warner (New York: Oxford University Press, 2011), 59-73.

"Jerry Lewis in *The Ladies' Man*" (translated as "Jerry Lewis nell' Idolo delle donne"), *Enciclopedia delle arti contemporanee*, ed. Achille Bonito Oliva (Turin, Italy: Mondadori Electa, 2010), 248-50.

"Katharine Hepburn in Holiday," *Film Theory and Criticism*, Seventh Edition, ed. Leo Braudy and Marshall Cohen (New York: Oxford University Press, 2009), 486-500.

"Orson Welles and the Direction of Actors," in *Action!*, ed. Paolo Bertetto (Fondazione Cinema per Roma, 2007), 164-77. Reprinted in *Caiman Cuadernos de Cine*, No. 38 (May 2015), trans. Juanma Ruiz, 12-20.

"Stanley Kubrick and the Aesthetics of the Grotesque," *Film Quarterly* (Fall 2006), 4-14.

"Acting in the Cinema," *The Cinema Book*, ed. Pam Cook (London: BFI, 2007), 114-19.

"Love and Death in *A.I. Artificial Intelligence*," *Michigan Quarterly Review* (Spring 2005), 256-84.

"Citizen Kane: The Magician and the Mass Media," in *Film Analysis: A Norton Reader*, ed. Jeffrey Geiger and R. L. Rutsky (New York: W. W. Norton, 2005), 340-60.

"The Future of Academic Film Study" (with Adrian Martin), *Movie Mutations: The Changing Face of World Cinephilia*, ed. Jonathan Rosenbaum and Adrian Martin (London: British Film Institute, 2003), 119-32.

"The Man Who Caused the Mars Panic," *Humanities: The Magazine of the National Endowment for the Humanities*, Vol. 24, No. 1 (July/August 2003), 38-40.

"Hitchcock and Humor," *Strategies*, Vol. 14, No. 1 (May 2001), 13-26. Reprinted in *Hitchcock: Past and Future*, ed. Richard Allen (New York: Routledge, 2003). Also in *Critical Concepts in Media and Cultural Studies*, ed. Thomas Schatz (New York: Taylor & Francis, 2004) and *Hitchcock*, ed. Neil Badmington (London: Routledge, 2014).

"An ABC of Reading Andrew Sarris," *Citizen Sarris*, ed. Emmanuel Levy (Lanham, Md.: Scarecrow Press, 2001), 175-84.

"Introduction," *How a Film Theory Got Lost*, by Robert B. Ray (Bloomington: Indiana University Press, 2001), ix-xii.

"The Death and Rebirth of Rhetoric," *Senses of Cinema*, http://www.innersense.com.au/senses, April 2000.

"Il Noir" (Film noir), in *Storia del cinema mondiale*, Vol. II, ed. Gian Piero Brunetta (Turin, Italy: Einaudi), 1213-37.

"Lo Star System dopo la seconda guerra mondiale" (The star system after the Second World War), in *Storia del cinema mondiale*, Vol. II, ed. Gian Piero Brunetta (Turin, Italy: Einaudi), 1157-83.

"Film and the Reign of Adaptation," *Distinguished Lecturer Series*, No. 10 (Bloomington: Indiana, University Institute for Advanced Study, 1999).

"Authorship," in *A Companion to Film Theory*, ed. Toby Miller and Robert Stam (Oxford: Blackwell Publishers, 1999), 9-24.

"Hitchcock at the Margins of Noir," in *Alfred Hitchcock Centenary Essays*, ed. Richard Allen and S. Ishii Gonzales (London: British Film Institute Publishing, 1999), 263-77.

"Remaking *Psycho*," *Hitchcock Annual* (1999-2000), 3-12.

"La Chambre de mort," trans. Cecile Wajsbrot, *Trafic* (Paris), No. 27 (Fall 1998).

"American Film Noir: The History of an Idea," *Film Quarterly*, 49, No.2 (Winter 1995-96), 12-28.

"Straight Down the Line: Making and Remaking *Double Indemnity*," *Film Comment* (January-February 1996), 22-31.

"High Modernism and Blood Melodrama: The Case of Graham Greene," *Iris*, No. 21 (Winter 1996), 99-116. Hungarian trans. in *Apertura* (Fall 2013) www.apertura.hu.

"Vincente Minnelli," *The Oxford History of World Cinema*, ed. Geoffrey Nowell-Smith (Oxford: Oxford University Press, 1996). Also in *The Film Encyclopedia*, ed. James Monaco (New York: Peregrine Books, 1991), 379.

"The Actor as Director," in *Perspectives on Orson Welles*, ed. Morris Beja (Boston: G. K. Hall, 1995), 273-80.

"Return of the Dead," in *Perspectives on John Huston*, ed. Stephen Cooper (Boston: G. K. Hall, 1994), 197-206.

"Spies and Lovers," introduction to *North by Northwest*, (New Brunswick: Rutgers University Press, 1993), 3-19.

"The Trial: Orson Welles vs. the FBI," *Film Comment* (January-February 1991), 22-27.

"Six Artistic Cultures," introduction to *Modernity and Mass Culture*, co-authored with Patrick Brantlinger (Bloomington: Indiana University Press, 1991), 1-23.

"Authorship and the Cultural Politics of Film Criticism," *Film Quarterly*, 44, 1 (Fall 1990), 14-23.

"Between Works and Texts: Notes from the Welles Archive," *Persistence of Vision*, 7 (1989), 12-23.

"Expressive Coherence and the 'Acted Image," *Studies in the Literary Imagination* XIX/1 (Spring 1986), 39-54. Reprinted in *The Cinematic Text*, ed. R. Barton Palmer (Atlanta: Georgia State University Press, 1989.)

"The Orts and Fragments in Between the Acts," *Critical Essays on Virginia Woolf*, ed. Morris Beja (Boston: G. K. Hall, 1985).

"Film and the Performance Frame," *Film Quarterly* (Winter 1984-85), 8-15.

"Dashiell Hammett and the Poetics of Hard Boiled Fiction," in *Essays on Detective Fiction*, ed. Bernard Benstock (London: Macmillan and Co., 1983; New York: St. Martin's Press, 1984), 49-72.

"Actor, Role, Star: James Cagney in *Angels with Dirty Faces*," *Mosaic* XVI/1 2 (Winter 1983), 1-17.

"True Heart Susie and the Art of Lillian Gish," *The Quarterly Review of Film Studies*, Vol. 6, No. 1 (Winter 1981), 891-104.

"Nature and History in *The Years*," in *Virginia Woolf: Revaluation and Continuity*, ed. Ralph Freedman (Berkeley: University of California Press, 1979), 11-28. Reprinted in *Modern Critical Views: Virginia Woolf*, ed. Harold Bloom (Boston: Chelsea House, 1987).

"Introduction," *Orlando*, by Virginia Woolf, trans. Gerry Franken (Copenhagen: Betziege Bij Press, 1976).

"Consciousness and Society in *A Portrait of the Artist*," in *Approaches to A Portrait of the Artist*, ed. Thomas Staley and Bernard Benstock (Pittsburgh: University of Pittsburgh Press, 1976), 172-84.

"Style and Theme in *The Lady from Shanghai*," in *Focus on Orson Welles*, ed. Ronald Gottesman (Englewood Cliffs: Prentice Hall, 1976), 140-45.

"Dracula in Chinatown," *The Boston Arts Review*, Vol. 1, No. 1 (Nov. Dec. 1974), 19-20.

"Phillip Larkin's Lost World," *Contemporary Literature*, Vol. 5, No. 3 (1974), 331-44.

"The Walking Shadow: Welles' Expressionist *Macbeth*," *Literature/Film Quarterly* (Summer 1974), 360-67.

"John Huston and *The Maltese Falcon*," *Literature/Film Quarterly* (Summer 1973), 239-49. Reprinted in *Reflections in a Male Eye: John Huston and the American Experience*, ed. Gaylyn Studlar and David Desser (Washington, D. C.: Smithsonian Institution Press, 1993), 119-35. Also reprinted in *The Maltese Falcon*, ed. William Luhr (New Brunswick: Rutgers University Press, 1996), 149-60.

"A World Without a Self: The Novels of Virginia Woolf," *Novel: A Forum on Fiction*, Vol. 5, No. 2 (1972), 122-34. Reprinted in the *Croom-Helm Anthologies of Modern Criticism*, 1994.

"The Imagists and the French Generation of 1900," *Contemporary Literature*, Vol. 11, No. 15 (1970), 354-74.

"Style as Meaning in *A Portrait of the Artist*," *James Joyce Quarterly*, Vol. 4, No. 4 (1967), 331-42.

## Film

Screenplay, co-director, co-editor, *A Nickel for the Movies* (1984). 16mm., 21 mins.

# INDEX

www.ingramcontent.com/pod-product-compliance
Lightning Source LLC
Chambersburg PA
CBHW061609120626
46550CB00004B/1669

* 9 7 9 8 8 9 9 7 6 0 0 1 3 *